MOSIENKO

THE MAN WHO CAUGHT LIGHTNING IN A BOTTLE

TY DILELLO

**FOREWORD
BY STAN FISCHLER**

GREAT PLAINS
PUBLICATIONS

Great Plains Publications
320 Rosedale Avenue
Winnipeg, MB R3L 1L8
www.greatplains.mb.ca

Great Plains Publications gratefully acknowledges the financial support provided for its publishing program by the Government of Canada through the Canada Book Fund; the Canada Council for the Arts; the Province of Manitoba through the Book Publishing Tax Credit and the Book Publisher Marketing Assistance Program; and the Manitoba Arts Council.

Design & Typography by Relish New Brand Experience
Printed in Canada by Friesens
Cover painting by Jennifer Mosienko
Back cover image courtesy Mosienko family
"Billy Mosienko" lyrics © The Kubasonics, used with permission
"Bill Mosienko (21 Seconds)" lyrics © Wordburglar, used with permission

LIBRARY AND ARCHIVES CANADA CATALOGUING IN PUBLICATION

Title: Mosienko : the man who caught lightning in a bottle / Ty Dilello.
Names: Dilello, Ty, author.
Identifiers: Canadiana (print) 20210253525 | Canadiana (ebook) 20210253533 |
    ISBN 9781773370620 (softcover) | ISBN 9781773370637 (ebook)
Subjects: LCSH: Mosienko, Bill, 1921-1994. | LCSH: Hockey players—Canada—Biography.
    | LCGFT: Biographies.
Classification: LCC GV848.5.M68 D45 2021 | DDC 796.962092—dc23

ENVIRONMENTAL BENEFITS STATEMENT

Great Plains Publications saved the following resources by printing the pages of this book on chlorine free paper made with 100% post-consumer waste.

TREES	WATER	ENERGY	SOLID WASTE	GREENHOUSE GASES
9	720	4	30	3,860
FULLY GROWN	GALLONS	MILLION BTUs	POUNDS	POUNDS

Environmental impact estimates were made using the Environmental Paper Network Paper Calculator 4.0. For more information visit www.papercalculator.org

Canadä

FSC
www.fsc.org
MIX
Paper from responsible sources
FSC® C016245

For Roy and Iris

CONTENTS

FOREWORD

I began following the NHL in 1939 (age seven) but was not allowed to go to a New York Rangers game until 1942 when I was ten because the games started at 8:30 p.m. and my parents wanted me up early for school.

I saw my first NHL game in 1942. My dad took my buddy Gerald Sussman and me. It was a nasty, rainy night and my father almost decided to nix the trip, but we talked him out of it.

It turned out that the Rangers were playing the Black Hawks, and I found myself rooting for Chicago because I loved their uniforms. Bill Mosienko only played two games for the club that season, and he wasn't there for the game I went to, although Doug Bentley was and some other good players as well.

While I never became a Black Hawks fan as such, I always liked them. There was something appealing about their game, apart from the jerseys. Maybe it was the fact that they were underdogs nearly all the time in the 1940s when I got really interested in major league hockey.

Mosie came into the picture when he was aligned with Doug and Max Bentley to form The Pony Line. They were so much fun to watch because a stick handler had to be very special to integrate his game into the nuances displayed by Max and Doug. Mosie was just the guy, but the fact that all three were so small presented problems when going up against strong opposition.

Big foes such as Black Jack Stewart of Detroit would pick on the Pony guys, and it was Chicago defender Johnny Mariucci who had to protect the trio. From 1946-47 season on, I saw every Black Hawk game vs. Rangers at Madison Square Garden and savoured Mosie's clean, fast play along with the Ponies until that day in November 1947 when Max Bentley was traded to Toronto.

This was tough on Doug but also rough for Mosie because he and Maxie made such beautiful music together. That brings me to the night of March 23, 1952, at Madison Square Garden.

By that time, I had become vice-president of the Rangers Fan Club and never missed a game, even what would seem like the most unimportant game of the campaign. Chicago finished last and the Rangers fifth, both out of the playoffs. Last game of the season, who cared?

Well, we Rangers fans cared, although only about 5,000 showed up. We didn't care that third-string goalie Lorne Anderson was in goal for New York. (Charlie Rayner and Emile Francis were injured.) Nor that defenceman Hy Buller was playing despite an injured ankle.

As it happened, Mosie had been visiting a friend in Toronto a few days before coming to New York. "We were thumbing through the record book," Bill said, "and I said how nice it would be to have my name in there with some of the hockey greats."

It didn't look like it would happen. The Rangers wanted to make the small crowd happy, and they sure did. We were delighted as the Blueshirts carried the 6-2 lead into the third period. For all intents and purposes, the game was over.

But it wasn't. When Mosie made it 6-3, it didn't matter. When he made it 6-4, it still didn't matter. It was Bill's 30th goal of the season, but we were more interested in the Rangers winning the game.

Still, it was getting serious from our viewpoint, and when George Gee set up Mosie and he pulled a new deke on Anderson for his third goal in 21 seconds, everyone suddenly woke up.

My recollection is that Mosienko almost had a fourth goal, but either hit the post or just missed faking out Anderson. "I had an open net," said Mosie, "but shot it wide."

Chicago went on to win—by that time we were rooting for Bill—and his post-game punch line was right on: "I caught lightning in a beer bottle."

I hope you enjoy this book.

Stan Fischler
Hockey Historian, Broadcaster, and Author of 100+ books on the sport of hockey

INTRODUCTION

It was late February of 2020 that the idea for this book came about. At the time, I was spending a week in Toronto visiting a good friend.

One day we had gone to check out a sports card and memorabilia shop. Tucked away in one of the glass displays near the front counter was an early 1950s Bill Mosienko hockey card. Not only did the card immediately pique my interest, but it brought back a memory from my childhood.

Although I was St. Vital kid, I had relatives in the North End of Winnipeg that I would visit with my dad a few times a year. My eyes would always be glued to the mural on the side wall of a bowling alley called Billy Mosienko Lanes every time we passed the junction of Main Street and Redwood Avenue.

Depicted on the mural is a smiling Chicago Black Hawks player who is holding up three pucks in one of his hands. I would ask my dad about its significance, and he'd tell me the story of Bill Mosienko's famous record of three goals in twenty-one seconds.

Three goals in twenty-one seconds? How is that possible?

That's where my curiosity about the legend of Bill Mosienko began.

Ironically enough, just the day prior to going to the sports card shop, my buddy and I had paid a visit to the renowned Hockey Hall of Fame, where Mosienko was enshrined many moons ago. While I was there, I checked out the display that had Mosienko's stick and three pucks from his famous record.

Long story short, I bought the hockey card and brought it back with me to Winnipeg.

As I was unpacking my things, I grabbed the card and studied it for a while. I thought about how Mosienko was such an excellent ambassador for the sport of hockey in Manitoba during his lifetime and that I should do something to commemorate his life.

The next day I called up Mosienko's son, Bill Jr., who I had known previously from writing the book, *Golden Boys: The Top 50 Manitoba Hockey Players of All Time*, a few years back. In the book, I had written a lengthy biography on Mosienko, so I was already pretty well-versed in his hockey career and later life.

But now, I wanted to dig deeper.

I told Bill Jr. my idea of doing something to commemorate his dad and suggested that I could write a book. I was quite elated to hear that he was warm to the idea and wanted to help in any way that he could.

A few days later, I travelled up to his and his wife's home near Lundar, Manitoba, to go through some of the family's stuff and to ask questions about his dad. Upon arriving, Bill Jr. pulled out a big trunk, and upon doing so, photos and newspaper clippings soared out like they were coming out of a time machine back to the 1940s.

When I left that day, Bill Jr. handed me something that would prove to be perhaps the most essential key to my research: a USB stick.

You see, Bill Jr. did all the hard work for me as he had already spent countless hours scanning old newspaper clippings and photos onto his computer and had categorized them perfectly.

In total, there were around three thousand items on that thumb drive that would get me started on this journey. And what a journey it was!

It just so happened that what would have been Bill's hundredth birthday was coming up on November 2, 2021. So I began working on the book with the idea of having it completed and released for around that time.

I ended up interviewing over a dozen of Bill's former teammates and opposing players for this book. And I'm very thankful I was able to talk to these people and get their stories down while they're still with us as they're all in their eighties or nineties. Unfortunately, a few of them passed away between the time that I talked to them and the release of this book, so I'm glad I was able to reach them when I did.

Even before mentioning what a great hockey player Mosienko was, the first thing that every former player said was how nice of a guy Billy was. That says something when literally every person says the exact same thing.

You'd think that playing so many years in the NHL would gain you some enemies, but nope, not for Bill. Even opposing players liked him a great deal!

With that, I learned early on in writing this book that while Mosienko was a world-class hockey player, he was more importantly a world-class person. A people person, Bill was a genuine guy that loved to just talk to different people, regardless of their background.

That's not to downplay his hockey career at all.

The son of Ukrainian immigrants, Mosienko grew up on skates in the tough working-class North End neighbourhood of Winnipeg. He spent all his time at the local rink near his house, honing his craft by skating and shooting pucks.

Shortly after becoming an adult, Mosienko burst onto the scene in Chicago in the early 1940s and scored twenty goals in his first thirty NHL games. With his boyish good looks and that million-dollar smile, Mosienko was a hit in the Windy City right from the start.

Although he was one of the smaller guys out there at 5'8", 160 pounds, he was extremely quick on his feet. Bill's smooth strides gave him the extra time and space needed as a right winger to get that pass off or fire a shot without much hindrance. He was without a doubt the fastest skater in hockey for the majority of his career.

Mosienko would go on to spend his entire fourteen-year NHL career from 1941 to 1955 in a Chicago Black Hawks uniform. During that time, he skated on the famous high-scoring Pony Line with two legends of the game: Max and Doug Bentley. In this book, you will read all about the Bentley brothers; for my research, I travelled to their hometown of Delisle, Saskatchewan, to get the complete story on the Pony Line.

Mosienko often challenged for the NHL scoring title and finished among the top ten scorers five times. He was inducted into the Hockey Hall of Fame for his illustrious career in 1965.

Even hockey fans today still know his name for his record of scoring the fastest hat-trick in NHL history, three goals in twenty-one seconds on March 23, 1952. After the game, he humbly told the press that he simply "caught lightning in a beer bottle."

It's a record that has stood the test of time and will likely never be broken—unless if they double the size of the nets.

Mosienko was also a two-time NHL Second-Team All-Star and won the Lady Byng Memorial Trophy in 1944-45 as the league's most gentlemanly player. He also skated in five NHL All-Star Games and won a Western Hockey League (WHL) championship in 1955-56 with his hometown Winnipeg Warriors.

This is my seventh book about hockey history, and I have to say that I've never worked harder on a book project than the one you have in front of you. I've never gone this deep into researching someone's past, and I hope it shows as I tried to honour the life of Bill Mosienko as best as I possibly could.

This book became a personal project for me to learn everything I could about one of the greatest hockey players this province has ever produced and one of the best ambassadors for the game that there ever was.

I sincerely hope you enjoy learning about Bill's story. I sure enjoyed writing it.

TOBANS

Dnipro, Ukraine. Population: 1,000,000. That's where the Bill Mosienko story begins.

A beautiful historic city situated on the Dnieper River, after which it is named, Dnipro is located in the heart of Ukraine, roughly 400 kilometres southeast of its capital, Kyiv (Kiev). Archeological findings suggest that the first fortified town in present-day Dnipro territory dates to the mid-sixteenth century. The city was first known as Ekaterinoslav until 1925 and was later called Dnipropetrovsk from 1926-2016.

It was in the year 1880 that Daniel Mosienko was born in Ekaterinoslav, which at the time was a part of Russia. So actually, the Mosienko story begins in the old Russian Empire.

Ekaterinoslav started to grow considerably in the years shortly after Daniel was born, thanks in part to the railroad built through the city that connected it to larger cities such as Odessa and Moscow. The city later became a vital industrial centre of Soviet Ukraine, one of the key centres of the nuclear power, arms, and space industries of the Soviet Union. Because of its military industry, it functioned as a closed city until the 1990s.

It was in Ekaterinoslav that Daniel met Natalia Zemenchenko, a native of Kishtowski, Russia. The pair had a quick courtship before getting married and starting their family. Daniel's family otherwise was tiny, with just a brother named Karnay. Sadly, Karnay, who was a dancer, died on stage while performing at age 21. Tragedy seemed to follow the Mosienko family, and this was the first case of it. Shortly after his brother passed away, Daniel and Natalia moved 550 kilometres south to the port city of Sevastopol, which lies on the Black Sea. It seemed that they moved there for work as Daniel, who was a boilermaker by trade, got a job at the historic Sevastopol Shipyard where he worked as a foreman.

Sevastopol is an important and historic port on the Black Sea. The city became part of Ukraine back in 1954. In the twentieth century, it was the home port of the USSR Navy's Black Sea Fleet. Over time, both Russian and Ukrainian fleets were based in the city.

Today, Sevastopol sits in the Crimean Peninsula (Crimea), a territory currently being disputed by Russia and Ukraine. Since the annexation of Crimea in 2014, Sevastopol has been administered as a federal city of the Russian Federation. With that said, Ukraine and most of the United Nations member countries continue to regard Sevastopol as a city with special status within Ukraine.

The Sevastopol Shipyard was founded as a dockyard for the Imperial Russian Navy in 1783. The shipyard has mostly been used to repair and maintain warships throughout its history, although it has occasionally built ships.

While working at the shipyard from 1905 to 1910, Daniel worked as a builder on several notable Black Sea Fleet ships, including the warship *Kreiser Ochakov* and steamer *SS Johan Zlatoust*.

Daniel and Natalia eventually sought to try to leave Sevastopol and emigrate to Canada. By this time, they already had six young kids. When they all packed up and left, very little was brought with them, except for a few briefcases holding some clothes, jewellery, and money. Daniel heard from another family emigrating to Canada that there were jobs in Saskatchewan on the railway. That was enough to pack up everything and start a new life across the pond.

On October 22, 1912, just a few months after the *Titanic* sunk off Newfoundland's coast, the Mosienko family boarded the *SS Pallanza* of the Hamburg America Line, that took them across the Atlantic Ocean from Rotterdam, Netherlands to Montreal, Canada. On the ride over, the Mosienkos met the parents of future NHL star Alex Shibicky, who were also emigrating to Canada. Roman Shibicky (Alex's dad) convinced

Daniel and Natalia to join them in travelling to Winnipeg, where he said there were prospects for a job.

Although the *SS Pallanza* didn't sink as the *Titanic* did, the Mosienkos' trip to Canada was also marred by tragedy. Only one day after reaching the Grosse Isle Quarantine Station in Quebec on November 6, one of Daniel and Natalia's young sons named Ivan (John) sadly perished at age one. They were now down to five kids.

Grosse Isle was a small island on the Saint Lawrence River that served as a depot for European immigrants coming to Canada. On arrival at Grosse Isle, immigrant ships were not permitted to sail onwards unless they had assured the authorities that they were free of disease.

It was here that an immigration official likely changed the spelling of Mosienko's last name from Museyenko or Moiseyenko, which are both much more common last names in Ukraine. But "Mosienko" was just how the spelling sounded to the official when they asked the family for their names. Similarly, the Shibickys, who were being processed simultaneously, had their last name changed from "Schileitzky" to "Shibicky" while going through immigration.

After spending a week on Grosse Isle, the ship finally cleared immigration and carried onto Montreal. From there, the Mosienko and Shibicky families got off and boarded a train that took them to Winnipeg.

It was on the train ride from Montreal to Winnipeg that tragedy struck once again. Partway through the trek, Natalia realized she didn't have enough milk for her newborn baby and couldn't get her message across to the train officials as no one in the family spoke English. The baby ended up passing away shortly before the train pulled into Winnipeg.

A family of eight had now shrunk to six in a span of only a few days. The four kids remaining were Tina (born in 1900), Alice (1904), Anita (1908), and Mickey (1909).

Winnipeg's North End was—from 1890 to 1930—a tough working-class hub for central and eastern European immigrants. The location was known in those years for its high incidences of extreme poverty and a relatively high prevalence of diseases such as typhoid fever and cholera.

As a city, Winnipeg was deeply segregated, with the North End cut off from the rest of the city by the vast CPR yards and distinguished by its "foreign" character. A 1912 publication described the North End as "practically a district apart from the city," adding that "those who located north of the tracks were not of a desirable character." The largely eastern European working-class residents of the North End were called "dumb hunkies," "bohunks," and "Polacks," and antisemitism was rampant.

It made for very tough living, and for the Mosienkos it would be no different. The Mosienko family settled in the North End right after getting off the train, and the first known address for them in Winnipeg was at 94 Granville Street in Point Douglas.

Daniel and Natalia faced many more difficulties after settling in Winnipeg beyond losing two children. This included learning a new language and adapting to a new culture, but they also faced great economic hardship. Through all this, Daniel did his best to make ends meet for his family, working hard as a boilermaker at the CPR Weston Shops for $1.00 a day.

Upon arriving in Canada, Daniel and Natalia continued where they left off, making babies. A pair of sons, Sonny (1913) and Fred (1914), were born in short order, perhaps to make up for the two that were lost on the trek to Winnipeg. Another son, Nicholas, came along in 1917, followed by a daughter, Nadaliene, in 1919. The eldest daughter, Tina, died in 1919 from influenza during the Spanish Flu pandemic.

On November 2, 1921, William (Bill) Mosienko entered the world. He was born in his parents' home at 94 Granville Street. Alex Shibicky's father, Roman, was named Bill's godparent as the two families were still close. A few years later, brothers Harry (1923) and Jim (1924) were born, making Bill the third youngest of thirteen children.

When Bill was very young, the family moved to a house at 1402 Selkirk Avenue. The big home was a white building with red trim and was conveniently located right behind the CPR Weston Shops where Daniel worked. One hundred years later, the building is still there, looking pretty close to how it did in 1921.

The specific area of the North End that the Mosienkos were in was

Mosienko family photo (Bill is seated to the left of the baby).
COURTESY: BILL MOSIENKO FAMILY

made up of strictly Ukrainian, Polish, Russian and German immigrants. Survival instincts were more substantial than their knowledge of English, French, or the Canadian lifestyle. Here, Bill's parents felt somewhat secure. Living among folks who also came from the old country made it slightly easier for Daniel and Natalia to adjust.

But the kids didn't have much cultural heritage. Their parents' culture and way of life didn't interest the kids as their dreams and mannerisms were old-fashioned. And if the kids tried to be like the English or French people who lived in the more affluent neighbourhoods, their parents would frown at that.

A hatred between European immigrants and the second or third generation French and English continued as Bill was growing up. There was always the feeling of superiority among the English and French communities, while the immigrants were always the lowest on the totem pole.

Even the younger generation's attempts to rise above the ethnic bar-
riers were frowned upon by the older generation. If a girl from their
neighbourhood dated an English boy, for instance, she was called frivo-
lous by her people, while the boy's parents would speak negatively about
the girl as well.

Daniel would often tell his sons, "This is English country. The only
way a Russian immigrant's son will make good is for him to be better
than the English."

But being better was not easy. To make one's mark in the world, one
needed a college education. But the poor immigrant parents didn't have
the money to send their children to college.

Then, in the 1930s, the Great Depression made everyone's life painful,
and immigrant families were the hardest hit. The North End was no different. During the Depression, the Manitoba government would allow
people to rent vacant plots of land for one dollar an acre. Many North
Enders took advantage of this and had big gardens, the size of a football
field, where they would grow potatoes that were all dug and watered by
hand. There was no running water either in the homes; you had to use
a water pump that would be at the end of your street.

The boys of these working immigrants either played sports to occupy
their time or joined gangs. In most cases, parents didn't care what their
kids did in their spare time, and most boys were left to their own devices.
Those that wanted to read books couldn't go to the library because the
nearest library was six miles away.

Daniel barely made enough to take care of his family. With that said,
he was one of the lucky ones as there were barely any jobs during the
Depression. People who were fortunate to have employment worked long
hours, so Daniel would sometimes work ten to sixteen-hour days at the
CPR Weston Shops to help his family get by.

The Mosienko family had been getting through the Depression until
the summer of 1931, when tragedy once again caught up with them.
Sonny was only eighteen when he drowned in 1931 at Ingolf, Ontario,
in Lake of the Woods. Sonny had worked for the CPR but was recently
laid off, so he had come to Ingolf with his mom and two friends for a

short holiday and to pick berries. While swimming with his buddies, Sonny was pushing a raft but lost it and quickly got beyond his depth. Realizing this, he started back to shore, and, as he could not swim, disappeared under the water before his friends could reach him.

It appeared that one of the currents caught Sonny, and he drowned. A reminder that it doesn't matter how strong you are once the water gets you.

Sonny was very beloved by the family, and his loss affected everyone for years. Through all this, the family remained optimistic and slowly, as the years progressed, circumstances improved.

"Dad never talked much about those early years in his life because it was too painful," said Bill Jr.

Early on in my research I came across some articles and a voice recording where Bill talks about his early life in Winnipeg. It was amazing to hear his voice across time. Despite the hardships going on, the North End was always a great crucible of hockey talent. Before the Mosienko boys started playing, it had produced the likes of Dick Irvin, Art Coulter, Alex Shibicky, Babe Pratt, Wally Stanowski, and Joe Cooper, to name a few.

Life was tough at that time. Hand-me-downs and few, if any, luxuries. Most kids wore used skates. Many of the kids couldn't afford skates, so they wore their shoes inside adult skates. How tough was that! But it kept your feet warm when it was thirty below outside.

Bill's first hockey pants were strips of wood or bamboo sewn into a pair of cutdown trousers, which is undoubtedly a testament to what the Great Depression was like.

Bill skated for the first time just down the road from his home at the Rocketeer Rink, which was just west of the Acme Vinegar Factory on the corner of Selkirk and McNichol Avenue. In the late 1920s, the factory burned down, and the rink went with it.

The rink was moved to the west side of Shaughnessy Street between Selkirk and Pritchard Avenue and became known as the Tobans Rink. Tobans was only a stone's throw from the Mosienkos' front step, and it quickly became the neighbourhood hangout spot for all the young kids.

Tobans was initially built out of old wooden boxcars by the fathers of Bill and fellow hockey great Fred Shero. Working for the CPR, they carried over these old wooden boxcars and some of the lumber to construct the rink. In the early years of Tobans, the delivery of goods and services was done by Eaton's wagons, coal and wood wagons, and fire prevention wagons (courtesy of the fire department)—all pulled by horses. Bill later recalled, "We used to drag barrels of water over the field to flood it for making ice."

Bill's older sister, Alice, bought him his first pair of skates when he was five years old during the winter of 1926-27 after he quit using a pair of skates that were hand-me-downs from an older brother.

The kids would start skating in November after the first snowfall and skate and skate until only the bare ground stopped them in the spring. Mosie was no exception and would skate all over, from rinks to frozen roads and sidewalks. Anything to improve his skating.

Speed skating seemed to be Bill's first big passion in life as he won numerous speed skating tournaments as a youngster. In Bill Jr's collection of his dad's stuff there's even a banner from winning first place for Lord Nelson in the Grade 7 Boys division of the 1935 Winnipeg Schools A-A Skating Relay Races. His speed skating background was no doubt a big factor in how he went on to become the fastest skater in the National Hockey League. It's something that was just embedded in him from the beginning.

Although speed skating and racing around the rink with his friends was something that Bill loved, he soon loved the feeling of a hockey stick in his hands and shooting pucks into a net.

It's at Tobans where Bill honed his hockey skills against his brothers and friends. Bill, Harry, and Jim used to play hockey together all day long as they were all close in age. The boys would get called in for lunch or supper, and they wouldn't even take their skates off. They'd go to the table, eat, and then be gone to the rinks again the second their plate was clean.

Bill would skate and skate at the rink until his chums wearily slumped down on the snowbanks and wondered if he would ever stop. And it was Bill's mother, Natalia, who continually had to bundle up and trek through the snow to drag her offspring home for dinner and do it all over again to get him home to do his homework before sending him off to bed.

When Bill was a youngster, Tobans would have a curfew hour when the kids would be kicked off the ice for the night. If they ignored the call, the staff would throw the kids' shoes outside. That didn't seem to bother anyone, or Bill at least, as he lived right across the street.

On the days when organized teams occupied the rink, the boys had no problem making up teams for street hockey in front of Bill's home with a tennis ball or broomball as there were tons of kids anxious to play. There weren't many cars driving by to pause the games back then either. Finding worn-out brooms also wasn't a problem as most of them were the good ones from home. Bill and his brothers would make darn sure they were intact when they returned them at home—you wouldn't dare break the handles or face the wrath of your parents.

Right from the beginning, Bill was always one of the smallest boys in the neighbourhood. He was also always the first boy out on the ice every day. In the early morning hours, you could hear him shooting the puck around the boards, and the neighbours would wonder where he got that energy from. He then would be off to school, and from there, every spare minute of his time went to hockey and skating.

Any night that he wasn't playing a scheduled game, Bill was always mixing it up with some of the boys on his home rink. He was a welcome player in any game and played with a strong desire for the game every time he stepped onto the ice.

That strong desire for the game was there right from the start.

Tobans Athletic Club started when a CPR boxcar was placed near an ice rink to serve as a change room . A shack was later built and remained there until around 1948. Later, a good-sized clubhouse, made up of a large room that could be used as a dressing room (when required) or a dance hall on Sunday nights, a smaller room which was an everyday room, and a canteen opening up to both rooms, was built.

With no sewer and water, Tobans would have the city firemen come out and give the rink a foundation of water to work out (usually in late November). For any additional layers, members would have to haul water in huge barrels on sleighs from the pump on Magnus Avenue. This was a lot of work and usually took place on Saturday because hockey games were on Sunday.

The clubhouse was heated with coal or wood through a couple of pot-bellied stoves. The club never had a proper furnace, but when they finally got sewer and water, Tobans ended up with some electric base-board heaters to protect the water and sewer lines.

One of the original Tobans members, Walter Novak, let the kids use his outside water tap and a very long hose to sprinkle the ice. He lived on Pritchard Avenue across the street from the clubhouse. Many times the boys would have to thaw out the hose to complete the sprinkling.

Over the winter, the Tobans clubhouse was active with whist drives, bridge nights and ping pong tournaments. During the summer, they made use of the rink lights to play touch football in the rink. Volleyball and horseshoes were also played there. Sunday night was dance night at Tobans—with a three-piece band playing. There were also hayrides in the summer and sleigh rides in the winter.

Baseball and soccer were played in the Florence Nightingale school-yard and later in "Shaughnessy Stadium," located approximately where Northwood Community Club is now, (half a block west of Shaughnessy, between Burrows and Alfred).

Bill and his friends were always creating new games and sports to play around their neighbourhood. As you can see, kids growing up in the Depression years made their own fun. There was no such thing as television, video games or computers in those days!

Another popular activity would be the Saturday three-mile walks to the bush northwest from Tobans to pick chokecherries, saskatoons and Nanking cherries—and the odd raids of farmer's fields for cantaloupe and watermelon. The farmers never did miss anything as the boys would leave the plants in perfect condition—there was no waste.

Nowadays, the area is all developed, but back then, past Sisler High

School, it was all prairie. There weren't nearly as many houses as there are today. Kids could skate for miles in early spring right on the road from Magnus and Shaughnessy towards the northwest prairies. Picture a sheet of ice for miles—it was no doubt awesome.

In the summer, they would head out in the same direction to the "Pits" for a swim. This was a dugout that had accumulated quite a bit of water and served as a cooling-off place. A few of the kids even created a little nine-hole golf course on Magnus Avenue. They used Fred Shero's dad's lawnmower to cut the tall grass.

Bill and his friends were also instrumental in getting their section of the North End named "Shaughnessy Heights." Any time they were asked by people growing up, "where are you from?" they would answer "Shaughnessy Heights"—and it eventually stuck.

The Tobans Rink would last until around 1953 when Northwood Community Club on Burrows Avenue started up. Today, the land that Tobans was on has long since been built over with houses. You can't even tell that it was once the spot where so many young kids had their start in hockey.

When Bill was ten years old, he began playing amateur hockey around Tobans and the Old Exhibition Grounds rinks with his buddies. The Old Exhibition Grounds used to be called the Winnipeg Industrial Exhibition Grounds. It covered a swath of land north of the sprawling Canadian Pacific Railway yards, hard-by the ancient Arlington Street viaduct that is bordered by Sinclair Street to the east, Jarvis Avenue to the south, McPhillips Street to the west, and Selkirk Avenue to the north. The Old Exhibition rinks were pretty basic compared to Tobans as they had no boards. Having to try and find your puck in the snowbanks was a daily occurrence there.

Through an old photo in the family's collection, I discovered which hockey team that Bill played for first. The photo depicts an eleven-year-old Bill with a hockey team on March 18, 1933, at the former Osborne Stadium (now the Great-West Life building) with the Legislative Building in the background. At the bottom of the photo, it reads "St. Barnabas Wolf Cubs hockey team 1932-33." St. Barnabas Anglican Church is a

St. Barnabas Wolf Cubs hockey team 1932-33. This photo was taken on March 18, 1933, at the former Osborne Stadium with the Manitoba Legislative Building in the background (Bill is standing, second from the left). COURTESY BILL MOSIENKO FAMILY

church that Bill's family attended for a time on McPhillips Avenue, and Bill got to travel around the city a little bit on this church team. It must have got his competitive juices flowing as he signed up for organized hockey for the first time the following year.

The Mosienko family home was ablaze with excitement one night early in 1934 when Bill romped in and exclaimed, "We won, we're unbeaten!" Mosie was twelve years old that year, his first with a puck team, and was darn proud of being a member of the 1933-34 Tobans Athletic Club "Playground" squad. In years before, he'd eagerly awaited the time when he'd be old enough to play, and here he was now with a whole season under his belt and with the best team at that. Tobans won all of its games that season. It's not very often that a young kid plays his first organized hockey season and doesn't lose a game the entire year.

"Gee, I wonder if I'll ever be a real star, like Joe Cooper," Bill thought at the time. Cooper, who lived in the neighbourhood, was fast becoming one of the best players in the region and was not too far from professional status.

Bill's blinding speed was evident even as a twelve-year-old. The other kids had an awfully tough time keeping up with him. And with that, young Billy realized pretty quickly that with money scarce and opportunity scant, hockey was his chance for advancement in life.

In the Playground Hockey League finals, Tobans defeated Wolseley at the Old Exhibition Grounds outdoor rink. Afterwards, Bill and his younger brother Harry, who was also on the team, met the great Chicago netminder Charlie Gardiner. Back in Winnipeg after backstopping the Black Hawks to the 1934 Stanley Cup, Gardiner presented Tobans with their trophy and gold medals.

"It was a real thrill meeting Gardiner," Bill later recalled.

Sadly, Gardiner passed away less than two months later from a brain hemorrhage brought on by a tonsillar infection.

In the Paperweight division the following year, Bill and his Tobans squad again went undefeated in the season, winning their division, but this time lost out in the city championships.

A little-known fact is that for these first two seasons of organized hockey, Bill was a defenceman and didn't really take part in the goal-scoring.

Oh, how that would change.

As mentioned previously, Bill's first hockey pants were strips of wood or bamboo sewn into a pair of cutdown trousers. However, proper equipment or not, it made little difference to the boys' enjoyment of the game. Even when Bill's team faced a team from the better neighbourhoods, they never felt inferior. Even as the other team from a wealthier neighbourhood strutted into the rink with new and expensive equipment.

For Bill and his friends, rolled newspapers around legs to protect their shins were common. Some kids would stuff newspapers in their shirts, too, although they would never stay in place. Mittens were worn instead of gloves, but they would freeze in the minus-twenty-degree weather.

Some of the boys played without skates, while others had no sticks. They just kicked the puck around. The game always started with a shaved tennis ball that was frozen so it wouldn't bounce. But it never lasted. How can one expect a frozen ball to survive under the constant hitting and kicking of the rowdy bunch of boys? It would shatter like heavy pottery, and then they would kick the broken pieces until they were lost.

"Let's get a puck. I've got 10 cents," someone would say.

A rubber puck cost 25 cents, and that was a lot of money in those days. For some people, it was an hour's wage. The kids would all run home and return with a few cents.

There was a glass jar behind the counter at the local grocery store that was full of rubber pucks. And some of the boys thought of plans to steal the jar so they could play hockey forever. Playing with a rubber puck was a luxury, and since they were able to have fun without frills, they could do without a puck. And so, sometimes they used frozen horse manure as a puck.

On Saturdays, horses appeared on the streets pulling Eaton's delivery wagons that brought the week's supply of cheese, vegetables, meat, and dry goods to stock the local stores. The boys would take turns trailing the wagons and waiting for the horse to give the kids a deposit. The kid would then shape the manure into a puck and let it freeze. Once frozen, it was hockey time. When the puck shattered during a game, the boys would duck and close their gaping mouths for fear of taking in the flying fragments.

This was how the kids in the neighbourhood learned the game of hockey—by playing with each other and trying to stickhandle around everybody. There was really no one around to teach the finer points of the game. Television and instant replays were certainly not available to show the techniques of Howie Morenz, Charlie Conacher, and Busher Jackson.

Sometimes, Bill and his friends would walk for miles to a theatre so they could see a few minutes of a news film about an NHL game. But most of their hockey news would come from checking the sports pages of the *Winnipeg Free Press* or *Winnipeg Tribune*. A few photos would show the results of a hip-check or a defenceman on the ice, blocking a shot, or other action. But how much can one learn from pictures showing players frozen in mid-air? The only other way would be gathering around a radio on a Saturday night and hearing Foster Hewitt describe the game.

Everyone loved the Toronto Maple Leafs and the famous "Kid Line" of Joe Primeau, Busher Jackson, and Charlie Conacher because that's the team that was always on the radio. And the boys imagined themselves as Primeau, Jackson, and Conacher on the outdoor rinks.

"Jackson is the best in the world!" Jim Mosienko would say. "He can check hard and score too."

"What about Conacher?" Bill would chime in. "He has that blistering hard shot and can score at will."

"But you certainly need a guy like Primeau at centre to set them all up," Harry remarked.

The debates were endless on who was better, despite no one physically seeing them play.

NHL great Alex Shibicky grew up in the neighbourhood as well. The boys' parents were life-long friends. Roman Shibicky first worked as a repairman for the CPR with Daniel Mosienko after moving to Winnipeg. He later started a grocery store out of his family's home on Pacific Avenue in the North End.

Alex was a highly touted hockey prospect that first joined the New York Rangers in 1933. He won a Stanley Cup for the Blueshirts in 1940 and was credited as the first NHL player to use the "slapshot." He was a few years older than Bill but used to come by and see the Mosienkos occasionally over on Selkirk Avenue in the summer, once his hockey season had wrapped up.

On one hot summer day after one of Alex's first seasons in the NHL, he drove up to the house as the Mosienko brothers were doing something in the yard. Picture it, Alex coming out of the car with a snazzy suit on, while Bill and his brothers were all wearing hand-me-down clothes with holes.

"Hey Alex, how'd you get a suit like that?" Bill asked.

"From playing hockey!" Alex boasted.

Shibicky then pulled out a wad of money from his wallet and thumbed through the bills for the kids to see. Alex then said, "Come see my car out front too!"

The boys were all in awe of Alex. And seeing Alex and his rewards from playing the game of hockey made a big impression on Bill. Alex and Bill would go on to become lifelong friends.

Joe Swarek was a childhood friend of Bill Mosienko that lived just a few houses over on Selkirk Avenue. Joe was closer to Bill's younger brother Jim as they were the same age, both born in 1924. Shortly before he passed away in 2008, Swarek put together a booklet detailing the history of the Tobans Rink and distributed copies to his old neighbourhood pals from childhood.

In the booklet, he writes about the days he started playing hockey at Tobans around 1930. He notes how the rink boards were constructed out of boxcar boards and that they were quite thick and solid and lasted for many years.

"I recall having to clear the snow off the ice before we could do any skating or play our games," said Swarek. "We started out with home-made wooden shovels—then progressed to metal ones. We sure could have used the modern-day snowblowers then."

In photos of the Tobans Rink, it's clear that they got quite a bit of snow in the winter, and snow would be piling up a few feet over the boards all around the rink. Picture a wall of snow six feet from the top of the boards around the whole rink.

The first lights over the rink were strung across the rink's width with reflectors protecting the bulbs. They were similar to the old lighting used over pool tables, so as you can imagine, it was quite a chore to replace any burnt-out bulbs. Swarek described the hockey experience:

> As kids, we would raise the pucks high to try to hit these lights—without much success, I might add. Mind you; we didn't have regular curved sticks at that time. We did curve a blade when about half of the blade was broken. It sure made a difference in shooting.

I remember our first 'pucks' were provided by horses. These 'pucks' were hard as a rock when frozen, and they hurt to get hit with it. We did progress to tennis balls and regular pucks as one could afford them.

The favourite spot for street hockey when the boys weren't allowed on the rink was on the road in front of the Mosienko home. "Whenever Bill was not playing organized hockey, he would be out on the road with us, along with brothers Jim and Harry," recalled Swarek.

Swarek also notes that there was always hockey going on all around the neighbourhood, so it's no wonder the North End churned out some high-end talent:

> During the 1930s, I remember watching the Senior Hockey League comprising of Tobans, Mets (Redwood & Prince), Maple Leafs (Boyd & Arlington), Tyros (Burrows & McPhillips), and CACS (McGregor & College). The games were played every Sunday afternoon at alternating rinks. I remember my dad and I would walk (cars were not affordable and transportation was by streetcar) to the various rink to watch our Tobans team—it was excellent hockey. There was also the Bulldogs (Old Exhibition Grounds) and Hermits (Boyd & Railway tracks) with rinks. As you can see, there was a huge concentration of rinks in a small area that produced many fine hockey players in its day.

Swarek notes that many strong hockey players, not just Bill, came up through the Tobans system as he was growing up.

> Billy Mosienko's brother Jim was an outstanding player, too. He wasn't the accomplished player that Bill was but had good potential—and with proper coaching, he could have made it. He just needed a coach to take him under his wings. I believe that Jim and two other Tobans guys Kaz Gaçek and Borden Semenchuk, could have played in the current watered-down version of the NHL. I remember going out with Jim Mosienko and Fred Shero

to the Exhibition Grounds for tryouts—I went twice with them but got discouraged when no one showed up. I wonder what potential I had to make it—I was a good skater and stickhandler. We'll never know.

There were other potential NHLers around Tobans in those years, but many did not make the effort to try, while others had to make a living. Hockey wasn't paying much at that time, and opportunities were scarce.

Joe Swarek went into the service during World War II from December 1943 to January 1946. When World War II began, many of Tobans members joined the service, and the club was boarded up. An enterprising group of fellows, led by Paul Mykytiuk, took it upon themselves to take down the boards and re-open the clubrooms. There were no funds to work with, so they had memberships printed and solicited members as best as they could. Soon enough, there were enough members to elect an executive and plan for the future.

When the other members returned from the war, things started to hum once again at the club, and hockey and baseball teams were soon organized. Originally called Toban Athletic Club, the directors had to change it to Toban Community Club so they could enter its various teams under the umbrella of the Associated Community Clubs of Winnipeg.

Tobans quickly boasted many junior teams in various age groups and a senior team. Tobans was also the first athletic club to create a newspaper in the city called *Toban Clarion*, which Swarek helped produce. There were two issues printed—September and October 1948.

Swarek was always proud to consider Bill Mosienko a lifelong friend:

> I remember when Billy was building his bowling alley. I had the privilege of accompanying Jim (Bill's brother) to view the progress. The upper alleys were about complete, and the lower area was being started. I felt a sense of pride to see a friend make a commitment to the North End from where he came. I also knew Billy's wife, Wanda, whom I knew as Wanda Swita when she was a classmate of mine at Florence Nightingale School. Both were down to earth people.

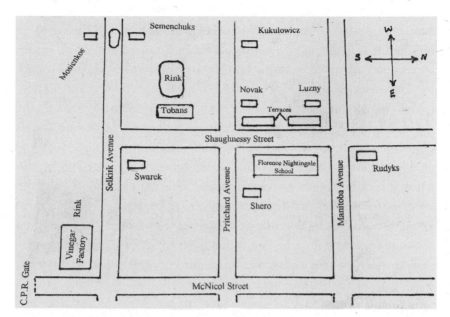

This is a map of the Tobans area that Joe Swarek drew up. You can see the close proximity of the Mosienko house to the hockey rink. COURTESY JOE SWAREK

I can picture Billy when he was home from hockey, walking to catch a streetcar or bus (which was three blocks away) and spending time with any neighbour who happened to be outside. He had a kind word for everyone and enjoyed speaking with all. He was a humble human being.

I have fond memories of my 'growing up' at Tobans and the lasting friendships that were manifested.

There was a "dream" that the directors at Tobans had in the late 1940s to expand its facilities and make it an elite community centre in the city. Unfortunately, many of the grassroots members moved out of the area—got married—pursued other challenges—and were not available to continue their dream of Tobans. And so the community club started to go downhill.

Northwood Community Club sort of replaced Tobans as the spot for minor hockey teams in the area. Northwood started around 1953 on Burrows Avenue with an old railway car as a clubhouse, and then a new building was built in 1956. The community club is still around today.

After Bill's season of Paperweight hockey with Tobans as a thirteen-year-old, he thought he ought to be good enough to perhaps get on with a better team. He went to tryouts for the Panthers and Sherburns squads, but both rejected his services because of his size.

"It's not that you aren't good enough kid, you're just too small, and this is a rough game. Grow a little more and come back in a couple of years."

After he'd received this kind of advice a couple of times, young Billy realized he'd just have to take matters into his own hands.

One afternoon he managed to sneak into a practice of the Sherburns. The squad's coach could hardly believe what he saw when the little fellow took the ice. He had lightning in his skates and was almost too small to keep track of. The coach had to eat his previous words of advice as Mosienko made the team with ease.

"I guess you could say I cheated a bit to make Mr. Jim Lightfoot's fly-weight team," recalled Mosienko in a 1958 Winnipeg Warriors program. "One day, I overheard him telling some of the chosen players to report at a certain time for a closed practice. Well, I got a bright idea, and showed up at the appointed time, told the coach I was supposed to be there. I made the team all right, and I often think that might have been a real turning point in my career!"

The Sherburn Athletic Club was based out of the Sherburn Rink, a giant ice-skating rink located at the corner of Portage Avenue and Sherburn Street, where the Addictions Foundations of Manitoba building currently is. In those years, the Sherburn Rink contained two hockey rinks and another large skating surface. The poles on the rinks carried lights that allowed for night-time games and public skating.

After seeing him play, Les Russell, who operated the Sherburn Athletic Club, quickly put Bill's name on a Canadian Amateur Hockey Association card. Bill stayed loyal to Russell and would play with the Sherburn Athletic Club team for four seasons from Flyweight to Midget, and two seasons of Juvenile hockey.

The year that Bill played Midget, he was teammates with Ernie Dickens, who would go on to win a Stanley Cup in 1942 with the Toronto Maple Leafs and play with Bill in Chicago for four seasons.

Jim Lightfoot, who coached Bill for four years, went on to become one of Bill's biggest fans and supporters throughout his career. He later attended all his games with the Winnipeg Warriors after Bill's National Hockey League days were through.

"I guess I did all my growing at once," Mosienko said after recalling his time with the Sherburn club.

Borden Semenchuk is ninety-two years old today. He's a little hard of hearing and can't see all that great, but other than that, he is relatively healthy. Borden was seven years younger than Bill and grew up living directly across the street from the Mosienko family on Selkirk Avenue.

What's neat is that after all this time, Semenchuk lives on Boyd Avenue, just a couple of streets over from his childhood home. His son, Ron, lives only five doors down and makes sure to give his old man a visit a few times a day.

I visited with Borden one afternoon, and we chatted about his childhood growing up in the North End. Like all the other kids in his neighbourhood, the Tobans rink quickly became the hub for Semenchuk and his pals. Semenchuk recollected:

> I got into hockey as a kid because I was forty-seven steps away from Tobans. There were also four boys that lived to the right of us and three Mosienko boys that lived across the street. We basically had a full hockey team right there.
>
> I remember watching games at Tobans on Sunday afternoons and seeing the orange and black sweaters. At that time, Charlie Coman (ten years older than Billy) and the three Novak brothers: Joe, Eddie and John played there.
>
> If you weren't on the rink, you were in the shack hanging out with buddies or playing cards. In the summer, we played baseball or volleyball on the Tobans rink.

Despite growing up through the Depression, Borden loved his childhood and wouldn't change it for the world. "We didn't even bother with Christmas presents because we didn't know any better. Who knew that we were poor? We certainly didn't."

Semenchuk was beaming when I asked him about the Mosienko family. He said they were all excellent neighbours and loved growing up with the three brothers as close friends:

> Once we were playing horseback (one kid gets on another kid's back), and my shirt got really torn, so I took it to Mrs. Mosienko, and she sewed it up right away. My mother didn't notice until she saw it in the wash and then asked me what happened. We all used to play games together like 'Germans vs. Russians,' which was a type of capture the flag game. Once when we were playing, someone's head got cut by a thrown stone accidentally. Billy's older sister, Alice, was a nurse that lived upstairs. She took care of the wound. Casualties also occurred when we played cricket. And once, my mother fell down the stairs and cut her knees. Billy brought her a 'strong' drink and called the doctor for us.
>
> Bill was seven years older than me, but he always played baseball with us and 'Muchka Ball' (pronounced Mush-Ka). The weaker hitters would line up, and then when the big hitters hit the baseball, the weaker hitters had to run and avoid getting hit by whoever caught the ball. Since Alice, Billy's sister was a nurse and quite a bit older; she would always buy the sports equipment that we used. She was great to us kids.

Borden recalls skating with Bill many times on the Tobans rink despite their age difference. He notes that Bill would play with anybody as he just wanted to be out on the ice all the time:

> And Christ, he could skate that bugger. Even when he was a kid. But late at night, he'd be the only guy left skating on the ice, going round and round. He worked hard at it, and he deserved what he got out of the game. He really worked for it.

Semenchuk was closer with Jim and Harry growing up as they were closer in age than he and Bill.

I remember the family talked about Sonny for years after he drowned, so they must have really loved him. Harry used to take me to hockey games. He really liked me. But then he left, joining the Canadian Forces during World War II, and later moved to Sarnia, Ontario, where he got married. I missed him a lot when he left. I was able to play with Jimmy in the Catholic League in the early 1950s. Jimmy was a decent player but not as gifted as Billy.

Fred Shero was three years older than Borden:

Once he borrowed my hockey stick and accidentally broke it. He repaid me with a helmet, stockings, and pants. That's where I got my gear to play hockey!

Another time we hitchhiked to go berry picking. While we were out there, I stepped on a broken bottleneck. I was only eleven years old. Fred carried me to a nearby house. No one was home, so then he carried me to a second house. Fred was big and strong. I didn't end up getting stitches but had to be pulled in a wagon for two weeks until my foot finally healed!

Semenchuk went on to play junior hockey with the Winnipeg Rangers and Winnipeg Black Hawks in the MJHL. With the Black Hawks, he made $10 per home game as he skated on the "Kid Line" with Steve Witiuk and his long-time centreman from age twelve to twenty-one, Kaz Gacek.

When Borden joined the MJHL's Winnipeg Black Hawks, the club had been given a load of sticks that were used by the Chicago Black Hawks players the previous season. You see, Chicago sponsored the Winnipeg club and looked after everything. It was common in the 1940s for NHL teams to sponsor junior teams in various Canadian cities to get the first crack at signing their players. This was long before the days of the NHL Entry Draft.

"One thing I remember about the Black Hawks is that they placed all of the players' hockey sticks in a pile, and Billy's stick had about a good foot cut off. It was the shortest stick by far. He was short and skated very low to the ice, so you could pick out his bloody stick easy."

At 46 inches long, Mosienko's stick was very short. It was nearly six inches shorter than that of his Chicago teammate John Mariucci, for example.

Although junior hockey wasn't great to Borden, he managed to attend a Chicago Black Hawks training camp in Regina in 1947-48 with his linemates Witiuk and Gacek, as they were all property of Chicago in those years. They tried out as a line, and even though they all get sent back to Winnipeg after a week, Witiuk would go on to have a brief stint in the NHL with Chicago in the early 1950s. Semenchuk later attended a Denver training camp in the Western League one year.

Shortly afterward, Borden decided to forgo hockey to work at the CPR. "Back then, we had two choices, play hockey or work for the CPR. I only weighed 150 pounds and was 5'9", so I wasn't the strongest player. I couldn't hit anybody, but wow, could I get hit!"

As mentioned previously, Semenchuk is a lifelong North Ender and is darn proud of it. He's the last of the old guard of strong Tobans hockey players that grew up in the 1930s.

Also growing up at Tobans around the time Bill was coming up was a kid by the name of Fred Shero. Yes, the same Fred Shero who would coach the Philadelphia Flyers to back-to-back Stanley Cups in the mid-1970s.

The son of immigrants who fled Russia to escape religious persecution, Fred was born on October 23, 1925, in Winnipeg's North End. He lived a few doors away from Florence Nightingale School and diagonally across from the Tobans rink, where he started his own hockey career.

When he wasn't helping his dad with carpentry, Shero would be out vying for a spot in hockey's various age groups. Jim Mosienko's prodding helped instill confidence in his abilities. Shero later said, "he gave me the push that eventually led me to the major leagues." Fred Shero was best friends with Jim growing up as they were the same age.

Fred played quarterback for the Isaac Newton School football team that was city champ one year, and played hockey, soccer, and baseball. He also boxed at the Grain Exchange club. And naturally, he was a tough customer on the ice.

"I remember playing against Fred Shero in an inter-room game at Isaac Newton High School," said Joe Swarek. "I remember carrying the puck over the blueline, and next thing I know, I'm on the bench feeling a little dizzy. I had been nailed by Freddy with my head down—and that was a no, no—a lasting lesson I had learned. I did not make that mistake ever again."

Shero joined the Royal Canadian Navy for World War II. When the war ended, Shero made the NHL as a defenceman with the New York Rangers for two-and-a-half seasons. But he'd be better known for his coaching days in Philadelphia that followed his own playing career.

"Shero was a tough kid, but he didn't show it much," Bill Mosienko recalled in a *Maclean's* article from 1974. "If somebody tried to push him around, look out."

A story about Jim Mosienko is one of Fred's fondest from his child-hood in Winnipeg.

"Jim and I were the same age, but he was one of those rare natural athletes who seemed to do everything without effort," recalled Fred Shero in his autobiography, *Shero: The Man Behind the System*. "At the age of twelve, he was considered the best athlete in town."

One night, Jim, Fred Shero and Wally Gacek were walking to a team's juvenile tryouts at the Olympic Rink and talking about their chances of making the team. As they got within a few blocks of the rink, Freddie looked at Jim and Stan and said, "You two will make it because you're good players, but I'm not going to make it."

"Don't worry, Freddie, you'll make the team," Jim calmly replied.

Freddie didn't believe him. "Aww, Jimmy, you guys are so much better than me—there's no chance I'll make it."

Boys came from all over town to try out at the Olympic Rink. The boys got on the ice, and the coach called the players one-by-one and to see how they skated and ran them through some quick drills that revolved around skating and shooting.

Right away, Jim went over to the coach, who stood by the rink with his assistants. Jim grabbed the man's hand and shook it vigorously. "Hi, I'm Jimmy Mosienko. How the heck are ya?"

Nobody shook the coach's hand in those days. But Jimmy's outgoing manner had a way of reaching people. Jim quickly made the team when he showed the coach he could skate and shoot. The same went for Wally Gacek.

Fred went through the drills nervously, and when the coach turned down Fred, Jim gave the thumbs-down sign to the coach and said, "Freddie and I come as a package. We'll play together on the same team." The coach had to settle to Jim's terms.

All the Mosienko boys were like that, and that story is just one example of what kind of people they all were.

Bill attended Florence Nightingale School as a young boy. It was within walking distance to his house on Shaughnessy Street, between Pritchard and Manitoba Avenue. The school was demolished in 2002 and built over with houses. He later attended Lord Nelson School, and finally, Isaac Newton School as the trio of schools were all within walking distance of his home.

In September of 1937, Bill won a half-mile run at the Old Exhibition Grounds for all junior boys in the area. He also won a speed skating event that year at the Olympic Rink during the Kiwanis Ice Carnival. At Isaac Newton, Bill won numerous track and field medals and played for their hockey team in 1937-38.

Bill dropped out of school after completing Grade 8 to go to work and play hockey. You see, back then, it was not unusual for the kids to drop out and help with the family income once they reached a certain age.

Bill worked at various places in his youth. Most notably, he worked for a tinsmith making spacers for rain pipes. He'd get paid by the piece so he could crank them out pretty fast after a while. The legend goes that Bill was twice as fast as the other workers. This attests to his speed not only on the ice, but at anything he did.

Bill had a knack for building things, and it's likely that if he hadn't become a hockey player, he might have been a general contractor. He always liked doing woodwork on the side throughout his life and would later build things such as desks and cupboards in mere hours.

While things were going great on the ice and at work for Bill, things weren't all sunshine and roses at home. His parents' marriage had deteriorated during the 1930s and 1940s. They still lived together, but they didn't get along.

Natalia was a sweet and caring woman, loved dearly by all her children. On the other hand, Daniel was very old-fashioned in his ways and very tough on his kids. Most of the kids didn't spend much time with him once they became adults.

"He was mean looking and a tough bugger," recalled neighbour Borden Semenchuk. "I remember the boys never wanting to get on his bad side."

Daniel didn't like that the boys were always playing hockey instead of working.

"There's no future for hockey players," he would tell his sons at the dinner table. He wanted them working hard labour and earning a modest wage like he was. He just didn't see hockey as a way of paying the bills and supporting a family. Natalia was much more supportive of the boys chasing their dreams.

The Mosienko boys didn't exactly do great in school anyway, although that's because they were always cutting out of class to go to the rink. Maybe that's part of the reason why Bill dropped out after Grade 8.

What really killed Daniel was losing his job as a boilermaker at the CPR as it was a big job at that time. Daniel had given someone a free ticket, which he shouldn't have done. His boss found out about it and fired him because of it. Shortly after, Daniel and Natalia split up for good. Neither remarried.

In the fall of 1939, Bill left the Sherburn Athletic Club after four seasons to try out for the junior Winnipeg Monarchs at the Olympic Rink at the corner of Church and Charles Avenue.

It was an essential step in Bill's young career as he'd finally get to play the best of the best for junior hockey players in the province and begin to get on NHL teams radars if he could succeed at this level.

By the time Bill had his tryout with the Monarchs in 1939-40, fellow North-Ender and Chicago Black Hawks defenceman Joe Cooper was well

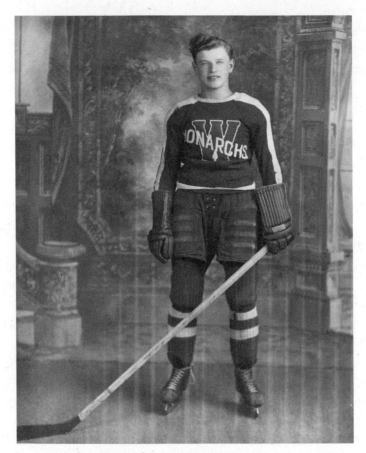

Bill with the Winnipeg Monarchs in 1930-40 COURTESY BILL MOSIENKO FAMILY

aware of young Bill's speed and dexterity. He'd watched him skate at the Old Exhibition Grounds and warmly recommended him to Chicago's ownership.

Mosienko lived only four blocks from Cooper, who was seven years his senior. What Bill was unaware of then was that Joe would later become his pal, teammate, and protector in Chicago, and later his business partner. But at the time, Bill was just in awe that an NHL player had taken an interest in him and believed that he could play in the big leagues one day.

It was also around the time that Bill was told that he made the Monarchs team that he faced some pressure from his father to take up a job offered to him at the CPR Weston Shops. Basically, all the boys in the Mosienko family worked with the CPR at one time or another. However, Bill remembered Alex Shibicky pulling up to his house in the car he bought from his hockey earnings. And like Alex, Bill wanted to pursue hockey as a way of escaping the railroad lifestyle that their families had grown accustomed to.

Confident that he would make it in hockey, Bill chose against a job on the railway and joined the Winnipeg Monarchs. He was betting on himself and seeing where it would take him.

ROAD TO CHICAGO

The story goes that Bill Mosienko wandered into the old Amphitheatre one fall afternoon in 1939 while the junior Winnipeg Monarchs were having a preseason workout and asked, yes asked, the Monarchs management if he could have a tryout.

A year prior, Bill had ventured to the St. James Canadians tryouts but was deemed too small and inexperienced. He'd played for the team in the preseason but had failed to impress the St. James coach. Bill was cut and returned to the Sherburn juvenile squad, where he led his team and the league in scoring. That chip on his shoulder for being rejected by St. James gave Bill some fire inside him to not let the next opportunity pass him up. Despite being known in the papers as quite the "speed merchant" during his years with the Sherburn Athletic Club, Bill was never formally invited to tryout for the Winnipeg Monarchs in the fall of 1939.

"Dad always told me that early on, nobody wanted him because of his small stature," said Bill Jr.

Well, that sure changed in a hurry.

It was a cold, fall day in late October when Bill snuck on the ice for the Monarchs tryouts. Bill had taken a streetcar to the Amphitheatre, which at one point was the only indoor artificial ice surface between Toronto and Vancouver. It was located where the Great-West Life building now stands in downtown Winnipeg, across from the Manitoba Legislative Building.

Monarchs coach Harry Neil and President Bruce Boreham weren't sure at first glance, but when they watched him go through the motions, they soon noticed his strong skating style and speed. From there, young Bill was a lock to make the team.

Coach Harry Neil liked the way Bill played and instantly put him on the club's fastest line. His linemates were Bill Benson and Paul Platz, and that season, the Benson-Platz-Mosienko combination were in there like income tax collectors, scoring goals galore.

In 1939-40, The Manitoba Junior Hockey League (MJHL) boasted nine teams: Winnipeg Monarchs, Kenora Thistles, Brandon Elks, Elmwood Maple Leafs, Canadian Ukrainian A.C. (CUAC), Portage Terriers, St. James Canadians, Winnipeg Rangers, and St. Boniface Athletics.

Ralph Allen, the sportswriter, who later became a war correspondent, tagged Bill that season as: "The Kid who skates with a pain in his belly." In the ninth game of the season, the Monarchs met up with the Brandon Elks for a contest at the Amphitheatre. In the *Winnipeg Tribune* Allen noted that

> The battle had hardly started when students of the game noticed a perfect right angle skating up and down the port wing for Monarchs. That's correct, a right angle. The kid named Bill Mosienko doing the eyebrow raising was doubled up as though in pain but still managed to cover large quantities of Amphitheatre ice.
>
> A few minutes later, the tiny streak snagged the puck in mid-ice and sailed in to score as pretty a goal as legendary broadcaster Foster Hewitt could dream up. Maybe the kid was skating in that funny position because he was shy. Or maybe he hid pucks in his sweater.
>
> The reporter's philosophical musings were interrupted by the PA system announcing: "Goal scored by Bill Mosienko."

Mosienko scored twice that night, including the winning goal as the Monarchs defeated Brandon 4-3.

The Winnipeg Monarchs went on to finish first in the South Division with a 16-6-2 record. In the division semifinals, the Monarchs defeated Portage two games to one with one tie, to set up a date in the division finals with the Kenora Thistles.

The Monarchs and Thistles were considered the top two teams in Manitoba junior hockey that season and the series was considered a dead-even split to bettors and reporters.

Bill and the Monarchs travelled to Kenora for Game 1. On the train ride, *Winnipeg Free Press* reporter Scott Young (father of Neil Young) noted that the Monarch players seldom mentioned Kenora, and beyond the odd remark, you never would know there was a big hockey game coming up.

In the first period of Game 1, Bill took a pass from Paul Platz and fired a shot past Thistles goaltender Chuck Rayner. Unfortunately, that would be the only Monarchs tally of the night as Kenora took Game 1 by a 4-1 scoreline.

Game 2 back at the Amphitheatre was a much tighter contest. Mosienko scored two goals in the third period to ignite the packed Winnipeg crowd, but it was just not meant to be. Down 4-3 in the final minute, the Thistles tied the game on a late goal and then won the game in overtime. The Monarchs season was over.

It's likely that had it not been for the Thistles, the Monarchs would have been a championship team that season. The Thistles were able to hold Mosie's line at bay very well during the series, thanks largely in part to Chuck Rayner's goaltending and Bill Juzda's sturdy defensive play.

The Thistles would go on to win the league championship and ultimately reach the 1940 Memorial Cup final, where they would lose out to the Oshawa Generals three games to one.

As an eighteen-year-old, Bill scored 21 goals in 24 games for the Monarchs that season, but he decided to leave the Monarchs after one year despite having two years of junior eligibility left due to money issues.

"I lived in the North End, and the Monarchs wouldn't give me $5 a week for car fare (streetcars)," Mosienko later recalled. "I needed that money to get to games and practice. Our family was poor, and I knew darn well Paul Platz and Bill Benson (his Monarchs linemates) were getting it. That made me mad. I left the first chance I got."

Bill wanted to try and earn some real money, so he took a chance to play professional hockey as soon as one came his way. And it was right around this time that he was being courted by both the New York Rangers and Chicago Black Hawks of the National Hockey League.

Bill had first signed a paper to go to a New York Rangers tryout camp. However, right before the Rangers were going to put him on their negotiation list officially, Chicago Black Hawks defenceman Joe Cooper spotted Mosienko playing at the Old Exhibition Grounds outdoor rink and was intrigued by how good Mosienko was and how he could fly on the ice. Plus, he knew how well that Mosienko had been playing with the Monarchs that season as the pair were pals who kept in contact over the years.

Cooper was so impressed that he followed Bill home that day and convinced him to sign with the Chicago Black Hawks. Cooper then wired Mosienko's name to Chicago, and the big-league club promptly added him to their negotiation list. Twenty-four hours later, the Rangers tried adding him to their list as well, but they were too late. The tryout form that Bill had signed with New York didn't hold any weight, and so the Rangers missed out on Bill Mosienko by twenty-four hours.

Bill later recalled, "Well, I signed with the New York Rangers first, but the Chicago team had placed me on its negotiations list twenty-four hours previously, and that means 'hands-off' for any other team. So I went with the Black Hawks."

What Cooper said in his initial telegram is unknown, but it was not only enough to get Black Hawks manager Paul Thompson to put Mosienko on the team's negotiation list but also convinced Thompson to make a special trip out west to check out the speedy prospect for himself.

As he watched Mosie go through the paces, the Chicago manager learned that the youngster had quit school two years earlier so that he could concentrate on hockey and bring more money to the family. He also noticed that Mosienko was aflame with eagerness to get into major league hockey and earn more as well.

Thompson showed a definite interest in Billy and told the Mosienko family that he might be able to find a place for their son in the Chicago organization that next season. They were happy and hopeful when the Windy City manager left, and the thought of a big salary seemed good.

A few days later, their joy ended when a wire from Thompson revealed that Canadian immigration authorities had decreed that Billy was too young to play professional hockey in the United States.

Bill burst into tears.

But Thompson wasn't done. He turned on all of his powers of persuasive eloquence and pointed out the fact that Mosienko's family needed whatever financial help he could get. A second wire came to the Mosienko household from Chicago a few days later, and this time Thompson had good news. He had gotten authorities to reconsider, and Billy was invited to attend the upcoming Chicago Black Hawks training camp in Hibbing, Minnesota.

Clearing Canadian immigration was only the first hurdle that Mosienko had to jump to play pro hockey in the United States.

Because Bill still had two years of potential junior hockey left, the MAHA (Manitoba Amateur Hockey Association) put up a strong fight to keep him playing junior hockey in Manitoba. E. Vic Johnson, president of the MAHA, expressed deep concern over the inroads being made on Manitoba players still of junior age.

Juniors were the only brand of hockey in Manitoba at the time that provided any source of revenue. Despite there being no professional hockey in the province in those years, the MAHA strived to put out the best product possible for the fans. And that's why they tried to keep high-end talents like Mosienko from leaving, at least until they were out of junior age.

The matter had to go to a joint special committee meeting between the CAHA (Canadian Amateur Hockey Association) and the NHL. Bill and a couple of other eighteen-year-old players only received permission to sign pro contracts after this meeting occurred.

Dr. W.G. Hardy of Edmonton was the chairman of the special CAHA committee dealing with the NHL. He gave this statement to the *Winnipeg Free Press* on behalf of the committee:

> After careful consultation with the Manitoba branch and Winnipeg Monarchs, the CAHA has decided to allow junior

players Andy Branigan and Bill Mosienko to be signed to professional contracts. It should be noted that the Manitoba branch and the Winnipeg Monarchs have concurred in this because they wish the boys to have every chance possible, even although allowing these boys to turn professional makes matters difficult for junior hockey for the Manitoba branch and Monarchs. Two things should be clear also: these boys are allowed to go only because we consider them exceptional cases and letting them go is not to be considered a precedent. Secondly, they are being paid for under the CAHA/NHL agreement authorizing payment of $250 to the club or branch which developed them.

When informed by the *Winnipeg Free Press* of the Mosienko-Branigan decision, MAHA president E. Vic Johnson said:

Less than a month ago, Manitoba hockey men were elated with what we had explained to us as a CAHA-NHL agreement which prevented pro clubs taking players of junior age. Junior brand is the only hockey played here, which provides revenue to promote minor hockey. Our senior hockey was ruined back in 1933 by a wholesale migration to the Maritimes, and unless something is done soon, our junior brand—the best in Canada up to now—will be in the doldrums alongside the senior.

The agreement still says the pro clubs will not touch juniors, but there is a clause which allows the NHL clubs to request consideration of special cases, and it's under this clause that sanction has been given for Vic Lofvendahl, Andy Branigan and Bill Mosienko. These youngsters all had contracts offered them far in excess of anything they could hope to gain from employment here. Two of these boys weren't even employed. As an association, we couldn't stand in the way of a boy making a decent living. That's not our point. Our concern right now is a way of preventing continued raids from ruining our minor set-up. Neither club officials nor the MAHA can stand the rap at the $250 price. Unless the pros look elsewhere, our fertile field here will dry up and dry up quickly. Our branch contributed more than $2,300 last year to the promotion of minor hockey in Manitoba, and the bulk of this money was derived from junior playoffs. If the junior brand starts to slip, the gates will certainly slip, and that's why we are viewing with alarm designs on our junior players when there is so much senior hockey being played in Canada.

With the CAHA decision, Mosienko turned pro in the Chicago organization with Paul Platz and George Johnston, while Andy Branigan joined the New York Rangers family. They were all graduates of the Winnipeg Monarchs. Vic Lofvendahl, a Kenora Thistles junior, signed with the New York Americans and skated for one of their minor league clubs that season.

Chicago Black Hawks president Bill Tobin announced the signing of the Manitoba trio in a telegram.

Bill later recalled, "I had two years of junior left. But we were a very poor family. Money and food were hard to come by, so I took the first opportunity to turn pro. I'm too embarrassed to say how much I got that first year, but I sent home most of what I made."

The Chicago Black Hawks went to Hibbing, Minnesota for training camp in October of 1940. Second-year Chicago coach Paul Thompson was relatively young at age thirty-three. Only two seasons earlier, he'd been manning the left wing for the Black Hawks, as he'd been doing since 1931. In 1938, Thompson and the Black Hawks had won a surprising Stanley Cup. With a record of 14-25-9, that year's Black Hawks possess, to date, the lowest regular-season winning percentage of any championship team in the four major professional sports leagues and are the only ones to do so with a losing record.

Aiming to win another Stanley Cup, Thompson's team convened in northern Minnesota three weeks ahead of the opening game of their 48-game regular-season schedule, a November 7 meeting with the New York Americans at Chicago Stadium.

Twenty-five players travelled to Hibbing. Those who didn't accompany the coach on the train from Chicago came south via Winnipeg. Paul Goodman was the incumbent in goal, though the Hawks were excited by a young local prospect named Sam LoPresti. Defensive stalwarts Earl Seibert, Jack Portland, and Art Wiebe would be challenged by another Minnesotan, John Mariucci from Eveleth, and a recently graduated mining engineer from the University of Alberta, Dave MacKay. Returning forwards included Mush March, Johnny Gottselig, Phil Hergesheimer, and Doug Bentley. The latter's brother, Max, was given a good chance of making the team. There was also a young eighteen-year-old Billy Mosienko.

Bill Mosienko's name first appeared in the Chicago sports pages on October 16, 1940. It had to do with Mosienko's delay in reporting to the Hawks training camp at the Hibbing Memorial Arena in Hibbing, Minnesota, as they referred to him as "Baby Face Bill" in the article.

Mosienko told the story years later to *Blueline Magazine* with a laugh:

> I'd never been very far away from Winnipeg up to that time. I wasn't quite nineteen. Of course, I had never been to the United States, and somehow, after talking to different people, I got the idea I should take along just enough Canadian money to get me across the border. I had my transportation and figured pretty closely on what meals should cost me up to the time I got to Hibbing. Well, at the border, immigration authorities found some flaw or something in my visa, and I had to stay overnight at Emerson while it was straightened out. I hadn't figured on a hotel bill—and I was practically broke. I called Bill Tobin—collect—at Hibbing, and he wired me extra money and went to work on my visa problem.

Bill was only 5'7" and 140 pounds or so when he finally arrived in Hibbing, but Tobin never cared that Mosienko was a bit on the small side. After all, he also signed Doug Bentley and, later, Max, after one or two other teams dismissed them as "too small."

"It was a good thing for me turning pro so young, but I wouldn't advise every youngster to go down the same path," Mosienko recalled years later in the *Winnipeg Free Press*. "I was pretty solidly built for my age and could take a lot of punishment. I had good speed and was able to dodge the big guys. I didn't have any fear of getting hurt in those days, and I'd go in there and take them out, big or small, just to prove I could stay up there. I knew if things got out of hand, we had plenty of big guys to protect me."

Joe Cooper was in Hibbing too and served as Bill's protector as he navigated his first professional training camp. Joe was a tough and very physical defenceman. It came to him naturally as growing up in the North End, he had hard-working immigrant parents who were dead set against him playing hockey, to the point that he had to hide his skates from them.

Thompson was enthusiastic about the future of his franchise. He told the *Chicago Daily News* that this team was shaping up to be "the most evenly balanced in Chicago history." The team's tempestuous owner agreed when he came to town for a visit midway through camp. Never before, Major Frederic McLaughlin declared, had a team of his looked so good so early. This despite the fact that the Hawks hardly skated the first week of the preseason. The ice was iffy in Hibbing that October— what there was of it.

The crew at the Hibbing Memorial Arena was no doubt doing its best to get a freeze on for the hockey players, but they had their troubles that first week. Five days into camp, the Hawks still hadn't seen a serviceable surface. Thompson ended Wednesday's drills before they really got going as "after five minutes of skating," *The Canadian Press* reported, "the ice had worn down to the floor."

The players took to the outdoors and quickly found the Hibbing Golf Course. Wednesday saw Mush March score a hole-in-one on the Hibbing course's 190-yard seventh hole. March had spent the summer as a club pro in Valparaiso, Indiana, so it wasn't as big of a surprise that he got a hole-in-one than if first-time golfer Bill Mosienko potted one.

By the Thursday, coach Paul Thompson's patience was almost at its end. He figured that if the Hibbing Memorial Arena couldn't get it together by Friday, he'd take his team and head five hundred miles east to Sault Ste. Marie, Michigan, where former Chicago defenceman Taffy Abel managed the rink.

On Friday, with the team packed and ready to go, Hibbing's icemakers came through in the clutch, and the Hawks skated for the first time with sticks and pucks. "The frozen surface stood up under two 90-minute tests," *The Canadian Press* noted. "Jubilation was rampant."

Art Wiebe was the season's first casualty, suffering a gash over the right eye along with what *The Canadian Press* termed "a slight brain concussion." No worries, said coach Thompson, he'd be back on the ice the following day.

During the second week of camp, the ice was fine and held up the entire time. On Monday, a thousand or so spectators showed up to watch Chicago's first open scrimmage. Coach Thompson played referee, "allowing some fouls to pass unnoticed, but was quick to stop play on offsides." It was nineteen minutes before anyone could score, with Johnny Gottsclig beating Paul Goodman.

As planned, the Hawks left the following Monday for St. Paul. They had another week of drills ahead of them there, along with a series of exhibition games against the local St. Paul Saints of the American Hockey Association. However, when the Black Hawks first arrived in St. Paul, they learned that the refrigeration plant had broken down and that the ice wouldn't be ready for another day or two. It was a total gong show, but the Black Hawks did get those exhibition games in before carrying on to Chicago for the start of the season.

Mosienko performed so well at the Chicago training camp that he was offered a professional contract. Bill quickly signed it and then headed by plane from Minnesota to Chicago's AHL farm club in Providence, Rhode Island, for conditioning. It marked the first time in his young life that Bill would be hopping on an airplane.

Bill landed in Providence, Rhode Island, in late October and began skating with his new team. He was to be paid $75 per week with Providence and would be skating on a familiar All-Manitoba line with Paul Platz and George "Wingy" Johnston. Upon arriving in Providence, Bill met a fellow rookie named Max Bentley, and a friendship soon developed between the pair.

When the season started, Bill settled in nicely as a top-scoring forward on the team. He was scoring at nearly a point-per-game pace while enjoying his new surroundings in a different city and country than what he was accustomed to.

A news release from the Providence Reds on December 12, 1940, shows a radio interview with the young pro Mosienko who had just recently turned nineteen. Here's the transcript of the interview:

> And fans, we have right here this evening, Billy Mosienko—the "Littlest Red of them all"—Billy's a smiling lad—with blue eyes—very boyish-looking with blonde hair. He's a youngster in every sense of the word—and, (maybe he won't like this) but you'd never take him for a gladiator in the bruising game of hockey—not in his street clothes, anyway—but out there on the ice—well—that's a different story. Youthful Bill can skate with the best of them, and judging from his showing in his first professional year, young Mr. Mosienko will be heard from—and a whole lot before he finishes what promises to be a brilliant hockey career. So Bill—how do you feel after listening to all that?
>
> MOSIENKO: Oh gosh! But I'm not the "Littlest Red."
>
> WARREN: You're not, Bill? Well, you're the youngest, aren't you?
>
> MOSIENKO: Yes, I guess I answer that description all right.
>
> WARREN: Well then, Bill, now that we're all agreed on that point, just how old are you?
>
> MOSIENKO: I'm 19, Warren.
>
> WARREN: Well, you were only 18 when you reported in Providence, weren't you?
>
> MOSIENKO: Yes, I had a birthday while I was in my first week here.
>
> WARREN: And how about that birthday party on the airliner. You know, it isn't everyone who can celebrate a birthday while flying up there among the clouds.

MOSIENKO: Yes, that was quite a surprise, Warren. They had a cake with candles, and we all had a fine time while flying home from Philadelphia. I think we were right up over New York City at that time.

WARREN: How long have you been playing hockey, Bill?

MOSIENKO: I started when I was only 11 years old, and I've been playing ever since.

WARREN: Well, that isn't very long—but I suppose it seems like a long time to you. Does it?

MOSIENKO: Yes, it does, sort of.

WARREN: Where did you play last year, Bill?

MOSIENKO: I played with the Winnipeg Monarchs last year.

WARREN: Pretty good club, were they?

MOSIENKO: Most of the players turned pro from that club this year.

WARREN: It must have been a good team! Are there any other players with the Reds who were with the Monarchs?

MOSIENKO: Yes, Paul Platz was with the Winnipeg Monarchs last year.

WARREN: He's pretty good, too. Isn't he Bill?

MOSIENKO: He's good all right.

WARREN: Well now, Bill, you belong to the Chicago Black Hawks, don't you?

MOSIENKO: Yes.

WARREN: How did you come to join the Black Hawks?

MOSIENKO: Well, I signed with the New York Rangers first, but the Chicago team had placed me on its negotiations list twenty-four hours previously, and that means "hands-off" for any other team. So I went with the Blackhawks.

WARREN: Well, New York's loss is Chicago's gain—or rather a gain for Providence—is that right, Bill?

MOSIENKO: Well, if that's the way YOU want to put it.

WARREN: How many goals did you score last season, Bill?

MOSIENKO: 21 goals and eight assists in 24 games.

WARREN: That's a pretty good record, Bill—In fact, I should say that it's very good. Maybe that's the reason why the New York Rangers and Chicago Blackhawks were after you—is that it?

MOSIENKO: I suppose it is.

WARREN: They tell me that this is your first trip away from home. Is that right?

MOSIENKO: That's right.

WARREN: How do you like it—are you homesick?

MOSIENKO: Well, I'm not exactly homesick, but I sure would like to see my mom.

WARREN: I'll bet you would, Bill—How many are there in your family?

MOSIENKO: We have a very large family. There's Alice, Mike, Fred, Nick, Nadaliene, myself, Harry, and Jim. That's in order to according to ages.

WARREN: Nice going, Bill. Nine all together. Any other hockey players?

MOSIENKO: Yes, my two younger brothers.

WARREN: Are they pretty good players?

MOSIENKO: Yes, in their class. They're improving all the time. Maybe they'll be in the pro game in a few years.

WARREN: Well, how do you like it here in Providence?

MOSIENKO: I like it very much. Especially the weather. They say it's very cold at home now. That's down in Winnipeg, Manitoba. Everything is great here—Bun Cook and all the players as well as manager Lou Pieri.

WARREN: Have you seen the saltwater yet, Bill?

MOSIENKO: Yes, Eddie Malfetano took some of us down to Point Judith last Monday.

WARREN: How did you like it?

MOSIENKO: Very impressive. But I don't think I'd like to try swimming in it.

WARREN: Not in this weather anyway, Bill. What are you going to do against that New Haven club tonight?

MOSIENKO: I'm going to do my best. In fact, we're all going to try very hard to win. We want to get up there in first place just as soon as we can, and we want to stay there.

WARREN: Well, I certainly wish you the best of luck Bill Mosienko. And best of luck to Bun Cook and the Reds in their game with the New Haven Eagles at the Auditorium in Providence tonight at 8:30 o'clock. Fans, you've been listening to Bill Mosienko, who is the youngest member (He's only 19) of the Providence Reds Ice Hockey club. Thank you, Bill, for coming down here to this *Everybody's Sport* program.

All in all, things were going very well for Bill in his first pro season. He had adjusted to the much more physical game than he had been playing previously in the junior ranks. Through thirty-six games with Providence, he had scored thirty-three points.

In February, the Black Hawks bought the Kansas City Americans of the American Hockey Association (AHA) to use as a farm club. Mosienko was called up to the Black Hawks on February 8 and then immediately sent to Kansas City. Chicago sent veteran Pep Kelly to Providence in place of the new recruit.

Mosienko left Providence on a Tuesday morning, and by Wednesday morning, he was practising with his new team in Kansas City.

Calling Mosienko up this way and then sending him down, the Hawks were living up to the letter of its agreement with the Reds, for they sent a player back to the Providence team in place of Mosienko. But this was hardly the way Providence management expected the agreement to work out, anticipating that the Reds would have the best of the surplus Chicago players. Mosienko was certainly one of these.

"It was in January 1941, and Johnny Chad (a Hawks winger) was injured," recalled Mosienko years later. "They brought me into Chicago, but by the time I was there, another, more experienced replacement had been found. In the meantime, they had bought the Kansas City team for a farm, so I was sent there for the rest of the season. I was called up by Chicago from Providence to fill in for Johnny Chad, who was injured. But I don't remember even seeing the inside of the Stadium at that time. When I got to Chicago, Chad was in the lineup after all, and the first thing I knew the Hawks had breezed me right through town, and I was in Kansas City."

Mosienko said that the switch from Providence to Kansas City broke his heart at first. He'd just gotten to know some people in Rhode Island, and here he was again in a new city with new teammates. The only saving grace at Kansas City was player-coach Johnny Gottselig, an NHL veteran of thirteen seasons. It was Gottselig who really helped Bill along during his time there.

Bill penned this letter to Providence coach Bun Cook after arriving from Providence to Kansas City. Bill must have thought the world of Cook for giving him his start in professional hockey:

> *February 12, 1941—from Kansas City, Missouri—*
>
> *Dear 'Bun,'*
> *I sure would have liked to have seen you before leaving Providence, but seeing that I did not, I would like to express my thanks to you, Mr. Pieri, and the rest of the fellows, for the wonderful way I have been treated.*
> *I'm still pulling for the Reds, coach, so wishing that you turn out another championship.*
> *I'll say, so long now, to the swellest coach and fellow that I have ever met, but hoping, that we shall meet again.*
>
> *Sincerely, Bill Mosienko.*

Bun Cook kept that letter nestled in a personal hockey scrapbook for the rest of his life.

Manager Gottselig was immensely pleased with Kansas City acquiring Mosienko. He told the press, "This will be a sample to Kansas City fans of the kind of talent we'll have next year. Mosienko is the youngest professional in organized hockey today and should prove the same kind of a star here that he was in Winnipeg and Providence. He hasn't reached his peak yet and is still developing."

Bill scored four points in Kansas City's final eight games of the regular season. In the league semifinals, Bill and his Kansas City Americans swept the Minneapolis Millers in three straight games to advance to the league finals against the St. Louis Flyers.

In the opening game of the league finals in 1941, Mosienko, the nineteen-year-old rookie, poked in two goals in the final period to propel his team to a 3-1 win. Scoring the winning goal at 13:05 of the third period, Mosie swiped the puck behind the Flyers cage and snuck it into the net before the goalie knew a play had been made.

Sadly, Bill and his boys lost out in the fifth and decisive game. It was an unfortunate end to an otherwise stellar rookie campaign.

"We had a good year at Kansas City, went to the finals—three games against Minneapolis and a full five games before losing to St. Louis," said Mosienko. "I remember my first playoff bonus check after those twelve games was $52."

Bill returned to Winnipeg for the summer and hung around the North End with his family and old pals. In the fall of 1941, he once again boarded a train for the Chicago Black Hawks training camp in Hibbing, Minnesota.

An article in a Chicago newspaper during training camp notes that "Nineteen-year-old Bill Mosienko, who plays the position of right wing, earned his right to try for a major league berth through sheer force of merit. Bill tips the beam at 160 pounds, stands 5'8" in height and close in on the nets is the possessor of a wicked and accurate shot."

After another strong showing in camp, management decided that Bill needed to spend a little more time developing his skills in the minor ranks. They didn't want to rush their future star to the big stage and were willing to be patient with Mosienko.

Bill took being sent down to Kansas City in stride and sought to do everything in his power to get called up to the NHL at some point during the season. In the meantime, he would continue to learn under the tutelage of Johnny Gottselig.

"I was fine starting my career in the minors. I just wanted to get ahead, really wanted to get ahead in hockey. That was my one ambition. I wanted to succeed so badly," Mosienko recalled years later. "I had to sacrifice a lot of things. I could have gone out and had a good time, but I stuck to hockey and worked hard because it was the only way I knew where I could make what I wanted out of my life."

As fate would have it, Bill would get his wish in late January of 1942. To that point in the season, Mosienko had potted 31 points in 33 games for Kansas City.

On January 26, Bill and the Americans had just finished practice one morning at the Pla-Mor Ice Palace in Kansas City. The night prior, Mosienko had broken a scoreless deadlock in overtime to give his team a 1-0 win over the Tulsa Oilers.

Mosienko was getting undressed at his stall and chatting with team-mate Cliff "Fido" Purpur, who hailed from Grand Forks, North Dakota, only a two-and-a-half-hour drive from Winnipeg. The pair had grown close over the 1941-42 season and would often visit each other long after their careers were over. Suddenly, player-coach Johnny Gottselig barged into the dressing room with a big smile pasted across his face.

"It's you for sure," Purpur whispered to Bill. "That overtime winner last night just sent you to the NHL. I know it."

Bill just smiled and stayed quiet.

It was early 1942, and NHL teams were losing players to World War II left and right. Rumours were circulating that some Kansas City players were going to be called up at any moment.

Finally, after what seemed like forever, Gottselig walked up to Bill and beamed, "I just got the wire from Chicago, Bill. You're going up!"

Gottselig gave Bill a big hug. "You earned this, and you are ready for the big time. Now show the National Hockey League what Bill Mosienko can do."

Mosienko said goodbye to his teammates and left the rink to grab his belongings from the apartment he was renting in Kansas City. From there, it was off to the train station.

Next stop: Chicago.

PLAYING FOR STANLEY

Upon reaching the Windy City, Bill only had time to drop his things off. And then just like that, he was off with his new team to head to Detroit for his first National Hockey League game.

The twenty-year-old Mosienko would be joining a Black Hawks team that was mixed with both new and old guys. Future Hall of Famer Earl Siebert, Mush March, and Bill Thoms provided the veteran leadership on the squad. There were also many players in their first few pro seasons, such as Mosienko, Max and Doug Bentley, Alex Kaleta and John Mariucci, to name a few. On defence there was Bill's mentor, Joe Cooper, who served as the team's backbone.

For Bill's first NHL game, the evening in question was January 29, 1942.

It just so happened to be "Syd Howe Night," honouring the great Red Wings scorer who would go on to be inducted into the Hockey Hall of Fame in 1965.

Syd, the man of the night, played a blistering game, scoring both goals in a 2-0 Detroit victory.

Bill had played an excellent first game, and as one hockey scribe said after watching Mosie's first game, "You could almost hear the music when you watch that guy skate."

Mosienko's first appearance at Chicago Stadium was a few nights later, on February 1, against Montreal. Although Chicago lost 3-2, Bill had an assist, which marked his first NHL point.

Bill smiles his trademark smile shortly after joining the Black Hawks.
COURTESY MOSIENKO FAMILY

Bill played his first couple of games in Chicago with a lump on his ankle the size of an egg. It was the result of a collision in his final match down in Providence. It bothered him a little bit but wasn't nearly enough to keep him from making his big-league debut.

When Billy first arrived in Chicago, he didn't move immediately into the historic Guyon Hotel, where all his teammate idols lived. It wasn't diffidence; it was thrift. He couldn't afford what the others could, at least not yet. So he rented a room at a place around the corner.

He still hung around his teammates, especially his idol Joe Cooper, who referred to Mosie around the team as "my boy." To get Bill involved with the rest of the guys, Cooper taught him how to play the Black Hawks' card games while on the train or in their hotel rooms. Playing cards soon became a career-long hobby for Bill to pass the time and bond with his teammates.

In Bill's fifth NHL game on February 8 against the New York Rangers, he had his "Welcome to the big leagues" moment. Late in the first period, Bill scored his first NHL goal on Sugar Jim Henry. A few seconds later, he scored another. Two goals in twenty seconds—was this an omen of what was to come?

The Rangers ended up rallying to win the game 4-3, but all the talk afterwards was about Chicago's new star. Coach Thompson told reporters, "Billy shoots as hard as Art Wiebe—a real board-breaker. His speed is the greatest in the league, and his skating takes your breath away. He can stop, start, swing, and turn like lightning, but it's that hard, sharp shot that is driving the defensemen crazy."

Bill's old family friend from the North End, Alex Shibicky, was skating left wing for the Rangers that night.

"Not bad, kid," Shibicky told Mosienko after the game. "You're here to stay now, I think."

Basically, for the first week in Chicago, Bill appeared on the tail end of the lineup and still managed to pick up a couple of assists despite the limited ice time. When Thompson put Bob Carse, Red Hamill, and Bill on one line before the game against New York, the goals started coming.

It's quite the difference a couple of games can make. Before he started his first game in Chicago, manager Paul Thompson had told reporters, "Mosienko will go back to the Amerks as soon as Doug Bentley recovers from his injury."

But Thompson never sent Billy back down that season: "From now on, we will carry sixteen players on our squad. This same arrangement will probably hold true through the Stanley Cup playoffs too."

The team started carrying sixteen skaters solely because of Mosienko. The one extra player watched the games from the stands and entered when there were injuries or illness. The "odd man" served to keep every one of the players, old or young, on their toes, for there was always the danger that the sitting-out process would become permanent, with a possible trip to the Kansas City farm looming.

Mosienko came onto the team and was not only the hottest player in Chicago but in the entire league, too. The Chicago newspapers were quick to talk to Bill and give readers all the info about their new player. The *Chicago Daily News* wrote, "Bill never loses sight of the fact that for his family he is the main provider, and he means to provide more and more. And girls, who are not shy about meeting hockey players, don't get between Billy and the nets. There will always be girls, and goals have to be got now."

On February 12, Bill scored two goals and two assists as the Black Hawks defeated Detroit 4-2. He could have had three more goals had it not been for some brilliant saves by Red Wings goalie Johnny Mowers. Mosienko came within an eyelash of performing the hat trick. With only seconds remaining to play, he made a clean breakaway and had only Mowers in front of him. As the *Chicago Tribune* reported, "The youngster smartly drew the latter out of position and had him cleanly beaten, but his shot hit the post."

After this game—Bill's seventh—it was made official: he was going to permanently stay in Chicago. Thompson said, "Mosienko is positively a fixture and will hold down one of the right-wing berths as long as he's able to get into a uniform."

Through those first seven games, Mosienko had netted four goals and five assists for nine points. Not a bad start to the young man's NHL career by any standards. Coach Thompson remarked that, "Bill easily could have had a half-dozen more goals to his credit too, with any kind of luck, for he's been robbed of at least that number by some clever work on the part of the opposing goalies."

Billy became a sponge when he entered the NHL, trying to soak up as much knowledge as he could. During games, he was always looking up to coach Paul Thompson on the bench for tips on where to position himself on the ice and weaknesses for opposing goalies.

An interesting anecdote is that Bill was ahead of his time regarding protection on the ice. He was one of the first NHL players to wear a helmet on the ice. He did so at the urging of his mother and sister, who didn't want to see him get hurt while playing at the pro level.

When he came to the NHL, Mosie was told that he would be called a coward if he continued wearing a helmet. But he didn't care. He was fine with letting people say what they wanted to say.

"My mother and sister think I ought to wear it. They're afraid I'll get hurt, skating the way I do, headfirst and body low. If I'd crack my head, it would hurt them more than me."

Billy wasn't afraid of anyone, no matter how big and tough they were. He also knew that he had protection from his teammates if it was needed.

Bill initially wore a helmet when he joined the pro ranks at the suggestion of this mother. COURTESY MOSIENKO FAMILY

"Oh, I feel all right up here," Bill told the *Chicago Daily News*. "There's always Cooper or Siebert or Wiebe or Mariucci saying, 'Go on in there. We'll take care of you.' Even when I was with Providence, there were big defensemen to back me up. I don't take much of a beating because of my size. I never need to take a body check if I keep my head. And that's what I have to do or get laid up. I can duck 'em. I don't want my brains mixed up. I'm pretty light. I start a game at 154 pounds and come off the ice weighing 148, so I'm always losing six pounds a game."

Kansas City's player-coach Johnny Gottselig checked out one of the Hawks games when they were in town and marvelled at the courage and determination that kept his young prodigy focused on playing a skill game instead of getting involved in the rough stuff.

"He's the real deal, isn't he?" Gottselig smiled at Thompson after the game.

"It sure looks that way," Thompson agreed. "You brought me a gem with this one."

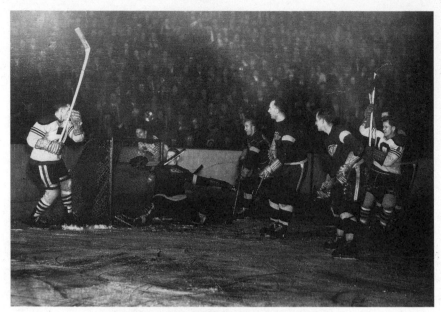

Mosie (#10) beating the Detroit Red Wings netminder
Connie Dion for a goal.   MOSIENKO FAMILY

On February 12, Bill had another big night when he scored two goals and two assists in a 4-2 win over the Detroit Red Wings.

Mosienko had his first setback on February 15 during the second period of a contest with the Boston Bruins. He was the victim of a hard board check by Boston's Jack Shewchuk and had to be carried off the ice after lying motionless for a couple of minutes. The check resulted in a badly wrenched right ankle, which kept him out of action for seven games. The sidelining injury was the first of many to come in Bill's long career.

Bill went right away for an x-ray on his ankle, and for the next few days, he underwent heat treatments at Garfield Park Hospital, which was just a few blocks from Chicago Stadium. The *Chicago Daily News* wrote,

> Billy appears to be raising a mustache, but denies that—at least when the pretty nurse brings him his lunch.
>
> Art Wiebe and Cully Dahlstrom dropped in daily to visit their teammate and check out his right leg. It was golden-hued almost

to the knee with several black bruises around the ankle. The whole leg was greatly swollen, and Bill told his pals it hurts plenty.

"I just tried to stand on it," Bill grins, "and it isn't ready yet."

"You've got a real gold brick there," says Dahlstrom as he inspects the injury with a professional eye. "You'll probably miss the next Sunday game here, and then maybe you'll be ready. Wish I had some of those bruises to make my knee look good. The darn thing isn't right yet, but outwardly it looks all right."

"Pretty sore?" inquires Wiebe.

"If I hadn't got my skate caught in the boards, it wouldn't have been so bad," explains Billy. "I just about got away from Shewchuk, and then the skate tip caught in the boards as I fell down lengthwise. I thought: 'There goes my leg. It's broken sure.'"

"You laid there awful still and quiet," interjects Wiebe.

"Oh, I wasn't out," reassures Billy, "but I thought my leg was a goner, and I groaned. I wasn't moving until I had to."

"You were pretty sick, weren't you?" Wiebe solicits.

Billy just grins at that. "Gee, I hope I get back in soon," he says.

"Oh, it isn't so bad up there in the organ loft," Dahlstrom soothes. "You can't make any mistakes up there."

Wiebe threw in, "but you can see a lot, and you can hear the fans pouring it on! What they say!"

Art and Cully are going skating, and from the hospital window, they can see a park employee spraying the ice.

"Getting it ready for us, eh Art?" says Cully. "S'long. Let us know if you want anything."

A nurse brings in Billy's meal, and he really ties into it.

"I'm gonna lose weight if I don't," he explains. "I take heat twenty minutes, then rest twenty minutes. And, boy, do I sweat. They have to change the sheets four or five times a day. They're really cooking me."

"But it isn't bad. Only I wish I was playing. Tough one last night, wasn't it? (He referred to the loss last game in Detroit.) Those babies really fly at home. But we'll get going again."

The ever-resilient Mosienko started skating again after only two days. He told the paper, "It doesn't feel so bad anymore, but I don't have much push in the leg."

He returned to action on March 8 for a contest against the Brooklyn Americans. The injury didn't slow down Mosienko's scoring at all and he picked up right where he left off, scoring a goal and an assist in a 6-1 blowout win. His linemates Bob Carse and Red Hamill greatly welcomed Billy's return as their point totals had dropped in his absence.

The *Chicago Daily News* wrote, "Little Billy Mosienko, back for his first game since his ankle was hurt, was a hornet all night, but he didn't score until the third frame when he beat Rayner at 1:25."

The Black Hawks were going through plenty of injury problems late in the season but would qualify for the playoffs despite losing nine of their last eleven games. They finished with a 22-23-3 record, which put them fourth in the league and a date in the first round of the 1942 playoffs with the Boston Bruins.

"We will go into the playoffs, I hope, with ten forwards and four defensemen, but we still are not 100% able at four positions," said Chicago coach Paul Thompson. "Joe Cooper's broken rib is still wrapped up in a harness. Doug Bentley's trick knee and that twisted arm of Art Wiebe's are not right yet, and Bill Mosienko's ankle is not in top shape. We had two really bad breaks in the cases of Mosienko and Cully Dahlstrom. Of course, Cully is lost for the season and will need a knee operation if he's ever going to play hockey again. Both he and Billy were going like houses afire when they were hurt. The biggest consolation to me is the return of Earl Siebert. He's our key man."

Mosienko finished his regular season with 14 points in 12 games with Chicago. He was hoping to score some big goals in the playoffs for his new big-league team.

For the best-of-three first-round matchup, it was an all-Eveleth, Minnesota battle in net as Chicago's Sam LoPresti went up against Boston's Frank Brimsek. In Game 1 at Chicago Stadium, the Hawks battled hard but fell 2-1 in overtime.

In Boston for Game 2, the Hawks chances were discounted sharply when a sinus attack put big Earl Siebert, their star defenceman, out of action. Despite that, they were superior most of the game. Bill opened the scoring in the fourth minute of the second period by backhanding in a puck after taking Bob Carse's well-aimed pass at the edge of the crease. Mosie's marker served as the game-winner as the Black Hawks won 4-0 to force a third and decisive game.

Game 3 was also played at Boston Garden. Telegrams from the Windy City wishing the team good luck were posted all around the club's dressing room. However, right from the get-go, Boston had a firm grasp of the game, going up 3-1 by the second period. The Hawks clawed their way back in it and got to 3-2 on a goal by Mosienko, but that was as close as they would get. Boston's Frank Brimsek stood tall in goal and held the Hawks snipers at bay to win 3-2, eliminating the Chicago Black Hawks from Stanley Cup contention.

Bill's NHL contract for that 1941-42 season was worth $3,000 with the Black Hawks. That was good money for a twenty-year-old back then. Because he was called up late in the season, he only made $1,119.50 of that. He also earned around $700 from playing in Kansas City earlier that year. Bill hoped that the money would do his family good back home.

As Mosienko had done the previous year when the season ended, he quickly packed up his belongings and earnings from Chicago and hopped on a train back to Winnipeg for the summer.

With World War II reaching crucial stages in 1942, Bill got a job working at a Winnipeg defence plant over the summer. He soon realized that it was going to be challenging to get across the border in the fall and play with the Hawks for the upcoming 1942-43 season.

To their credit, the Black Hawks were hard at work over the summer months, filling out various special exemption forms for Mosienko. However, they were not successful.

Chicago held its training camp in Hibbing, Minnesota, in late October. Mosienko and fellow Winnipegger George "Wingy" Johnston received word during camp from Canadian authorities that they would not be allowed to cross the border and play hockey in the United States that season because of wartime travel restrictions. These restrictions were partially in place to provide people from leaving the country to avoid having to join armed services.

It was a big blow for Bill as he was really hoping to play his first full season in Chicago. It was also tough on the Black Hawks losing a couple of key players that they thought would be able to play. But at the end of the day, it was World War II, and players were dropping like flies from NHL teams enlisting into various armies.

Bummed that he wasn't going to be able to play for Chicago that season, Bill walked into an Army enrollment center in Winnipeg in November, a few days after his twenty-first birthday, and attempted to enlist.

Bill was examined by a doctor and quickly determined to be "Category 'F' Permanently Unfit," according to his Certificate of Medical Unfitness for Enrollment. The form doesn't give a reason for Bill being "unfit" for the army. All it says is, "Identification Marks: scar inner right ankle, scar left cheekbone."

There are a couple of theories, however, for Bill being deemed Category "F."

First, Bill had bad asthma when he was young, and it carried into his hockey career. He carried a contraption with him in the trunk of his car called a "Pneumostat" that served as a portable inhaler in those days.

He also had high insteps, which always made it difficult to get skates to comfortably fit his feet. No skate would fit him properly, so he had custom skates made for himself. These custom skates would be two sizes too small for his foot, so it felt like his skates were a part of his foot, which gave him more control on the ice.

Also, his smaller size perhaps had something to do with it. His measurements on the form had him listed at 5'5", 151 lbs, which is a little smaller than the Chicago Black Hawks had him listed at the season prior. However, what's most likely is that Bill was a prominent hockey player and that someone with influence prevented him from joining the army so he could attempt at rejoining the Black Hawks.

Yet, getting across the border again would prove to be very difficult for Bill while a war was going on. Bill had medical rejections from all three

Canadian armed services and showed them to border officials, but they wouldn't budge. He simply wasn't going to be able to cross the border that season. Still, Chicago held out hope that Bill could play some games for them when the team was in Montreal or Toronto.

With the NHL not a possibility, Bill began to look at other options to get some hockey games in that winter. One option was staying home and playing some senior hockey in Winnipeg. Another was going to Quebec City to play in the senior ranks with the Morton Aces.

Future Montreal Canadiens star Billy Reay had given Bill an open invitation during the summer to come join him in Quebec if things didn't work out crossing the border.

A *Winnipeg Tribune* article soon noted that:

> The Morton Aces (Quebec City) of the Quebec Senior Hockey League will have quite a Manitoba flavour this season. Billy Reay has been signed as playing coach, whole other players with the team who are well known throughout this province are Butch Staham, Eddie Bruneteau, Lude Check, Bill Robinson, and Bill Mosienko.
>
> Billy Reay helped Jimmy Morton build the Quebec Aces. He put in a bid for Bill Mosienko, who was running into difficulty with the Selective Service. Mosienko couldn't cross the border to play for the Black Hawks.

Mosienko decided to go to Quebec City in the new year and take a war production job at the Morton shipbuilding plant. He helped construct corvettes and frigates for the Royal and Royal Canadian Navies as part of the convoy escort construction programmes.

Jimmy Morton, the business manager of the Morton Aces, announced on January 28, 1943, that Mosienko had finally arrived in Quebec City to join the Aces. The following day, Bill was presented to a crowd of 1500 spectators that welcomed him with open arms to their city.

Bill slotted in nicely on the Aces with some familiar faces from his hometown as he skated on the team's top line with Billy Reay and Eddie Bruneteau. In eight regular season games with the Aces, Bill scored eight points.

Bill spent part of the 1942-43 season with the Morton Aces in
Quebec when war restrictions prevented him from crossing the
US border to play with Chicago. COURTESY MOSIENKO FAMILY

Hawks coach Paul Thompson arranged to have Mosienko report in
Toronto the morning of the game on February 27, 1943. He came on a
one-game agreement and then would be returned to the Quebec Aces
the following day.

The night before, he had played for Quebec against the Army team
and lost 2-1.

"Good luck, Bill," said Jimmy Morton, and the Acemen joined in a
well-wishing chorus.

Mosienko picked out his two favourite sticks, two pairs of skates,
waved his hand, and departed.

Bill would be playing for Chicago the next day, hop the train, and
play for the Aces the following night, which put him at three games
in three days. But that was nothing for the young Billy, who was full
of energy.

Bill walked into Maple Leaf Gardens on the evening in question and
played in an NHL game that he didn't think he'd be playing that season.

He must have brought new life into the team as Chicago dominated all game. Bill was able to score after catching a pass from Bill Thoms at the blueline. He then did some nifty stickhandling before blasting the puck past Leafs netminder Turk Broda. Chicago won 4-1.

Bill then scored the next night in Quebec as well in a 4-2 victory over the Montreal Army. Not a bad weekend for the kid.

A few weeks later, on March 13, Bill met up with Chicago in Montreal to play the Canadiens. The game was a goal-fest that ended in a 6-6 tie. Bill had a goal in the second period.

He rejoined the Aces the next day as they were now playing in the Quebec league playoffs. However, Bill and the Aces lost to the Montreal Army team in the Quebec Senior League quarterfinals.

In the end, Mosienko scored twelve points in the twelve games he played in with the Aces (eight regular season and four playoff games). He also scored two goals in two games for Chicago.

Mosienko would stay in Quebec City for about a month after the season ended as he continued his job at the Morton shipbuilding plant. He then returned home to Winnipeg by train in May and picked up his old job at the defence plant for the summer.

One mystery that I was unable to solve was that Mosienko was given a Quebec Aces ring during his time there. The Aces had won the Quebec championship the year prior to Bill playing there and the two years after he was there, so maybe a ring was just given to him. Or perhaps as a thank you gift/souvenir to him playing in Quebec.

"I'm not sure how he got it, but dad sure wore it out, so he must have been very proud of receiving it," said Billy's son Brian Mosienko.

Over the offseason, the Canadian Manpower Board finally granted Bill permission to play with the Black Hawks while World War II was ongoing. He was excited to really show the NHL what he could do with a full season and not just a handful of games.

What Bill and just about everyone else didn't know was that a significant rule change was coming when the teams began play for the 1943-44 NHL season.

In the summer of 1943, the NHL was facing many challenges. Not only was there a depletion in the player ranks due to the war, but the game was also evolving from its early days, and the rulebook needed to be revised.

Frank Boucher, a future Hall of Fame player with the Rangers and current coach of the team, volunteered to rewrite the NHL rulebook during the summer of 1943 after consulting about it with NHL president Red Dutton.

In Boucher's memoirs, *When the Rangers Were Young,* he wrote that the NHL rulebook "was close to incomprehensible. The book had no index, there were repetitions and contradictions, and there were even different penalties for the same rule infraction."

Boucher worked toward consistency, including consistency between the professional and amateur versions of the game. The NHL liked what Boucher had done and adopted his new version of the rulebook, word for word, in the fall of 1943.

One new rule really stood out—the implementation of the redline.

In the two seasons before the fall of 1943, defencemen began moving beyond their own blueline to break up passing plays by opposing forwards. Before that, defencemen never went farther than about halfway between their goal and the blueline.

This resulted in the birth of "dump-and-chase hockey," as forwards would shoot the puck past the defencemen and then skate by them to get it. It wasn't long before the defencemen on the attacking team joined in, and soon all five players were inside the defending team's blueline, causing "endless jamming sessions in front of the net." The reason was that a forward pass was not allowed from one zone to the net, so a defenceman could not pass the puck up to a forward beyond his own blueline to get it out of his own end. It had to be carried over the blueline. Thus, one team would be stuck in its own end for long periods of time, and when the puck was finally cleared, the same thing would happen at the other end of the ice.

Boucher discussed this problem with his peers, Art Ross and Hap Day, and one solution they considered was to allow a forward pass as far as the opposite blueline. But this was considered too radical, and Boucher came up with the red line at centre as a compromise.

"If one blueline's too near and the other's too far, what about halfway in between?" Boucher suggested. "We can put a line at centre ice, and we'll paint it red to avoid confusion."

The immediate result was that breakaway passes became an offensive specialty, and goal-scoring soared.

Boucher wrote that "this was a development that intrigued the fans but horrified a lot of traditionalists who claimed the red line was making a mockery of defence, if not destroying the whole structure of the game."

Eventually, defences adjusted, and the breakaways faded. But the game regained its up-and-down flow, which was Boucher's intent all along.

"This rule is considered to mark the beginning of the modern era in the NHL," according to the NHL's *Guide and Record Book.* In 2005, sixty-two years later, the two-line pass would be legalized for similar reasons.

This rule change was instrumental in increasing goals and increasing players' point totals. Bill Mosienko, who had the top breakaway speed in the league, thrived under these new rules. And his upcoming point totals would prove that.

In October, Bill boarded a train from Winnipeg to Minneapolis for the Black Hawks training camp. A bit of a change was that he decided to leave his hockey helmet behind in Winnipeg. He was going to play this season helmetless, which made his mother very nervous!

The Hawks bought Clint Smith from the Rangers at the start of training camp. A twenty-nine-year-old centreman who was exempt from military service, Smith was a reliable scorer who would replace Max Bentley as the team's top centreman. Max had enlisted in the Army and would be missing the entire season.

They also signed a rookie netminder named Hec Highton. Goalies were hard to come by during the war as many served in the armed forces, like Johnny Mowers of Detroit and Boston's Mr. Zero, Frank Brimsek.

A familiar face from Kansas City, Johnny Gottselig, was now back in Chicago and playing his final NHL season.

During training camp in Minneapolis, coach Paul Thompson put

Doug Bentley, Bill Thoms, and Mosienko on the top line together. "They really flew in workouts," remarked Thompson after a practice. "When Minneapolis sports fans attend the Hawks intra-squad exhibition here next Wednesday, they will see the fastest line in the NHL."

Thompson wasn't just trying to sell tickets; he was being honest. Reporters noted the Bentley-Thoms-Mosienko line as being the fastest unit since the days of Joe Primeau, Busher Jackson, and Charlie Conacher in Toronto.

From Minneapolis, the Hawks came back to Chicago for the season opener. The season began fine, and things were looking great after the team's first seven games. Unfortunately, Bill Thoms was having deep stomach pain one night after a game and needed an operation for his ulcers. He would go on to miss the rest of the season. In his place, Clint Smith stepped in and provided great chemistry on a line with the two youngsters Bentley and Mosienko.

With that, there was no doubt that Chicago was scoring at a great pace when the season started, but they also had sub-par goaltending from Hec Highton and were losing games because of him. It was clear early in the year that a change needed to be made. Hawks president and general manager Bill Tobin decided to bring back goaltender Mike Karakas, who had been demoted to the minors in 1939-40 for his lacklustre play. Karakas proved to be just what the Hawks needed and gave the team a chance to win every night. He was the main reason that Chicago was able to squeak into the final playoff spot.

The line of Doug Bentley, Clint Smith, and Bill Mosienko that season established an NHL scoring record of 219 points for the line, eclipsing the mark of 183 points in 44 games set by Cooney Weiland, Dit Clapper and Dutch Gainor of Boston in 1929-30. The new record was then broken the following year by one point by the Toe Blake, Elmer Lach, and Maurice Richard line.

Mosienko scored at a prolific rate all year long in his first full NHL season. He instantly became a superstar and was well-known throughout the league by the time the year concluded. Bill led the NHL scoring race early in the year into December and would ultimately finish with 70 points in 50 games, which was good for eighth in the league.

Mosienko with linemates Clint Smith and Doug Bentley
(circa 1943-44) COURTESY MOSIENKO FAMILY

In the league semi-finals, Chicago met the Detroit Red Wings. The Wings finished second in the league with 58 points, while Chicago finished fourth with 49 points. The teams split the year's ten-game regular season series. The other semi-final featured first-place Montreal against third-place Toronto.

Chicago came into Detroit and rallied to win Game 1 at Olympia Stadium 2-1. Mosienko and Doug Bentley scored goals thirty seconds apart in the third period to give Chicago the win. Detroit then bounced back to win the next game 4-1.

The series shifted to Chicago Stadium for Game 3, and the Hawks shut out Detroit 2-0. Bill's mentor Joe Cooper had the game-winning goal. After the game, coach Paul Thompson predicted his club would defeat Detroit in six games the way things were going.

Prior to the start of Game 4, Clint Smith's wife back in Vancouver had a baby girl. It must have motivated him as the Chicago Stadium crowd of 17,533 was treated to a goal-fest for the home side. Smith exploded for two goals and an assist, Doug Bentley had a hat-trick and two assists, and Bill Mosienko had one goal and one assist. The Hawks trounced the Red Wings 7-1 and were one win away from the Stanley Cup final.

Unfortunately, Mosienko and veteran Mush March both suffered injuries during the game and didn't play in Game 5. Mosienko had a separated right shoulder, and March had torn ligaments in his right knee. The team doctor said that March would be out for the rest of the playoffs, while Mosie might only miss the one game.

"This had to happen just when we had 'em down," Paul Thompson said mournfully. "Our misfortune will give the Red Wings a mental lift. It'll be a fight now to get by them even if we do have three games to get that one victory."

And fight they did.

In Game 5, the Hawks rallied to eliminate. For the second straight game, Doug Bentley scored a hat-trick. Back-to-back hat-tricks in the Stanley Cup playoffs are an extreme rarity and has only happened a few times in the league's history.

Throughout the series, various newspapers reported that Detroit was simply unable to cope with the blinding speed of Chicago's number one line of Doug Bentley, Bill Mosienko and Clint Smith.

Detroit Red Wings manager Jack Adams was quoted in the *Montreal Gazette* after the series as being very impressed by the Bentley, Smith, Mosienko line: "The best in hockey today, by far, and probably as good as the majority we've seen in 10 years."

"Bentley and Mosienko can skate like heck, and whether they make Smith look good or not, he sets up some great plays for them and can take the 'bit' himself when he has to," said Jack Adams. "But that still goes for Karakas. They never replaced him, not even with LoPresti or Goodman or anybody else. When the Hawks last won a Stanley Cup, who was in the nets? Karakas, with a broken toe and everything else."

Their hard work paid off: the game ended in a 5-2 win for the Hawks, who would advance to the Cup final. Meeting Chicago in the finals would be the top team in the NHL that year, the Montreal Canadiens.

The Habs had just knocked off Toronto in five games, with Game 5 ending 11-0 in Montreal's favour.

Mosienko celebrated with his team after the game and then packed his luggage and departed for Montreal with the rest of his teammates. A separated shoulder wasn't going to stop him from a chance at winning the Stanley Cup. He was going to play and give it his all.

Going into the final, Thompson said, "All I can say right now is we'll give 'em a helluva battle."

Then, with a wide grin, Thompson shook his head slowly and told reporters, "I still can't figure what happened to that Red Wings team. I can't understand it. Just look at the players they have like Hollett, Simon, Liscombe, Brown, Carveth, Howe, Grosso, Armstrong. They don't come much better, and yet they folded."

President Bill Tobin told the *Montreal Gazette* "Montreal will be tough. We'll be at a disadvantage. They have a wider sheet of ice there, and naturally will play the corners better than we will. But the way we played in our last three games, you can't tell what is liable to happen."

The Canadiens had been the top team in the NHL all season long, taking first place by nearly thirty points. In the ten games that the Canadiens and Hawks played in the regular season, Montreal won eight and tied the other two. It was going to be an uphill battle for Mosienko and company.

Still, the team's spirits were high as they travelled to Montreal by train for Game 1.

"Can you believe we're going to be playing for the Cup?" boasted Joe Cooper.

Cooper, Mike Karakas, Doug Bentley, Clint Smith, Cliff Purpur, and Mosienko were all huddled around a table. The boys had their usual card game on the train going for a couple of bucks and bragging rights.

"We just need four more wins," said Doug Bentley. "I know it's against Montreal, but I think we can take them. Nobody beats us ten times in a row!"

"I think we can," said Cooper. "That is if Iron Mike (Karakas) can bring some of that magic he had in 1938 the last time Chicago won this thing."

Bill greatly enjoyed playing cards with his Chicago teammates (Left-to-right: Bill Thoms, Bob Carse, Bill, Leo Miller, Joe Cooper, Bill Carse). COURTESY MOSIENKO FAMILY

Karakas chuckled. "I feel like I'm twenty-five years old again, so you never know!" he said.

"I didn't know if I would ever get back to the finals again," said Cooper. "When (Alex) Shibicky and I lost the 1937 final to Detroit, it really stung for a long time losing in the final game like that after getting so close."

Cooper looked at Bill and Doug and said, "What I'm saying is don't take these moments for granted because who knows if you'll ever get back there after this. Let's be great together and win because I sure as hell aren't getting any younger."

Mosienko just smiled. "I'm in the moment, Coop," he told his mentor.

"Yeah, yeah, you're in the moment all right, Billy," said Clint Smith. "Just lay down your cards already!"

"Full house!" Bill declared as he showed his pocket kings.

The boys all had a laugh as Mosie scooped the $4 pot.

Mosienko was still recovering from his shoulder injury and definitely wasn't at a hundred percent. But he was there on the ice for puck drop in Game 1.

The Murph Chamberlain, Phil Watson, Ray Getliffe line emerged as the stars in Game 1 for Montreal as they took the game 5-1. The line backchecked, slowing up the Hawks with their heavy bumping, and bagged four of the five Canadiens goals on the night.

Most of the time, too, they were in against the top Chicago line of Smith, Bentley, Mosienko. They stopped that line cold on all but one occasion when Clint Smith scored a powerplay marker.

The Canadiens were already two up at the time and replied with another goal of their own just forty-seven seconds later. They added a few more in the third period as the Hawks defence weakened.

After the game, both teams hopped on the same train from Montreal to Chicago for the next two games of the series.

Things were relatively quiet on the Chicago side of the train. Simply put, they all needed to be better in Game 2 to have a chance at getting back in the series.

But Game 2 did not go well at all. Maurice "Rocket" Richard scored a hat-trick en route to a 3-1 win for Montreal.

The game had to be delayed almost twenty minutes after Richard's final goal at 15:33 in the third period. The Hawks argued that Clint Smith was held on the play by Elmer Lach, and therefore the score should not count. Referee Bill Chadwick didn't see it that way, and the partisan Chicago crowd reacted by showering the ice with playing cards and newspapers, amongst other things. Play was finally resumed when veteran Hawk Johnny Gottselig appealed to the fans to cease their behaviour.

After the game, NHL president Red Dutton issued a stern warning to the Chicago fans that the Black Hawks match would immediately be forfeited if the crowd behaved like that next game.

Referring to the barrage of newspapers, confetti, programs, coins, and other articles—including a pearl-handled jackknife and a woman's compact—Dutton said he had been empowered by the league board of governors "to forfeit any future game to the visiting club if a repetition of this kind occurs in any of the forthcoming games."

He added: "I definitely intend to exercise my authority."

The Chicago fans were to be on their best behaviour two nights later when the Hawks and Canadiens met once again at Chicago Stadium for Game 3.

A crowd of 17,694 jammed the Stadium for a very closely contested battle that saw a great goaltending duel between Mike Karakas and Bill Durnan. Bill Durnan was a brick wall in Montreal's goal, especially when turning away shots from the always dangerous Bentley, Smith, Mosienko line, yet Chicago led 2-1 in the third period. They then gave up two quick goals to lose 3-2. The winning marker came at 6:42 of the final period when Phil Watson took a pass from Ray Getliffe and fired the puck over Mike Karakas from ten feet out after the latter had fallen to the ice.

Montreal now had a 3-0 stranglehold on the series and would be returning to Montreal to try and win the Stanley Cup at home.

When the puck dropped for Game 4, Chicago was ready to give it their all and were determined not to get swept. They came out firing and, for once, controlled the game.

George Allen opened the scoring for Hawks after five minutes of play. The Canadiens had just survived a slashing penalty to Mike McMahon, and the teams were at full strength when Cully Dahlstrom fed Allen a pass from a scramble. Allen made no mistake on a short, hard drive to make it 1-0.

Elmer Lach tied it up three minutes later, with a golfed shot from fifteen feet out that didn't leave the ice as it passed Mike Karakas. Lach was in front of the net when Toe Blake's hard pass came out to him from the side. He knocked it down and golfed it into the net all in one motion.

In the second period, the Hawks blitzed the Habs for three goals. The three Chicago goals came in less than three minutes, all of them on powerplays while the Canadiens were shorthanded through successive penalties to Toe Blake and Phil Watson. Johnny Harms, George Allen and Doug Bentley had the goals for Chicago.

With his team down 4-1 at the second intermission, Montreal coach Dick Irvin shifted his lines around to try and give his team a boost.

Chicago seemed to tighten up and get real defensive in the final frame.

Elmer Lach popped one in at the midway point of the period to make it 4-2. Then, Maurice Richard scored twice in a minute to make it 4-4.

Coach Thompson was in dismay on the Hawks bench. The Hawks managed to hold on and bring the game to overtime, but they looked defeated.

In the overtime, Bill Durnan stopped the first penalty shot ever in the Stanley Cup finals, awarded to Virgil Johnson.

Toe Blake scored the Stanley Cup-winning goal just nine minutes into the first overtime to give the Canadiens a thrilling 5-4 come-from-behind win. It was the Canadiens' first Stanley Cup since 1931 when they also beat the Black Hawks.

After the Black Hawks and Canadiens shook hands, Bill and his teammates quietly departed to the dressing room. NHL president Red Dutton then stepped onto the ice to present the Stanley Cup to Habs captain Toe Blake.

The Hawks were simply outmatched in the series by a superior team. Maurice "Rocket" Richard made his Stanley Cup debut with a five-goal performance in the series, including a hat trick in game two. The Punch Line of Richard, Elmer Lach and Toe Blake scored ten of the Canadiens' sixteen goals.

Bill finished with four points in eight games during the playoffs. He only registered one assist in the finals, which is a good indication that his shoulder must have been troubling him throughout the series.

All in all, however, it was a fantastic season for Bill. He had established himself as a top-scoring NHL forward and had his sights on big things in the league.

Coming into the 1944-45 campaign, things were looking bright for the Windy City club. They were coming off an appearance in the Stanley Cup finals and had high hopes of going one step further this season.

However, a significant blow came to the team before the training camp even commenced. Due to the National War Labour Board restrictions on crossing the Canada-US border, the Black Hawks would lose their top scorer Doug Bentley for the year, while Doug's brother Max would miss his second straight season due to World War II. Hawks winger George Allen also had to miss the season for the same reason as Doug.

A telegram from Paul Thompson came to Chicago's scout in Winnipeg and former NHL superstar, Baldy Northcott, at his sporting goods store. It said, "Will be in Winnipeg Sunday night. Will arrive on first section of Canadian Pacific and am making direct connection to St. Paul. Important I see Cooper and Mosienko so please have them up on the tracks as I only have few minutes. Regards Paul Thompson." It was dated September 22, 1944, only a few weeks from when Cooper and Mosie would be heading to training camp.

What Thompson needed to talk with Mosienko and Cooper about is unknown, but it may have had to do with figuring out how Bill was going to be able to play in Chicago in the upcoming season.

Like his pal Doug Bentley, Bill knew that he would have trouble getting across the border. Again, the Hawks fought for him with the immigration officials and at the start of the club's training camp, Bill was sent from Winnipeg to Windsor, Ontario, by train as he awaited his new passport.

After a two week wait, Mosienko telegraphed Thompson that his passport had been given to him by Canadian officials. Bill finally arrived in Hibbing after the first couple weeks of the Hawks training camp.

At ninety-four years of age, Tony Dorn of Thief River Falls, Minnesota, is the only person alive today who was at the Black Hawks training camp in the fall of 1944. He was invited to camp as a seventeen-year-old and looked to make the most of his time with the pros.

After the camp, Dorn was signed by the team and played the winter of 1944-45 in the East Coast League. In doing so, Tony became the first hockey player from Thief River Falls ever to be signed to a professional contract.

Today, Dorn still lives in Thief River Falls. We had a lengthy chat on the phone as he was quite excited to relive his time at an NHL camp that was over seventy-five years ago.

Here is Tony giving his recollections of his time with Bill and the Black Hawks in Hibbing:

> In those days, Chicago was the team of the Midwest as they usually got the first crack at players from Minnesota, which was the only hotbed of hockey in the United States at the time.
>
> In 1937, in the years leading up to World War II, the Black Hawks owner tried to ice an All-American team. Minnesota was

pretty strong on the range with a lot of good players, so some of them got to join the team sometimes and got chances they usually wouldn't have gotten. Then the war came along, and everyone went their different directions, getting listed and drafted and so on. So that All-American team plan was stymied.

But this is why Chicago held their training camps in Hibbing, Minnesota, all those years.

My hometown of Thief River Falls had a team in the States-Dominion League in the early 1940s, so I was coached quite well by those older guys, and with that, I was big for my age. How the Hawks got a hold of me, I have no idea. All I know is I got a letter in the middle of summer inviting me to Hibbing for camp and to bring my own skates.

When I came to Hibbing on a Sunday afternoon, I saw a sign in the back of the lobby at the Hibbing Memorial Arena that said "Black Hawks," so I walked back there, all naïve to everything. The coach, Paul Thompson, quickly saw me and introduced me to the players, but the names really meant nothing because I was only seventeen. We didn't have television or anything, so there were no names that I was really supposed to know. However, during camp, I got to know who they were and enjoyed being around them a great deal.

I remember Mosienko came late to training camp that year. His pal Joe Cooper was there, and I was Joe's roommate during camp. Cooper was a fun guy that smoked a lot of cigars. I thought he was very generous to me. After all, I was just a kid at seventeen, and I was awestruck by being at camp, and he was patient with me, which was a big help. He had told me that he had been through Thief River Falls before as he was from Winnipeg and was aware of our hockey program.

When Bill finally arrived at camp, I was amazed at how great he was at hockey. Without a doubt, Bill was the fastest skater on the team and probably the entire league. I remember him being a very happy-go-lucky type of guy.

There were a lot of great guys on the team. After the team's practices were done for the day, the Black Hawks players wanted to sneak out during camp to go up to the town of Chisholm, where the bars were and hang out.

We all stayed at the Androy Hotel in Hibbing. All the old hotels in that time had a fire escape at the back that you would have to pull down. So the guy on the second floor would go out on his landing and push it down. Our room was close to the spot where I could go out and push the fire escape down to the ground level, so my job would be to watch for when they would come back to sneak them back in.

The locals had cars, so everybody on the team had a chance to go while rookies like myself stayed behind. I remember helping guys like Cooper and Mosienko get back in through the fire escape late at night.

There were a few rookies at camp, myself included, and I skated well enough to make all the cuts and still be there into the fourth week. But I knew at that time that there was no place for me on the team.

Paul Thompson and Bill Tobin took me into their office and said, "We know you're planning on going into the service in a year, but we'd be happy to have you continue on with us and play this season in the Eastern League if that's alright. For now, go home and get some warm clothes, and we'll send you a ticket to New York.

Dorn spent that 1944-45 season in the Eastern League with the New York Rovers, Washington Lions and Philadelphia Falcons. Staying at a hotel across from Madison Square Garden, he got to practice a lot that year with the New York Rangers. Dorn turned eighteen in March of 1945 and promptly enlisted in the Navy, ending his pro hockey career for the time being.

Now, looking back on everything, Dorn relays that, "It was a very exciting time for me in my life being a colleague of Mosienko and the rest of the Black Hawks for a few weeks. I've always been able to hold on to the fact that I competed and skated with some of the best players in the world for a spell and came out all right! It was a heck of a ride."

The record shows that Mosienko arrived in Hibbing on October 19. President Bill Tobin joined the team for an intramural exhibition game on October 23, where the group was divided into two sides. Mosienko and Dorn skated on the same team for this game.

At camp, coach Thompson said that the team had the best practicing conditions in six years and that the sessions were marked by few injuries. He looked forward to the upcoming season and believed his side was a contender.

To open the season, Bill would skate on the team's top line with Clint Smith and Pete Horeck. The club would name Smith team captain, and after the first game of the season, an 11-5 loss to the Toronto Maple Leafs, head coach Paul Thompson was replaced by former Black Hawk captain Johnny Gottselig. Thompson would stay on as the team's manager.

Chicago would start the year off poorly, to say the least. After ten games, they had a record of 1-8-1.

In their eleventh game, a Mosienko hat-trick led the way to the club's second win with a 6-5 victory over Detroit. It was the first Hawks hat trick that season. Mosienko's three goals, two of which tied the score and the last winning the game, pulled the Hawks out of last place. A crowd of 14,754 voiced strong approval of the Hawks performance.

So did manager Paul Thompson, who permitted himself a grin and gave the team a day off. "They've been working pretty hard," he said. "Three games in four days."

Even goalie Mike Karakas, who was usually quiet and reserved, was bubbling over. "That Mosienko," he grinned. "He really tore it up, didn't he?"

The Black Hawks team had a tradition of buying the player a fancy hat after they scored a hat-trick. This was Bill's third hat-trick since being in the league, which meant his third fancy hat!

Unfortunately, the losses continued piling up for Chicago. On New Year's Day, 1945, the team was in last place with a 3-16-2 record.

During the time that I was writing this book, Steve Wojciechowski was the oldest living former NHL player. Steve Wochy, as he goes by now, played fifty-four games with the Detroit Red Wings from 1944 to 1947.

He skated in the 1945 Stanley Cup final with the Red Wings, where they ultimately fell to the Toronto Maple Leafs in seven games.

At ninety-seven, Steve still lives on his own at his house in Sault Ste. Marie and still drives. He has a hard time hearing, and his hip hurts all the time, but aside from that, life is good.

"Mosienko was a hell of a good hockey player and played on a great line with those Bentley brothers. They were great," recalled Steve Wochy. "I played against Bill quite a bit that 1944-45 season, and although Chicago was a very poor team, Billy was their lone bright spot. That guy could really play and was hard to keep up with, that's for sure."

On January 2, 1945, a major trade occurred when Chicago traded their outstanding defenceman Earl Seibert and Bill's pal Fido Purpur to Detroit for Don Grosso, Cully Simon, and Byron "Butch" McDonald. After team owner Frederic McLaughlin died of heart disease a few weeks prior at the age of sixty-seven, it was just a matter of time before Bill Tobin would trade Seibert, as the two did not get along.

Don Grosso had been a high-scoring forward with Detroit, and so he was slotted in to play with Clint Smith and Mosienko on the top line. He would score fifteen points in twenty-one games with Chicago after the trade.

Things were looking so bleak that in January, coach Johnny Gottselig began scouting Eastern Canada and the United States for hockey talent. He even spoke to the press and said that Mosienko was the only player on the club's roster who could be sure of finishing the season with the Hawks. Gottselig said that Tobin was "prepared to cut loose any players except Mosienko in the interests of future campaigns."

Apparently, the players took that to heart as things turned around a bit for Chicago in February. They started winning some games and even made a push for the playoffs!

On February 21, Chicago blanked Boston 5-0. On Chicago's first goal, Mosienko went on a solo rush from his own zone to the Boston net, and it was nothing short of spectacular, noted a Boston newspaper. Bill skillfully swept around the usually brilliant Dit Clapper and then tucked it past the Bruins netminder.

A few weeks later, on March 4, Mosienko had four assists in the third period in a 6-4 win over Montreal to share an NHL record.

Sadly, it was a case of too little, too late that season for Chicago. The Hawks would struggle to score goals all season long, scoring a league low 141 while allowing 194, which ranked them fourth. The team would finish the season with a 13–30–7 record, and their thirty-three points was their lowest point total since 1938-39. They would fail to make the postseason, as they would finish three points behind the Boston Bruins for fourth place.

Mosienko led the team in scoring for the first time with 28 goals and 26 assists for 54 points in 50 games. His 54 points were also good for fifth in the league. He also had zero penalty minutes that year.

Mosienko almost took a penalty during a late-season game with Montreal. Billy dodged a body check tossed by Ray Getliffe but went spilling into the boards, nevertheless. Mosienko leaped to his skates and tore after Getliffe, but the Canadiens left winger said, "Here's what tripped you," and chipped a penny up out of the ice.

Bill's efforts were good enough for the NHL to name him a Second Team All-Star. He would have been the First Team All-Star right wing had it not been for Rocket Richard scoring 50 goals in 50 games that season.

Bill also won the Sideliners' Club Award for most popular player from a group of rabid hockey fans who sit in the highest balconies whenever the team played in Chicago Stadium. Each member was allowed to vote for the most popular Black Hawk, but it cost 25 cents to vote.

Finally, because of the way that Mosienko played and conducted himself on the ice, coupled with the fact that he didn't spend a single minute in the penalty box that season, he earned the Lady Byng Trophy as the NHL's most gentlemanly player. In doing so, he became the first Manitoban to win the award. Andy Hebenton and Butch Goring are the only other Manitobans to win it since.

The *Canadian Press* reported that:

> By an almost unanimous vote, Bill Mosienko has been awarded the Lady Byng trophy of the National Hockey league, to mark the third year in a row that Chicago Black Hawks players have

taken the trophy for best-combining sportsmanship and playing ability. Black Hawk players had the award clinched from the start, and if Mosienko hadn't taken it, the trophy would have gone to linemate Clint Smith, who wound up in second spot ahead of Detroit's durable Syd Howe. Smith took the honours last year, and Max Bentley of the Hawks was the winner the year before. The wide margin of 14 points prevented Smith from becoming the first man since Frank Boucher was in his prime to take the award three times, for Smith won it in 1938-39 when he played for Rangers, as well as last year. Boucher took the honours seven times in the eight-year period between 1927-28 and 1934-35. Mosienko wound up with 95 points out of a possible 100. Smith had 81. and Howe finished with 75. Tied for fourth was Buddy O'Connor of Canadiens and Bill Cowley of Boston with 62 points each. Polling for the trophy is conducted by the NHL, with each club nominating two sportswriters from their respective cities to vote. Each nominator picks ten players, with 10 points going to a first choice, nine to a second, eight to a third and so on.

The Lady Byng Memorial Trophy, formerly known as the Lady Byng Trophy, is presented each year to the National Hockey League player judged to have exhibited the best type of sportsmanship and gentlemanly conduct combined with a high standard of playing ability. The original trophy was donated to the league by Lady Byng of Vimy, then–viceregal consort of Canada and was first awarded in 1925.

Lady Byng and her husband, the Viscount Byng of Vimy, who commanded Canadian forces at the Battle of Vimy Ridge and who was Governor-General of Canada from 1921 to 1926, were both keen sports fans, especially of ice hockey, and they attended many Ottawa Senators games. They donated the trophy because Lady Byng appreciated gentlemanly play and good sportsmanship and wanted to encourage and reward it.

Mosienko was thrilled with the Lady Byng. "It's a big honour," he told the press. "It affirms that I'm doing something right out there as I feel I conduct myself like a hockey player should."

Early in his career, Mosienko was frequently a target of big defence-men such as Toronto's Babe Pratt, who sought to rough him up and throw him off his game and wound up taking several penalties. Mosienko, on the other hand, was rarely guilty of infractions.

"I decided I couldn't do my team any good in the penalty box," Mosienko later explained. "I never backed down, but I was small, and they got a lot of penalties trying to get me down. I had speed, though, and we had several fellas on our team like John Mariucci who used to watch out for us little guys."

Over the summer, Bill had his hands on the newspaper almost every day, thumbing through the pages as he read updates on what was going on in the war. He knew that once the war was over, his pal Max Bentley would be released from the army, and Max's brother Doug would also be allowed to play for the Black Hawks again.

On September 2, 1945, Japan surrendered on the deck of the American battleship *USS Missouri*, effectively ending World War II. With that, Max and Doug would be returning to Chicago for the 1945-46 season, and no one was more excited about that than Bill. He knew that he'd likely be paired up on a line with them with the way he'd been playing the past few seasons. However, I don't think that Bill, Max, Doug, or anyone in hockey, for that matter, would know just how well the trio would click together.

THE PONY LINE

The Black Hawks picked Regina, Saskatchewan, to be the home for their training camp in the fall of 1945. Team president Bill Tobin had arranged for a preseason training junket of western Canada in an effort to popularize his team in that area.

After being in the United States Coast Guard for the past two seasons, Johnny Mariucci returned to the team. Max Bentley, who had missed the last two seasons, was also back, and so was his brother Doug, who had missed the previous year.

Training camp was rolling along well. The Hawks swiftly dispatched their minor league Kansas City squad in a pair of exhibition games in Regina.

They then travelled to Saskatoon to play Eddie Shore's Springfield Indians in an exhibition game at Saskatoon. The trip is described in Ed Fitkin's book *Max Bentley: Hockey's Dipsy-Doodle Dandy*.

The day before the game, Max Bentley walked up to Tobin and said: "Some of my relatives and friends would like to see this game, Mr. Tobin. I'd like to get a few passes."

The Bentleys hailed from nearby Delisle and had lots of family that wanted to make the thirty-minute drive to Saskatoon for the game.

"Sure," said the unsuspecting Tobin, "how many do you need?"

"Well..." mused Max, "there's The Boss and Mom and my wife and Doug's wife and Reg and Scoop and..."

He went on and on. The flabbergasted Tobin, undoubtedly with exaggeration, said later that Max required seventy-eight passes. "I nearly

Chicago coach Johnny Gottselig giving pointers to Bill,
Max and Doug Bentley. COURTESY MOSIENKO FAMILY

swooned on the spot, but I figured I had Max stumped. I told him
everything would be fine if he shot me one duck for every pair of passes."

To Tobin's dismay, Max, without batting an eyelash, not only agreed
to the deal but the next day produced so many ducks that the Chicago
president practically lived on fowl during the rest of the training tour.

"He outsmarted me," Tobin confessed. "He got Doug, Mosie, Clint
Smith and every other player who had ever handled a gun, and they
went back into the lake areas where the ducks were so plentiful. They
just pointed their rifles, and the ducks dropped dead from fright. I had
to go through with the bargain—and I never saw so many members of
one family at a hockey game in my life!"

From Saskatchewan, the Black Hawks moved east as they met up with
the New York Rangers in Winnipeg to play a best-of-three exhibition
series at the Amphitheatre. The pair of games marked the first time that
Bill's family saw him play since he had become a star in the National

Hockey League. Bill's mother was very proud as she watched her son score five goals in the three games.

It was during these preseason tests that Johnny Gottselig, who had succeeded Paul Thompson as manager and coach of the Hawks, created the Pony Line.

"Now that Mush March has retired," Johnny told Max Bentley, "you and Doug have to fit in a new right winger, and I think we've got the answer in Bill Mosienko. He's the nearest thing to Mush I've ever seen, and two years ago, he and Doug were terrific together. The three of you ought to set the league on fire."

Max and Mosienko had played together briefly as Hawk rookies at Providence five years prior, so they were fairly familiar with each other's style. Practice sessions quickly lent credence to Gottselig's theory that Mosie would blend perfectly with the Bentleys. Though he, too, was on the small side, his dazzling speed and ability to take a pass in full flight indicated that, barring injuries, the Hawks would have one of the greatest lines in postwar hockey.

"With Doug and Mosie to pull the trigger," Gottselig told Max, "you should set a new record for assists this year."

Thus, the Pony Line was born.

Right from the beginning, Gottselig truly believed his new line could outskate anyone in the league. "We've got the most speed along with the Frenchmen," he told a Chicago newspaper. "That top line of ours (Bentleys and Mosienko) is apt to skate away from everything in the league. Understand, I'm not predicting we'll finish on top. Canadiens, Toronto, and Boston will be tough, but we'll make 'em play sixty minutes of hockey to beat us."

The iconic name was given to the line by the team's publicity director, Joe Farrell. Mosienko later recalled, "It was because of our size. We were small. And every time we'd go for the puck, we'd give it a little bounce."

Once the trio was first linked together, the chemistry between them was undeniable. Bill became like another brother to Max and Doug. In the Hawks dressing room, Max always had to sit in the middle of Bill and Doug because of a superstition.

The Pony Line in action   COURTESY MOSIENKO FAMILY

The Pony Line quickly electrified hockey fans around the circuit with their speed and dazzling passing plays. They were the key players in Johnny Gottselig's determined efforts to have the Hawks make good on the "Lightning on Ice" motto expounded by Bill Tobin.

"Chicago fans like their hockey fast, and that's what we're going to give 'em—speed to burn," Tobin declared. "The forward pass to the red line has increased the tempo of the game, and it should be great for the Bentleys and Mosie. We're going to stick to our 'Lightning on Ice' motto, and we're sure it will pay dividends."

It did, too. The fast-flying Hawks, paced by their Pony Line, shattered all previous attendance records for their home ice and proved a magnetic drawing card all around the circuit.

The largest crowd to that point that ever saw an NHL season opener or league game on a weeknight—18,727—witnessed the postwar Black Hawks outscore the New York Rangers 5-1 at Chicago Stadium. It was estimated that 5,000 fans were turned away after standing room and rafter space had been exhausted. Mosienko scored the last goal of the night at 5:32 of the final period. Eddie Wares took a long pass from the blueline, and Mosienko picked it up off the toes of goalie Sugar Jim Henry's boots and converted for goal number five.

The Hawks showed the results of their extended training camp as their short passing game was looking sharp. The outcome was in happy contrast to the opener the previous year, at which the former opening night attendance record—18,618—was set. That evening saw the Toronto Maple Leafs wallop the war-affected Chicago team 11-5.

"I hated playing against that Pony Line in Chicago," recalled Wally Stanowski, former defenceman for the Toronto Maple Leafs. "They were all small, and I hated to start against them because I needed to warm up a bit to start the game. That line was here, there, and everywhere, passing the puck, this and that. After a while you get used to it, but when the game's just starting, you're not warm enough to move the right way, and so they would get you off the start. They were a tremendous line."

With the Pony Line buzzing early in the season, Chicago won five of their first seven games. As Gottselig had envisioned, Mosienko had fit in perfectly with the two Bentleys. Yet, making the plays for Doug and Mosie called for hair-trigger precision on Max's part as the centreman.

Mosienko liked a hard, fast pass that he could take in full stride as he hit the blueline. Doug was the exact opposite. He preferred Max to hang on to the puck until they were over the enemy blueline, then flip through the defence. This gave Doug, cutting in fast, a chance to beat his man, pick up the puck and have only the goalie to beat.

"We were all so small," Max Bentley later recalled of the Pony Line as he, Bill and Doug were all around 5'8", "but we were fast and worked so well together that it seemed like somebody was always open. If Doug wasn't free, or Mosie wasn't, I would be. Sometimes they'd both be hollering for the puck, and I'd divide up the passes to keep both of them happy."

The Pony Line and the system the Hawks played under forced other teams to adapt or die. The Black Hawks were scoring 4.75 goals per game on average. According to Bill Tobin, this was accomplished by the simple procedure of sacrificing the defence for an overwhelming attack—like the boxer who takes a punch so that he can deliver two.

The magic number to the team's success, coach Gottselig told the *Chicago Tribune*, was scoring four goals a game.

"The days of defensive hockey are gone," explained Gottselig. "A goalie doesn't have a chance in these days of five-man rushes, and I don't care if he's a second Chuck Gardiner or another George Hainsworth."

But like the Hawks' Pony Line, other clubs started to come up with a big line, which in most cases is augmented by defensive forwards for whirlwind two-minute shifts. Boston had the Kraut Line (Milt Schmidt, Woody Dumart, Bobby Bauer), Montreal had the Punch Line (Maurice Richard, Elmer Lach, Toe Blake), Toronto featured Gaye Stewart, Syl Apps, Mel Hill, and New York was using Edgar Laprade, Mac Colville, Alex Shibicky. Only Detroit was hanging on to a defensive theory. Wings coach Jack Adams wouldn't revamp his style because of his star goalie Harry Lumley, plus the likes of Flash Hollett, Earl Siebert, Jack Stewart and Bill Quackenbush overshadowed any offensive combination he could muster among his forwards.

The Guyon Hotel was the favourite living quarters for Hawk players in Chicago. Bill, Doug, and Max all lived there for a couple of seasons, and although it wasn't in the safest area of town, the boys enjoyed their time at the Guyon for the most part.

It was in front of the Guyon, which was on the West Side of Chicago, that some of the Windy City's infamous thugs opened a car door, pushed a man out into the sidewalk, and roared away while Doug Bentley and George Allen stared with fascination from the doorway of the hotel. After the car had disappeared, they went over and examined the man who had been so unceremoniously dumped onto the pavement. They found that he was very dead. He had been taken "for a ride."

It was in front of the Guyon, too, that Hawks goaltender Mike Karakas had been involved in a hair-raising episode that season. Emerging from a cab one night after a game, Mike was about to enter the hotel when a stranger stepped up to him and said, "Got a match, buddy?"

"Sure," said Mike, and began fumbling in his pockets.

Suddenly he felt something hard jabbing into his ribs, and the stranger was saying: "Keep yer yap shut and get into the car."

Mike obeyed. He was scared stiff and had good reason to be. He had been snatched by hoods, and there was usually only one ending to such an affair. Mike didn't seem to care to think about it. He sat in the back seat of the car and prayed.

The thugs drove out of the city limits, and in a suitably dark area, they stopped. "Get out," one of them snapped, "and keep yer yap shut."

Mike did. The thugs grouped around him, and Mike murmured to himself, "This is it."

"How much money ya got?" one of the gangsters demanded.

"Here's my wallet," said Mike. "There's a few bucks in it."

"Anything else?"

"Well, I've got a watch, but I'd like to keep it."

"Let's see it."

Mike pulled out the watch, and the hoodlum examined it by flashlight. He noticed that it had an inscription on it.

"What's that say?"

"It says, 'Presented to Mike Karakas, Chicago Black Hawks—" Mike began, but the gangster cut him short.

"Geez," he exclaimed, "are you Mike Karakas?"

"Yes," said Mike curiously.

"Well," said the thug, "that makes it different. You don't need to worry, Mike. We ain't gonna hurt ya. Them Hawks would be a bunch of bums without ya."

By now, Mike was breathing a great deal easier. "Look," he said, "give me the watch and keep the dough. Just let me out of here."

"Sure, Mike. You're okay. Here's two-bits, so's you can catch a bus back to town."

And they left him standing there. He walked back to the highway, thoroughly shaken, and hailed a bus heading into the city. "And," as Mike told Max Bentley later, "those jerks were probably in the Stadium cheering for me the next game we played!"

Hoping to get more kids playing youth hockey in Chicago, Bill penned an article for a local paper called *The TIMES* during the season, giving as much advice about the game that he could muster. He wrote that,

> Effective skating often is the difference between major league and minor league players. No puck carrier must ever be hampered by his inability to do anything required of him on skates.
>
> One of the best tricks applied to elude a checker is a quick change of direction. An expert skating puck-handler sometimes can make a checker look like he's standing still.
>
> Perhaps the best way to fool a checker is to let him get close, then make a quick move in one direction. When he makes a move in the same direction, change quickly so as to be away before he can recover. This takes plenty of practice but can be accomplished with more than a little thought.
>
> It is important never to permit the opposition's defence to get you away from center ice. You'll always have a better shot for the goal from center ice. For this reason, if you're playing right wing, feint the defence to your right and then shift quickly to the left.
>
> It's a good idea to give your opponent the impression that you are going to crash into him. He'll set himself for the crash, and you are in command of the situation.

Mosienko got lots of feedback for the article, and afterwards, he was an even bigger target of autograph seekers after games than usual. Bill would stay and sign anything that was put in front of him and wouldn't leave until everybody who wanted his signature got one.

By mid-December, the Pony Line was leading the league in points, headed by Max, with Mosienko second and Doug third. But contrary to what Gottselig had envisioned, Max, instead of deriving a greater number of assists than goals, was setting the league on fire with his deadly sniping. He was averaging a goal per game, and speculation was rife about his chances of emulating Richard's feat of scoring fifty goals in a season.

The club was working on the theory that the best defence is a strong offence as the Hawks were constantly goal-hunting. They were now averaging nearly five goals per game; the Pony Line was 1-2-3 in the scoring race, and hard on their heels were two other goal-getting Hawks in Clint Smith and Red Hamill. They were also hovering around first place in the league.

There was a tremendous team spirit, too, among the Chicago players—from the veteran Mike Karakas in goal right down to the newest rookie, George Gee—and it was to manifest itself in no uncertain manner when rival clubs began to go out of their way to stop the Bentleys and Mosienko somehow.

The Black Hawks were beginning to irk the rest of the NHL teams. Their speed and aggressiveness had prompted some of the other teams to resort to "commando" tactics in an effort to slow them down. Basically, other teams were trying to injure the Ponies and keep them out of the lineup. The violent play was quickly becoming widespread, and Mosienko was the first to feel its impact.

On December 30, in a rugged game at New York, Mosie was sidelined with torn left knee ligaments as a result of a diving body check by Bill Moe. Moe took what was perceived to be an illegal low dive at Mosienko, although no penalty was called on the play.

The Hawks' physician, Dr. William Meacham, was in New York when Mosie was injured and told the *Chicago Daily News*, "He'll be out two weeks at least and four at the most. Trouble with an injury of this sort—torn knee ligaments—is x-rays do not help. The only local indication is an inflammatory condition. He just simply must rest, then we'll try to exercise the leg easily and determine whether it's healed sufficiently. A premature return and another bang on the knee might put him out for the rest of the season."

When Bill was injured, the league scoring race was as follows: Max Bentley, Bill Mosienko, Elmer Lach, Toe Blake, Clint Smith, Doug Bentley, Alex Kaleta. That's five Chicago players in the top seven, which is very impressive to say the least.

Bill Moe took Mosie out with a brand-new type of body check for those times when the defender left his feet when making contact. This is a play that is certainly illegal now in today's NHL, but back then, Moe never even served a penalty.

Chicago president Bill Tobin was furious to say the least, at the loss of his star. "They're being provoked into a physical defence of themselves," Tobin told the *Montreal Gazette*. "That's the penalty of success by a team that plays the type of hockey we do. It's only natural the ponderous, slow-moving teams would try to stop us by literally stopping our best men. I hope Red Dutton (president of the NHL) is here Sunday night when we play the Rangers again. I'm not going to ask him to attend, but he certainly should. What burns me most about that injury to Mosie is the fellow who did it—Bill Moe, a player that I'm sure no manager in the league would buy for $10. Imagine a ten-buck player damaging a $25,000 star just at a time when we need him badly."

The change of Hawk disposition actually dates back to Thanksgiving night that season when John Mariucci tangled with the Rangers' Bill Juzda, who persisted in riding and holding Mosienko. That's when they began to suspect the rest of the league was resolved to neutralize their swooping speed and skillful feints with physical force.

Coach Johnny Gottselig sent an angry protest to league headquarters, accusing the Rangers of employing "football on ice" tactics, and he bitterly declared,

> We'll be lucky to finish fourth, not first, the way they're giving us the works around the league. We've got one of the smallest teams that ever played in the NHL, but they're trying to bounce our little fellows right out of the league. I'll bet Doug Bentley has had more crosschecks, bodychecks and slashes tossed at him than any player in the NHL in the last 20 years, and he doesn't weigh 145 pounds with a couple of flatirons sewn in his underwear. Everywhere we go, we hear the same old cry from the opposition— sock and stop those Bentleys and Mosienko. Isn't that great? The three of them form probably the smallest line in Big Time history. Max goes about 154 and Mosie 158. We're not hollering for help. We have Mariucci to dress up anybody who wants to act tough.

A few days after the incident, Tobin demanded an investigation of the hit and the post-game gloating in the press, as well as a look into the possibility that referee Bill Chadwick had a bias against the Black Hawks.

Tobin said he referred to a December 31 article by James A. Burchard, a *New York World-Telegram* staff writer. In his account of the game, Burchard said:

> It's doubtful whether any of the multitude attending realized and appreciated the part played by Bill Moe.
>
> All Moe did was win the game. He scored no goals, and he got no assists. But he laid out Bill Mosienko in the first period with a flying block. From then on, the Hawks couldn't produce.
>
> He pulled a Gus Sonnenberg on Mosienko, which put the Chicago star Hors de Combat. It was a nifty check, just at the knees. Mosienko tried to skate once again, but he didn't last longer than 10 seconds. He retired for the night.

In a telegram directed to league president Red Dutton, Tobin asked for a "detailed investigation" into "Moe's deliberate charge on Mosienko."

"I have delated wiring you pending investigation into Moe's deliberate charge on Mosienko," Tobin stated. "As this has disabled him from four to six weeks, I now request your personal and detailed investigation."

Tobin said that he could not see "any justification or pride in the Ranger players and the New York press gloating over the fact that they crippled a player who was awarded the Lady Byng Trophy last year."

Tobin also asked Dutton to assign referee Bill Chadwick to Chicago for their next game in New York, and "I request your permission to interview him on charges made by our players to me as to his attitude toward Black Hawks players."

The entire matter was left up to Dutton, who was in Edmonton while all of this was taking place. The protest and referee Bill Chadwick's report were wired to him, and a statement from Dutton was supposed to come in short order.

The Black Hawks awaited action from Dutton with their official protest on the body check for about a week.

Hawks' coach Johnny Gottselig asserted that Moe aimed for the knees in making the check. In contrast, Rangers' head coach, Frank Boucher, defended Moe by saying, "Bill Moe stopped Mosienko with a fair body-check and bodychecking is part of a defenceman's job."

That remark didn't appease Johnny Gottselig, who told the *Chicago Daily News*:

> As we hit the half-way mark in the league, it seems to me every club in the circuit is trying to bounce our little fellows out of the rink. 'Sock those Bentleys and Mosienko' is getting more monotonous than the Chicory Chick song.
>
> It was one of the most illegal checks I've ever seen. But if we don't lose anybody else, I think we'll be all right…although we'll miss Mosie's speed for a few more weeks. The rest of the clubs can't skate with us, so they try to knock us around. Any manager in the league who lost one of his best players at a time when his team was in the thick of the fight for the lead and didn't complain over what he thought to be an illegal body check wouldn't have much regard for his team or players.
>
> If they want to play rough going forward, it's okay with us. We'll turn some of our big boys loose, and let me tell you something—Mariucci can dress up anybody in this league real good.

The Hawks media soon began referring to the Rangers as the "Clippers." At the same time, the Rangers media proclaimed Chicago as waving the "crying towel" throughout the aftermath of the incident.

Mosienko spent some time in the hospital after the injury but was soon released. When he was first spotted at the rink a few weeks after the incident checking in on his teammates, he chimed in on the hit he received:

> It's absolutely illegal. It was a low dive, and I wasn't looking for anything like that. I was coming from the left, and I gave Bill Juzda a decoy for a legal body check, but he wouldn't go for it. So I shot over to the right, and Moe went for it, but he took a flyer at me as I was going by and caught me at the knees. I thought maybe

it was an accident, but while I was on my way to the dressing room, he pulled the same thing on Max Bentley. He didn't get hurt thankfully because he was watching for it and rolled over Moe.

In the end, the catapult check of Bill Moe was ruled legal. Moe never missed any time, and there was no disciplinary action given to him. I have to say that today's video replay would have been a big help instead of having to go from eyewitness accounts. However, it was the 1940s and games weren't televised yet.

Despite Dutton's ruling, Tobin continued to express opinions on that score for the rest of the season, declaring that if Moe continued his knee-high block, he might shorten the careers of a number of stars.

"If Bill Mosienko and Syl Apps (two of the players the Moe clip had immobilized) were hit that way again, they might be through," Tobin asserted.

Chicago and New York met a few weeks later, and tempers boiled for the grudge match, all while Mosienko was all out with his injury. Fights flared, and blood flowed as three players were hurt in the contest that saw the Rangers win 3-2.

Three separate fistfights broke out as 15,421 Madison Square Garden fans stood on their feet and howled. The major antagonists were Phil Watson of the Rangers and Reg Hamilton of the Hawks, who both drew five-minute major penalties, which found members of both teams struggling in vain to pull them apart. The fight went on for a full two minutes before referee King Clancy was able to quell it.

It all started when Doug Bentley fought Alf Pike, while Alex Shibicky and Reg Hamilton fought each other. Hamilton and Shibicky started with a quick fight, and then Bentley and Pike went at each other and finally Watson and Hamilton joined in the battle royale.

You could say that it was a rough and tumble game from start to finish. Pike was cut over the left eye in the first period when he was checked into the boards and finally had to leave the game in the third period because it continued bleeding.

Watson suffered a black eye in his fight with Hamilton. And Bill Moe was checked out of the game with a black eye from an elbow courtesy of Red Hamill. Hamill got two minutes for the elbowing infraction. Payback if you will for what happened to Mosie.

A week later, the Rangers played in Chicago—and the game was billed as the real "grudge match" as a record crowd of 19,749 fans filled the stadium. All reserved seats were sold out two weeks in advance, and people, in turn, lined up for hours to get rush seats. An estimated 12,000 folks were turned away.

If the fans expected fireworks, they were disappointed as there wasn't much in the form of rough stuff. But the good guys won easily as the Hawks rolled to a 9-1 win. Gottselig was exuberant afterwards. The Hawks had exacted vengeance on the Rangers in humiliating fashion; the team was back on top again and, better still, Mosienko was almost ready to resume playing.

But the jubilation didn't last long. In the next game, a 7-2 conquest of Montreal, Doug Bentley was crippled by a knee injury and deemed out of commission for a month. He was injured in the second period after being bumped by Toe Blake. At the intermission, the Hawks players had watched the team doctor tend to their wounded Doug, and when they came out for the third, they were ready to even the score with a big melee. Goalies Mike Karakas and Paul Bibeault even got involved in the quarrel.

With the win that night, Chicago moved into first place in the league as they boasted a 17-10-3 record with twenty games remaining. However, only Max Bentley from the Pony Line remained healthy to play going forward.

On top of all that was going on at this time, four men from Chicago's team were issued warrants charging them with assault and battery. John Mariucci, Joe Cooper, Reg Hamilton, and trainer Eddie Froelich allegedly assaulted a former amateur boxer, Evo Somentes, during a game in the Boston Garden.

The trouble started when Froelich resented remarks made by Somentes, who was sitting behind the Chicago bench. The three players joined him in the fight that followed as a melee broke out. The four Hawks were supposed to go to court on January 30 to face their charges, but the news reports said that the incident soon got swept under the rug and that none of the players had to appear in court. The charges were dropped.

Through it all, Mosienko was working hard to get back into the lineup. He thought he might return to action a little sooner than initially anticipated, but then he had a setback at practice. He told reporters: "Damn it all, I want to be in there, but I don't know. I still can't put full pressure on my leg. Why just Saturday, for instance, I was skating all by myself over on one side of the ice at the Arena, and the other fellows were shooting at the opposite side. Well, a puck came over my way, and instinctively I guess, I started after it fast, and the awfulest pain shot up my leg."

Bill finally returned from injury nearly a month after the incident on January 27 against Boston after a nine-game absence. He didn't score any points that night, but he skated well and looked to be getting back to his normal self. Gottselig and Tobin breathed a big sigh of relief that their star right winger was back in action.

On the other hand, Doug Bentley would still be missing some time as Gottselig didn't want to rush him back into the lineup. In the coach's mind, Bentley's injury wasn't worth reinjuring and risk missing the play-offs as Chicago was right in the thick of things. With Doug out for an extended time, it seemed to hurt the Black Hawks as their wins became harder and harder to get.

Brother Max managed to ward off injury until early February when his luck finally ran out. On February 5, in a game with Boston, Max was checked hard by Jack Church and was left lying writhing on the ice as play swung to the other end. Max got up, tried to skate to the Hawk bench but fell to one knee in front of the box.

The Bruins scored on the play, and the Hawks were so incensed over the injury to Max that Johnny Mariucci skated up to Church, spun him around and smacked him on the jaw with a terrific right. One writer covering the game reported that it was "one of the quickest and most convincing knockouts seen in the Stadium, in or out of a ring" and that Church was "out cold for five minutes, the length of time Mariucci spent in the penalty box."

The rash of injuries, which might halt the current second-place Hawks from making a run at first, caused coach Gottselig to explode. "We certainly are getting the works around the league," he said. "Every injury to our line is the same, and why? Because guys who couldn't hit the Bentleys and Mosienko with a handful of beans are hooking, tripping, and tackling them."

"Church took me into the boards hard at Chicago, and I got some torn ligaments," Max Bentley later recalled. "Mariucci went over and flattened the guy with one punch, coldcocked him with a right to the jaw. I was being worked on downstairs when they carried the guy past our door, and it was lights-out for him. I thought, 'well, there's a guy who had to answer to Mariucci.'"

Thankfully, Max's knee injury was not as severe as initially feared, and he was able to rejoin the team after missing only three games. Doug came back the same night, too. That was March 6, and that marked the first time the Pony Line had been fully intact since December 30 when Bill went down. All told, they had missed twenty-six games as a unit, with Mosie being out for nine games, Doug for fourteen and Max for three.

When they were reunited, they still led all lines in the league for points with 131 as a trio. That's 14 more points than Montreal's famous 'Punch Line' of Maurice Richard, Elmer Lach and Toe Blake that had been functioning all season long without injury.

Late in the season, taking advantage of a two-week homestay, Gottselig ordered his players on a heavier diet to regain weight lost due to constant overnight road trips and assigned them to more shooting practice.

The heavy toll of injuries was undoubtedly a contributing factor in Chicago's dip to third place in the regular season standings at the end of the year and not first. "Iron" Mike Karakas held the fort in net as best as he could, but Chicago limped into the postseason, winning only three of their final fourteen contests. Yet so prolific had been their early-season scoring exploits that, upon the Pony Line's return, they still topped the league as a line at season's end with 159 points, 13 more than Montreal's Punch Line.

Chicago would meet up with first-place Montreal in the league semi-finals. It was to be a rematch of the 1944 Stanley Cup final that ended in a sweep for the Canadiens. It pitted the Punch Line against the Pony Line, and Chicago had high hopes that this series would be a lot closer than two years before. To everyone's surprise, it ended up being an even bigger disaster.

With scorelines of 6-2, 5-1, 8-2, and 7-2, none of the games were close. Montreal swept Chicago again and would go on to win their second Stanley Cup in three seasons after defeating Boston in five games.

Later in life, Billy said that Bill Durnan of the Canadiens was the smartest goaltender he ever played against: "Durnan had you covered from all angles."

Max Bentley won the 1945-46 league scoring championship with 61 points in 47 games. His brother Doug scored 40 points in 36 games. At season's end, Max was awarded the Hart Trophy as league MVP and was named the NHL's First Team All-Star at centre.

For the second straight season, Mosienko was named a Second Team All-Star at right wing after scoring 48 points in 40 games.

By now, it was clear to everyone around the league that the Ponies were only getting warmed up. They were here to stay. For them, it was just about staying healthy because they all knew that they could accomplish big things out on the ice together.

Journalist Tom Alderman recalled:

> The Pony Line was my first real hockey heroes. I saw them play in the flesh only once at ten years old. How quickly they skated, my Max and Doug and Mosie, small men in a big man's game, skating frantically to keep from getting killed, tossing the puck back and forth to the other. Max, his huge nose leading the way, threading a path up centre, past clutching arms and outthrust sticks, over on his left to brother Doug, morose Doug with his jet-black hair combed straight back, who liked to slither through the defence or at least let them think so until the last second when he'd slide it over to Billy on the right, that little baldish Ukrainian who'd sweep around the check with choppy, nervous strides. And the

goalie would look around to find three elfin figures taking turns shooting at him. Oh, they could score. They were wonderful. They would go on forever.

It was no surprise to anyone that Mosienko had quickly become one of Chicago's most famous athletes in the 1940s. He was very popular amongst fans, as well as in the lady department. Bill could have had his pick of just about any woman in the city. He was a very handsome and polite man that was kind to everyone he met.

He mingled with the Norwegian figure skater and film star Sonja Henie while she performed in the Windy City. She even asked him out on a date once, which he politely declined. You see, Billy had a girl back in Winnipeg that he had known since childhood. And he was set on marrying her.

It all started when they were kids. When young Bill would slip out the back door of his home to head to the Tobans Rink, he had his eye on the house across the way on Pritchard Avenue from which one particular brown-eyed girl might come with her skates.

That girl's name was Wanda Swita. She was of Polish descent and came from a family that consisted of her parents and two brothers.

When asked if they were childhood sweethearts, Bill chuckled and told a Chicago reporter, "Not exactly."

"I never got up enough courage to even ask her for a date until I was a pro hockey player. It's more like, you'd say, I admired her from a distance all my life—you know how a kid will do, with a popular girl. Nothing had ever happened to make me stop admiring her just as much or more, either."

The pair started dating the summer that Bill had returned from his first professional hockey season, and they would stay firmly together for the rest of their lives.

Wanda used to sit on the bar of Bill's bicycle, and they'd ride around the neighbourhood. They would also drive to Clear Lake for summer vacations, renting a cabin with bunk beds for sleeping.

The newlyweds!   COURTESY MOSIENKO FAMILY

The couple lived with Wanda's parents when Bill was home every summer. During those hot summers, Bill worked as a building contractor to earn some extra cash.

A few years of dating went by before Bill proposed. Wanda said yes right away from the tip of her toes.

After a six-year courtship, Bill and Wanda married in Winnipeg on July 13, 1946. Family members recall that it was such a blistering hot summer day that all of the guest's faces were beet red! But still, a marvellous time was had by all.

Wanda's family was Roman Catholic, so they wanted to get married at a Catholic church. However, because Bill wasn't baptized with a middle name as a kid, the Catholic church refused to marry them. So instead, they got married at the St. John's Anglican Cathedral on Anderson Avenue in the North End of Winnipeg.

Bill later got baptized and confirmed as an adult. He was a religious man and took his family to the church he got married in on most Sundays.

"Mom told me they were going to change their last name to just 'Mosie' after getting married, but the fame had already begun, so it was too late," recalled son Brian Mosienko. "There were a few other nicknames bestowed upon him like 'Wee Willie,' but Mosie was the most common one. Everyone referred to him as that."

Wanda would later join Bill in Chicago for the winter months. She knew that he enjoyed a huge steak and then a nap in the afternoon before each game. It was his routine as a player, and Wanda made sure he stuck to his routine. There would also be long absences from each other and loneliness in a new city while Bill was on road trips, but Wanda toughed it out.

Together, they met lots of lovely people in the big city of Chicago, and some even became lifelong friends of the Mosienkos.

In the 1940s, Canadian teams certainly had a significant advantage in obtaining hockey talent. That's why they won the most Stanley Cups in the Original Six era. Toronto and Montreal had a massive advantage over Detroit, Chicago, Boston, and New York, mainly because practically all worthwhile hockey talent came from Canadian rinks. There were exceptions to that, such as Frank Brimsek, Mike Karakas, and Johnny Mariucci, and those players were coming from northern towns in Minnesota, or Minneapolis or Sault Ste. Marie, Michigan.

The Canadian kids started young, and by the time they start showing real potential, they were scouted and signed by clubs like the Leafs and Canadiens.

Under organized hockey's setup in those years, each club was entitled to a reserve list of forty players still in amateur hockey. Each of these players was pledged to the respective club. He was contacted first by a scout, or representative, in the open market. Naturally, the Canadian clubs were there first when a boy showed exceptional promise.

A good example of this monopoly of playing talent was shown in the Toronto organization. They sponsored amateur teams throughout Canada and minor league pro clubs such as Buffalo in the American

League, Tulsa in the United States loop, and Hollywood in the Pacific Coast circuit.

This meant that the Maple Leafs constantly controlled 200 of the top amateurs playing on Canadian rinks. The Canadiens had a similar hold over the boys in Quebec.

Sure, the Black Hawks could have installed a similar farm system. In fact, in 1947, they had one with a pro team at Kansas City and sponsored amateur clubs in Edmonton, Winnipeg, and Moose Jaw. That gave them the right to place 160 amateurs on their reserve list.

But finding 160 prospects was the problem. Perhaps the Hawks needed better scouts and better contacts in Canada. But even then, it seemed doubtful that an American club could make too much headway against Canadian clubs.

So the Hawks were going to get the leftovers, except on rare occasions.

Doug Bentley had two tryouts with Boston but was called too frail and released. Paul Thompson, then manager of the Hawks, liked Doug and signed him to a contract. When he started clicking, Doug recommended his brothers, Max, and Reg.

Mosie was, of course, recommended to the Hawks by Joe Cooper and promptly signed. And Mariucci through a friend, Larry Armstrong, coach of the University of Minnesota's hockey squad.

The Hawks seemed to obtain its star players more by accident than by expert scouting.

In the end, the American teams took after the Canadian ones and started sponsoring minor hockey teams across Canada, mainly western Canada, so that they could get first dibs on top players. Teams like the Winnipeg Black Hawks, Winnipeg Rangers, etc. But they were still behind the eight ball in terms of acquiring prospects. It was an unfair game in those years and one that was later changed with the inception of the NHL Entry Draft in 1963.

There were several shake-ups in Chicago's player personnel when the 1946-47 season got underway.

The retirement of Mike Karakas had left a netminding gap, which Bill Tobin attempted to fill by trading George Allen to Montreal for

An ad for a Toronto Maple Leafs showing the Pony Line coming to town. (Note the ticket prices compared to today!)   COURTESY MOSIENKO FAMILY

goalie Paul Bibeault. Tobin also parted with Don Grosso, who was sold to Boston, and Bill's mentor Joe Cooper, who was sold to the Rangers.

With Bibeault in goal, veteran defencemen like Johnny Mariucci, Reg Hamilton, and Eddie Wares around, supplemented by rookie rearguards Leo Reise, Bill Gadsby, and Ralph Nattrass, the Hawks figured they had plugged their weaknesses, that they had come up with a defence that could back up the high-scoring antics of their forwards.

Bill arrived at training camp a week late but was in fine shape when he finally hit the ice. "Bill seems to have made up for his week late training start," said Gottselig. "I'm satisfied we're in fine physical and mental shape."

"We're starting off a little better balanced than last year. But I'm still worried about replacements. A few injuries and we would collapse because we're thin in depth."

Gottselig's words were prophetic. It turned out to be a miserable season for the Hawks in everything but attendances. Even though they trailed the field almost from the first drop of the puck, Chicago's rabid hockey fans poured through the turnstile in record numbers, so great was the drawing power of the Pony Line, and so bitterly did the Hawks battle.

Away to a disastrous start and riled by the concerted attempts of rival clubs to stop Doug, Max and Mosie, the Hawks finally began to retaliate with rougher hockey on a nightly basis to prevent the Ponies from being pushed around. And Johnny Mariucci was the Chicago avenger. The former Minnesota football star was as tough a competitor as there was in hockey. And he prided himself on his physical fitness.

One of his favourite demonstrations involved his Pony Line pals. Stripped to the waist in the dressing room, Mariucci would invite them to test their strength and the strength of his abdominal muscles by letting them punch him as hard as they could.

"C'mon, HIT me!" he would snort at the boys as they delivered their best Sunday punches. "You're just ticklin' me."

Mariucci was a rugged citizen, the "policeman" of the Hawks, the protector of the Bentleys and Mosienko. Anyone who mistreated the Pony Line could expect rough treatment in return from Minnesota's big Italian boy.

"After the war, Johnny Mariucci became the captain of the Black Hawks. He always considered it part of his job to protect Mosienko and the Pony Line. If you touched those guys, you had to face Mariucci," recalled former Chicago netminder Emile Francis.

"Mariucci was really tough," Max Bentley marvelled in retrospect. "Fooling around in the locker room, he'd tell Doug and me to punch him in the stomach as hard as we could. You could break your knuckles that way. He had a stomach as hard as cement."

"He'd go up to the biggest guys on the other team and tell them if they took a run at Doug and me and Mosie that they'd have to answer to him, and those guys knew he meant it."

Naturally, then, he was in plenty of brawls, the greatest of which came in defence of the Pony Line on the night of December 4, 1946, at Chicago. The Hawks were playing Detroit that night, and there was bad blood between the two clubs as the result of a rough game in Detroit the previous week. Trouble flared when Gordie Howe crashed Doug into the boards after the whistle had blown for a stop in play. Enraged by Howe's action, Max Bentley went after him with his stick. Sid Abel tore into Max, and Mariucci went after Abel, and Black Jack Stewart went after Mariucci.

It looked like the beginning of a tremendous brawl, but it was quelled in short order. However, the fuse had been ignited, and later in the game, Stewart and Mariucci tangled again. The Detroit defenceman's stick had cut Mariucci's forehead. He skated over to the bench but, as trainer Eddie Froelich put a patch on the cut, one look at big Mariucci's face, and you could tell that trouble was brewing.

Stewart was in the penalty box, and Mariucci skated over, opened the gate and said, "Okay, Stewart. Let's go."

In those days, there was only one penalty box to house penalized players. Not one for each team like there is today.

Anyway, the fight the two big defencemen staged that night was one of the best ever witnessed, people said. They slugged away at each other in the penalty box, kept on swinging and moving around in the players' corridor, and they fought for five minutes before the slugfest was halted.

"Mariucci was the toughest guy I've ever seen play the game of hockey—the toughest and the meanest. He did everything to protect the Pony Line," recalled the Hall of Fame defenceman Bill Gadsby. "When I came up with the Black Hawks in 1946, I watched John Mariucci slather cream over his body to reduce the pain he would endure just to play. He played on nights when he could barely walk into the dressing room. He was the toughest man I ever met."

Bill Gadsby joined the Black Hawks in 1946 and went on to an illustrious twenty-season career as one of the NHL's best defenders. When he retired, he was the leading career scorer among defencemen with 568 points. He was inducted into the Hockey Hall of Fame in 1970. Of Mariucci, Bill told me:

> It was either my second or third game in Chicago, and he and Jack Stewart of Detroit got in a fight. They hit each other for two to three minutes on the ice. I knew Stewart was a tough guy, and I knew Mariucci was a mean, tough bastard from playing with him.
>
> They went in the penalty box together. Both of them are cut up. Their noses, chins, and mouths are all bloody and bleeding. They started up again. And they beat the shit out of each other. They were taking turns hitting each other, just to see who was going to go down first.
>
> And I'm saying to myself, Did I pick the right profession? Am I in the right place? Man, oh man. What have I gotten myself into?
>
> It was a fight-filled game, and we ended up with a minute, minute and a half to go with three men on each side on the ice. I'm sitting on the bench, and Max and Doug Bentley come over to the bench. Max led the league in scoring that season, and Doug was in the top 10, so you knew they were going to be out there, those two guys, with the speedster Bill Mosienko.
>
> So Gottselig asked the Ponies, 'Who do you want out there with you?' And they said at the same time, 'Give us the kid.' They meant me.
>
> So I went out, and with one second left, I scored the winning goal against Harry Lumley. That's one of my all-time highlights in my career.
>
> But that John Mariucci took care of the Bentley brothers and Bill Mosienko, our best players in Chicago. Guys would hit them with a bad check, a stick check, or into the boards; Mariucci would go after them just like it had been his own son. And he would beat the piss out of them. He'd beat them up!

Mariucci used to get charley horses. He'd be all bruised up. He'd get a bottle of that Capsolin they had. It's a cream. It's hotter than a son of a bitch. I'd put it on sometimes, and I had to go get a wet towel and rub it off; it's so damn hot. He would take a shower in it! He'd slather it on both legs. And he'd play. He'd just hobble out of that dressing room and play. I've never seen a guy like that.

Gadsby was a hit in Chicago. He quickly learned from Mariucci and would play a very similar type of game for his entire career.

A few games into my career when the Bentleys invited me up to their room for a post-game beer and a sandwich at the old Hotel Manger in Boston, it was like being told you were officially part of the team. Nobody said that, but nobody had to. If the Bentleys were in your corner, you were in. Neither Bentley was taller than 5'9" and weighed more than 155 pounds soaking wet, but they were considered among the top ten players in the league in that era.

Max was nicknamed 'The Dipsy Doodle Dandy' by the press, and he was the fancier player of the two. He was a dandy passer with slick moves, and he could shoot the puck. Doug was more of a worker, moving along the boards, knocking away the puck and feeding it to his brother.

Mosie, as we called him, was as small as the Bentleys, and he could fly down the ice. In fact, he was probably the fastest skater in the NHL at that time. He would whistle for the puck, and Max would put the puck right on the tape of his stick.

Before the 1946-47 season even began, there was another instance of violence against Bill in an attempt to slow him down.

Mosie was injured with a bruised leg in a preseason game with Toronto. Fortunately, he was able to be back for the season opener. Still, coach Gottselig said:

There was no excuse for what happened. It was in the last period with about five minutes to go, Bill didn't even have the puck, but this big Bill Ezinicki crashed into him and knocked him against the goal post. It simply meant we had to keep him out of it for the rest of the game. I think there should have been a penalty, but there wasn't.

And at Detroit, well, they forgot completely about hockey and concentrated on banging into the kids, so when we got a 5-1 lead, I took 'em out and didn't play them as much as usual in the last period. Then when Detroit suddenly switched tactics and went on offence, trying to score instead of scar, you might say they drew up uncomfortably close, so I put the Bentleys and Mosie back in for insurance.

When the regular season began, the Black Hawks struggled right from day one. Even the Pony Line struggled to score at its usual rate, and soon enough, Gottselig broke up the line after a month and placed Mosie with Clint Smith and Red Hamill while the Bentleys played with Alex Kaleta.

Gottselig figured that Mosienko had played on a line with Clint Smith previously for two seasons and that they'd have the chemistry to create some chances. Having two scoring lines instead of one elite line was worth the gamble for Gottselig and Chicago to try and string together some wins.

Although the new lines scored some points, the Hawks continued to lose. By mid-December, they were last in the league with a 5-12-3 record.

After a particularly hard-fought loss to the Canadiens where the Hawks dropped their ninth game in their last twelve, Mosienko grumbled to reporters, "We're not that bad. Why, we'd get the goalie out of their net or off range, take a shot, and it'd hit the supports."

Red Hamill agreed with Mosie and said, "How long is this going to go on? Damn it. We're trying. Playing as hard as we can, but nothing seems to work."

The club tried to shake things up when they dealt Pete Horeck and Leo Reise Jr. to Detroit for Adam Brown and Ray Powell. The Hawks also made a move in net. It just wasn't working with Paul Bibeault, so they replaced him with young Emile Francis. Yes, the same Emile Francis who would later coach the New York Rangers in the 1960s and 1970s.

I spoke with ninety-four-year-old Emile Francis from his home in South Florida and he told me, "That Mosienko sure could fly. He was the fastest player in the NHL at that time and was just a terrific player."

Gottselig finally reunited the Pony Line on December 15 against Toronto. In their second game back together a few nights later on the 18th versus Detroit, Mosienko scored two goals and two assists in a 5-2 win. The Ponies embraced one another gleefully after each goal.

After the game, Gottselig lamented the fact that in his head, Mosienko wasted two months before finally reaching his top form. With that, he was also happy that things were going back to normal with his club.

"Things are just a lot easier when I'm slotted with Max and Doug," quipped Bill. "We all play very well together."

The *Chicago Tribune* remarked that Mosienko was "driving hard, displaying the same weaving and bobbing style and sharp cutbacks that made him famous in pre-injury days of a year ago."

Gottselig was so happy that he gave his troops a break from practice the next day.

The Hawks won their next few games, and as you guessed it, the Pony Line was back to their scoring ways. "I shook them up for a while," Gottselig told the *Chicago Daily Times*, "and finally, they pleaded to be put back together again. I did so four games ago, and we've finally hit our stride."

Chicago was roaring into Christmas, winning three of their last four games. And in the press, Mosienko was beginning to draw comparisons to the former Montreal Canadiens legend Aurele Joliat, who was also a smaller player that scored a ton playing with Howie Morenz.

"Mosienko skates and shoots like Joliat once did on the Canadiens wing," said *The Hockey News*. "Why, all Bill needs is a pair of Stanley Cups, and you could call him Joliat's doppelgänger."

Early in the New Year, Mosie had to miss a game because of a charley horse. He sat in the organ loft to watch the game with child actor Claude Jarman Jr., the twelve-year-old star of *The Yearling*, who was watching his first hockey game. Mosie explained the game to the tow-headed youngster. "I like the goalie (Emile Francis)," said Claude when Bill asked him to name his favourite of the night. "I sort of looked for a rough game, and I can see where it could get plenty rough."

Johnny Peirson is ninety-five years old today and the third-oldest living former NHL player. Splitting his childhood between Winnipeg and Montreal, Peirson grew up playing on outdoor ponds, honing his craft. It was while he was a student at McGill University in Montreal that the Boston Bruins organization gave him a shot by awarding him a professional tryout with their farm team, the AHL's Hershey Bears.

Peirson took up the offer because he figured a few extra dollars from playing pro hockey would help pay for his schooling. He was in for a surprise soon after he agreed to play with Hershey because a gambling scandal had erupted at the NHL level, displacing several players and opening the door for Johnny Peirson to join the Bruins full-time in 1948.

He thrived in Boston and was one of the team's more reliable forwards during the 1950s. He scored 326 points in 545 games over eleven NHL seasons, all with the Boston Bruins.

After his career was over, Peirson elected to stay in the game by getting into broadcasting. He started in 1969 as a colour commentator for the Bruins alongside Hall of Fame play-by-play announcer Fred Cusick.

Johnny spent more than twenty years working as a broadcaster before deciding to retire. Now living in Wayland, Massachusetts for the summers and Florida for the winter, Johnny still follows hockey and especially his Boston Bruins and catches up with the team from time to time. Peirson recalled:

> The Pony Line was a great line, one of the best of its time. In an era where there were some great lines like the Punch Line in Montreal with Toe Blake, Elmer Lach and Maurice Richard, and the line in Toronto with Teeder Kennedy, Sid Smith and whoever

could play the other side. There were some really popular lines, and the Pony Line was perhaps the best at scoring. Doug Bentley was probably the least known, but he was quite a player as well. I never really played against their line because they were too good for me. I guess I never matched up against them because we had more checking lines in Boston than we needed!

Mosie was a very talented player. He knew how to play the game, had finesse and class. My exposure to Mosienko was that he was a shifty player. I mean, he wasn't known for body checking or anything of that nature, but he could score goals and make plays. The guys that play in the NHL today are all power skaters, and back then, it was just Mosie and a couple of other guys who could really wheel on the ice. Now everybody does it!

I can't tell who plays left wing or right wing anymore watching hockey because they're all over the ice! In our day, if the right wing went over to the left side, he was subject to ridicule by their own coach. But hockey's a great sport. It's come a long way.

Although Chicago played some good hockey from mid-December to early March, they would lose eight of their final nine games. They finished the season in last place, missing the playoffs with a 19-37-4 record. Even with the NHL increasing the number of regular season games that year from fifty to sixty, the Hawks failed to reach its point total from the previous campaign.

Chicago allowed a league-high 274 goals, which was 81 goals higher than the next closest team. But they also had the second-highest offence in the league, scoring 193 goals.

Each member of the Pony Line managed to top the twenty-goal plateau, which was a significant milestone back then. As Max Bentley said once, "Coaches didn't give a damn if their team never scored as long as no one scored against them."

That season, Max played a full sixty games, Mosienko missed one, and Doug missed eight. Together, they had 75 goals and 104 assists for

179 points. Their 75 goals represented approximately 40 percent of the Hawks' total of 193.

For the second straight season, Max topped the NHL in points with 72. His brother Doug finished sixth in the scoring race, and Mosienko ninth with 25 goals and 27 assists for 52 points in 59 games.

During the season, Bill purchased a new car and discovered shortly afterwards that he'd have to pay a $600 duty on it if he drove it to his Winnipeg home at season's end. He returned the car and stuck with the one he had.

After the playoffs wrapped up with Toronto winning the 1947 Stanley Cup finals over the Montreal Canadiens in six games, the Pony Line was invited to augment an All-Star team to play a series of games with the Montreal Canadiens in western Canada. Bill and the Bentleys were a big hit and the leading scorers throughout the tour of games.

When Bill finally returned to Winnipeg, he and his new wife bought a house at 620 Parr Street, which was just a few kilometres from their parents' homes. They would soon have their sights on starting a family.

A mysterious letter from Carlsbad, California, reached the Mosienko family in 2003. Enclosed in the letter was a personal story written by Rosalie "Lee" Chereskin, who had once met Bill in Chicago back in 1946. It was a very fascinating and endearing story that I thought should be in the book, so here it is:

> It was the fall of 1946. I was a student nurse at the Mount Sinai Hospital School of Nursing and was sent to affiliate at the Illinois Neuro-Psychiatric Institute on Wood Street and Taylor Street in Chicago. I was 19. My father had died in September at age 51 from a heart condition discovered five months earlier, and my mother was a patient at the Chicago State Hospital for the mentally ill. Needless to say, I felt very old.
>
> In addition to being a student nurse, I was also a "Cadet Nurse." During World War II, the nurse shortage was so acute, with many of the RNs going overseas and to service-related installations, the

civilian hospitals were left grossly understaffed. Therefore, the government came up with a plan to attract young women into nursing. Billboards depicting a beautiful young girl in a Cadet Nurse uniform of gray and red with her gentle healing hand on the brow of a handsome young wounded soldier, plus ads in the newspapers and radio that advertised free tuition, books, and uniforms if one qualified, did the trick. Of course, the applicant had to sign a contract stating that if the war was still in progress, she would either work in a military installation or join the service.

Being extremely patriotic, dedicated, and serious, I looked forward to a long career in nursing and in the service of my country. Since Mount Sinai Hospital had no psychiatric ward and no contagious disease ward, we were given a choice as to where we would like to go for our affiliation, which was a three-month period. I chose Psychiatry thinking of my mother, who I loved very dearly and thought, with better knowledge, I could help her.

So off we went to "Neuro," to a dorm-like floor in the same building where the patients' wards existed downstairs. Being a teaching and research hospital, the patient census was low, and only select patients were admitted, those being patients that presented a particular challenge and from which the staff might learn. As we progressed in class and on the wards, I found myself identifying with some of the patients, thinking, "I could have said that, or I could have done that." Also, because of my mother, I was very sympathetic, and frankly, my heart poured out to them.

One day, we admitted a young fellow, 16 years old, from the Chicago Juvenile Home—maybe it was called Cook County Juvenile Home, I don't remember which. In any case, this boy had absolutely no belongings except what he was wearing, and every garment had "Juvenile Home" stamped on it. In addition, he came with no family or friends to be there for him. His name was Jerry O'Bannon. Jerry was a tall kid; his sleeves and pant legs were too short. A nice-looking kid whose problem was that of a severe stutter. He was assigned to me, my patient. Needless to say, my heart ached for him. In a way, I was kind of like his mother, and he needed me.

I knew he smoked. Everybody did in those days, and I knew he had no cigarettes. I knew he was scared in spite of the bravado he displayed, like coming to a hospital like this was no big deal. So, the first thing I did was offer him a cigarette and sat down with him. I didn't ask him any questions, he just tried to talk, but the stutter was very pronounced. He would say, "ugh, ugh, ugh, ugh" many times before he could get a word out.

At the "Home," some social worker referred him to the medical department, thinking that there may be some neurological reason for this severe speech impediment. In time, seeing Jerry every day, we became friends while he was undergoing various tests to find the cause of his problem. We took walks together outside of the hospital with the permission of his doctor, and we played ping pong and cards together. On one walk, he told me that he had gone with a social worker to buy shoes for him, and he ran away from her, "But I wouldn't run away from you, Marksy," he'd say (Marks was my maiden name). He'd try to teach me how to "hot wire" a car to steal it. And he'd talk about hockey. He loved hockey, and Bill Mosienko of the Chicago Black Hawks was a personal friend of his, he said.

Jerry's parents were not in the picture. His mother and father were alcoholics, and Jerry had lived in many foster homes, eventually getting in trouble with the law. He had no visitors. He had no belongings. His tests were coming back negative in the Neurology Department. Psychiatrists were discussing the possibility of the many changes and frights in Jerry's life possibly causing the stutter because as the days went by in the unthreatening atmosphere created by the hospital staff, the relaxed manner in which his psychiatrist dealt with him and possibly my association with Jerry, the stutter became less and less prominent.

Throughout this entire time, Jerry kept talking about Bill Mosienko, star player of the Chicago Black Hawks hockey team. Bill was a personal friend, Jerry said over and over again.

What will become of Jerry O'Bannon, I worried all the time. One didn't have to be a brainy scientist to play hockey, I thought. What if Jerry had the opportunity to learn to play hockey. He could make money doing what he likes, and a little stutter won't matter in the slightest. How could I make this happen?

What if I went to see Bill Mosienko and told him about Jerry? Maybe he would give Jerry a chance. At least it would do a lot for Jerry's confidence and ego to meet Bill Mosienko face to face. It was then that my plan began to take shape. I confided my plans to a classmate and friend, Ethel Rosenberg, and convinced her to come with me to Chicago Stadium and talk to Bill Mosienko.

On a Friday night after the Hawks game, Ettie (as we called Ethel) and I, dressed very officially in our starched nurses' uniforms, white shoes and stockings, caps with the black velvet bands showing that we were seniors, and Cadet Nurse Raincoats, talked our way down to the locker room of the Chicago Stadium. We demanded to see Bill Mosienko and said we had official business with him, and that we were nurses from the Illinois Neuro-Psychiatric Hospital.

Oddly enough, we convinced the guard to go into the locker room and tell Bill Mosienko that there were two nurses outside that wanted to talk to him about some official business. Believe it or not, Bill Mosienko came out of the locker room and listened to the whole story about Jerry O'Bannon. Bill was a good-looking young man with light hair and not too tall. He was kind and patient and let me talk about Jerry. I told him that the one constructive passion in Jerry's life was hockey. Would he please come to see Jerry? And would he act as if he knew Jerry personally? To our utter amazement and joy, Bill said he would come on Sunday afternoon. He told me the time, we gave him the directions, and I said I would meet Bill in the lobby and take him to Jerry.

On Sunday afternoon, Bill Mosienko came to the lobby of the Illinois Neuro-Psychiatric Institute, and I met him. In his hand, he carried a hockey stick signed by all the players on the Chicago Black Hawks team.

Together we went to OT (Occupational Therapy), where Jerry was making something. We came in, and Bill Mosienko said, "Hi Jerry."

Jerry O'Bannon turned around, and one could see the blood rising to his face when he answered, "Hi Bill." Bill gave him the hockey stick, and they talked for awhile. Bill was wonderful to Jerry and played along that they were pals the entire time. Then we went downstairs to the courtyard, and I took pictures so that no one could say that Jerry had fabricated this whole story.

It concerned me that I had never asked permission from any of Jerry's doctors to do this and was relieved when his psychiatrist said she wanted to do something like that but didn't have the nerve. Needless to say, I was classified as a "C" Psychiatric Nurse and told that I was too sympathetic with the patients.

My three-month affiliation was over, and I had to go back to Mount Sinai before the pictures were developed. I wanted to give Jerry a set. Unfortunately, when I finally got the pictures, I heard that Jerry was transferred to another institution or Juvenile Home and ran away. At least he had the hockey stick and my watch that he talked me out of to remind him that someone cared about him.

Rosalie (AKA "Lee") Marks Chereskin RN

Prior to the start of the 1947-48 season, Max, Doug and Mosie were included in the first annual NHL All-Star Game. What nobody knew at the time was that this game would mark the trio's final appearance together as the Pony Line.

The trio found out they had made the All-Star Game from a letter they received at the King's Hotel during their team's training camp in Regina. And at the training camp, each Pony Line member got a decent-sized raise from Bill Tobin for their prolific scoring the past two seasons.

"Boy, were we filling those seats in Chicago!" Mosienko said proudly years after the fact. "I told Max and Doug that we should bargain as a line at contract time. All or nothing. This was years before Koufax and

The 1947 NHL All Stars (Bill is bottom row, second from left)
COURTESY MOSIENKO FAMILY

Drysdale did it with the Dodgers. But Doug, well, Doug just wanted to play hockey. I don't think he cared much what he got paid."

The Pony Line boarded a train to Toronto from Regina, while the rest of the Black Hawks ventured back to Chicago.

The NHL's First Annual All-Star Game between the reigning Stanley Cup champions (Toronto) and a selected team of all-stars was played on October 13, 1947. Two-thirds of the game's proceeds were donated to the players' pensions and savings plan, and one-third was donated to local charities.

The Ponies and the rest of the players took in a Toronto Argonauts-Hamilton Tiger-Cats football game on the afternoon of the All-Star Game. That was followed by a dinner at the Royal York Hotel, where the players were given miniature engraved gold pucks. There were extra gifts for the Maple Leafs, who had won the Stanley Cup the previous spring. The Leafs received gold cufflinks from the Ontario government and a free lifetime pass to Maple Leaf Gardens from Conn Smythe. Sponsors gave each player a coat, a hat, a table lighter, golf balls, a tie, cigarette boxes, pocketknives, team photos, silver tea trays, engraved gold watches and silver watch chains.

It turned out to be a terrific hockey game, fast and rugged and vigorously contested. The Bentleys proved to be the stars of the game, with each of them scoring a goal in a 4-3 victory for the All-Stars over the Leafs. But the excitement and enthusiasm of winning was tempered by a serious injury to Bill Mosienko.

Checked hard by Jimmy Thomson of the Leafs as he cut across the Toronto blueline on his wrong wing, Mosie slid into the boards and suffered a broken ankle. He was helped off the ice and taken to the local hospital where he stayed for several days before transferring to Chicago's Saint Anthony Hospital.

"I was going around Thomson, and he went to check me. His stick caught my skate, and I crashed into the boards and broke my left ankle," Mosienko told *The Globe and Mail*.

Jim Coleman of *The Globe and Mail* reported that "From this seat, it appears that the injury will be sufficient to assure the Hawks of last place in the NHL standings."

Back home in Winnipeg at the same time that Mosie was in the Chicago hospital, Wanda was also in the hospital, giving birth to their first child, Bill Jr., on October 13, 1947.

"My mom had stayed back in Winnipeg because she was pregnant with me, and then dad broke his leg at the All-Star Game, so we all ended up being at the hospital at the same time!" said Bill Jr.

The Chicago management was stunned by Mosienko's injury. Who was now going to play right wing for Max and Doug Bentley? Johnny Gottselig said: "This is a terrible blow to us. He was one of our key players and a potential 60-point scorer. He'll be out until January, at least, and I don't know how we can replace him."

Gottselig was quite right. The Hawks tried, but their attempts to find a replacement for Mosie met with little success. They started the season with four rookies in their lineup: Metro Prystai, Art Michaluk, Cy Thomas, and Dick Butler, plus a recruit from Kansas City, Hank Blade.

Bill and Wanda out and about with a young Bill Jr. COURTESY MOSIENKO FAMILY

In the offseason, the Hawks had sent goaltender Paul Bibeault back to Montreal for George Allen, paving the way for Emile "The Cat" Francis to become the team's number one netminder.

After Bill's injury, the *Chicago Tribune* soon reported that Bill Tobin had $100,000 he was willing to spend to upgrade his lineup. The problem was that Tobin's rivals weren't eager to help Chicago out.

In addition to bolstering their forwards, Chicago was very interested in upgrading their netminding position. They fancied a deal with the New York Rangers as the Blueshirts had two NHL-level goaltenders in Chuck Rayner and Sugar Jim Henry. Chicago wanted Henry, who was stuck in the minors, but the Rangers wanted Alex Kaleta in return, who was the best of the team's forwards not named Bentley or Mosienko. No deal was made.

Fortunately, Tobin was able to acquire future Hall of Famer Roy Conacher from Detroit after a particularly interesting series of events. Conacher had become embroiled in a bitter contract dispute with Red Wings manager Jack Adams following the 1946-47 season. Adams offered $7,600 for the next season, but Conacher refused to sign for less than $8,500. Refusing to bow to his demands, Adams traded Conacher to the New York Rangers on October 22, 1947, in exchange for Eddie Slowinski and a player to be named later. Conacher, however, refused to report to the Rangers. Instead, he announced that he planned to retire from hockey, a decision he claimed to have been mulling over for a few years. The trade to New York was nullified as a result of Conacher's failure to report. Bill Tobin then received permission from Detroit to speak with Conacher and successfully negotiated a deal with the player. Tobin claimed the negotiation was easy, saying, "It wasn't hard to sign Roy. I offered him so much money that he couldn't refuse." Tobin did not reveal what he was paying Conacher but admitted that he spent $25,000 combined on the contract and to purchase him from Detroit. The deal was announced on November 1.

At the start of the season, Dick Butler, who hailed from Delisle, was tried at right wing with Max and Doug. Apart from the oddity of having three NHL players from such a small community playing on the same line, the Bentleys-Butler combination had little to offer as a unit. Nor did the Hawks, as a whole. They lost their first three games, all on the road, and after the third defeat, Bill Tobin held a conference with Conn Smythe, the boss of the Leafs, in the hope that he could make a deal that would help the Hawks.

Smythe was willing to help. He offered Tobin five players. But he wanted Max Bentley in return!

Tobin was flabbergasted. "That's like me asking you for Syl Apps when he was in his prime," he snorted.

"Well," Smythe said, "that's the deal."

"I'll talk it over with my mother," Tobin said, facetiously, and departed. But he was a worried man.

Get rid of Max? Break up the Ponies? That was preposterous!

But was it? When the Hawks lost their next three games, stretching their losing streak to six in a row, Bill Tobin was a distressed and desperate hockey owner.

Something had to be done. And in a hurry.

There had been rumours of a shake-up in the Hawks and of a big deal in the works, but even though his name had been mentioned as one of the players being sought by other clubs, Max felt certain that Bill Tobin wouldn't break up the Bentley brother act.

Still, the rumours persisted, and when Tobin, on the morning after the Hawks suffered their sixth straight defeat, called Max and said he'd like to see him in his office, Max began to have his doubts.

"Doesn't it seem funny that he only asked to see me?" Max said to Doug.

Doug nodded. "Maybe this trade talk has something to it," he mused. "If they want you to go, what about it? Are you going to?"

"I don't know," said Max. "What do you think?"

Doug shook his head. He sat silent for several minutes, deep in thought. Then he said, "If you do get traded, Max, it might be the best thing for the two of us."

"What do you mean?" Max said, surprised.

"Just this. Say you go to the Leafs, for example. One thing is certain—they won't want you to play 40 minutes a game like we've been doin' with the Hawks."

"What does that prove?"

"Well," said Doug. "We might last five years longer. The two of us."

Max nodded. "Yeh," he agreed. "Maybe you've got something there. But then again, maybe we're jumping to conclusions. I'd better go see Tobin."

"I'll go with you," Doug said. "Even though he didn't invite me."

When the Bentleys arrived in the Hawks hockey office, Bill Tobin and Johnny Gottselig were there, waiting. Johnny looked exceptionally glum and Tobin, too, seemed uncomfortable and, for once, almost at a loss for words.

The four of them sat around the big table in the back section of the office, the same table where they so often had played gin rummy together. Only this time, there was no frivolity. The usually jovial Tobin merely nodded a greeting, sat down and slowly lit a cigarette.

He looked from Doug to Max and puffed on his cigarette for some time before he finally leaned back and said: "This is one of the toughest decisions I've ever had to make, and I don't know yet if I can bring myself to make it. We're on the spot, really on the spot this time. I've tried everything to strengthen the team, but nobody wants money anymore. They're willing to trade, but they want players in return, and they want the best we've got."

"I've had one offer that I find hard to turn down," he added. "Smythe has offered me three forwards and two defencemen—five players of NHL calibre—but he wants you in exchange, Max."

Max looked at him. "Just me?" he asked.

"Just you," Tobin said. "Five players for one."

Doug interjected: "What are you going to do? Are you going to make the deal?" His voice seemed unusually tense.

Tobin lit another cigarette before answering. Then he said, "I don't know." He looked at Max. "What else we can do is beyond me. I've tried everything. You don't have to go, Max, but that's the situation."

Doug got up, tears welling in his eyes, and left the room. Johnny Gottselig shook his head and said, "Maybe this will cost me my job, but if I were you, I wouldn't go, Max."

Max said nothing. He sat and stared endlessly at the floor. Now that the decision rested with him, he felt numbed; somehow, he couldn't picture himself playing for any other team but the Hawks, or with anyone but Doug and Mosie. Yet, while it was true that they didn't want him to go, there was no other recourse open to Tobin.

The Chicago situation was desperate and called for desperate measures. Fate had decreed for him to be the pawn, and if he had to go, then, he thought to himself, he preferred to go to Toronto. Years before, as a kid listening to the hockey broadcasts, he had wanted to play for the Leafs. He wasn't as eager now as he had been then, of course, because in the intervening years the Hawks had become his team.

His mind was a jumble of thoughts, but finally, he straightened up and looked at Tobin.

"Okay," he said. "I guess it's the only thing you can do. I'll go."

Before the gaudiest deal in hockey history was consummated on Monday, November 4, 1947, Tobin and Smythe bickered for hours over the transaction. Smythe, too, was on the spot. The five players he had in mind to trade were all popular with Toronto fans and popular, too, with directors of the club. And, much as he wanted Bentley, there was the highly important matter of manpower to consider. Parting with five players and getting only one in return would be a tremendous gamble. Suppose Max ran into a serious injury and was lost to the team—what then?

Finally, however, the deal was made. Chicago parted with Max Bentley and rookie Cy Thomas. In return, they received Gaye Stewart, Gus Bodnar and Bud Poile, three Fort William (Thunder Bay) boys who played on the same forward line and were known as the Flying Forts, and two defencemen, Bob Goldham and Ernie Dickens.

When the trade was announced, it hit the hockey world like a bombshell. Front pages of scores of newspapers in both Canada and the United States gave it an extensive play with headlines like "Max Bentley goes to Leafs in exchange for five players," "One hundred thousand dollar tag on Max Bentley's head," "Hockey's hottest brother act broken up as Max Bentley traded."

NHL President Clarence Campbell stated he was "astounded" by the deal and stated it ranked with the Maple Leafs' purchase of King Clancy in 1930 as one of the most significant transactions in league history.

"It is the biggest deal in NHL hockey in a long, long time and only goes to emphasize the worth of such a player as Bentley and puts him on a very high plane," was NHL President Clarence Campbell's assessment of the trade that sent Bentley to Toronto.

Conn Smythe of the Leafs boasted after making the trade, quipping, "I'll trade five ordinary players for one great player any day. You can always find ordinary players."

Back in Delisle, Saskatchewan, Max and Doug's father, Bill, professed himself to be very unhappy with the trade. He didn't think either one of his talented sons would be able to replicate the success they'd had playing with each other.

Chicago hockey fans greeted the news with mixed emotions. They were stunned at the thought of losing Max, whose popularity was at its zenith. Phone calls and letters of protest poured in on Bill Tobin, and everywhere he went, people said, "How could you trade our Maxie? Anybody else—but not Max!" After all, Max won the league scoring title both years the Pony Line was together.

But, generally, Chicago hockey observers took the sympathetic, it-had-to-be-view. Actually, Johnny Gottselig and Doug seemed to take the news of the trade harder than anyone else. Gottselig's affection for Max was deep-rooted, and when sportswriters asked him to comment on the deal, he said, "There isn't a man in the Hawk organization who doesn't hate to see Max go. It came as a shock to Max himself, but he could see where the deal might give the Hawks quantity and quality of strength they need. Basically, we needed fresh blood, and no other club wanted any of our players except Max Bentley."

The Midwest Athletic Club in Chicago was the hangout spot for sportsmen and prominent figures in the Windy City of the 1940s.

"The Capone family had a great love for hockey and would ask the players for favours from time to time," recalls Chicago netminder Emile Francis. "The Chicago Black Hawks were a very close group, even the married guys, single guys, would all go together after the game. The single guys lived in the hotel, the married guys weren't that far away, and we'd all go to the Midwest Hotel to hang out. Someone told me once when we were there that someone in the restaurant wants to meet you, so they took me out there, and it was Matty Capone (Al Capone's brother). And he said I'm so and so, he had two bodyguards sitting in the booth behind him. He said, "I really like hockey, and I love the Black Hawks; can you get me a goal stick with all the Chicago players signing it?" He asked, "Will you be here next Sunday, and I said, "Sure, I'll be here." Sure enough, the next Sunday, I went and brought him the stick. He took his tie off and signed it, "To my good friend, Emile 'The Cat' Francis—Matty Capone."

Chicago coach Charlie Conacher chatting with his club. COURTESY MOSIENKO FAMILY

That summer, I went home to North Battleford, and my mom's ironing the tie of mine that's from him. She asked, how do you know him!? She must have thought I was in a gang or something, so I had to explain what happened!"

Mosienko never mentioned to his kids if he talked to any gangsters in Chicago, but their paths likely crossed at one point or another, and he probably had an interesting story or two tucked away.

Twenty-eight games into the season, Hawks coach Johnny Gottselig felt he wasn't motivating his troops anymore, so he resigned from his job. Replacing him would be all-time Leafs legend "The Big Bomber" Charlie Conacher, who wanted to try his hand at coaching at the NHL level. Charlie would also get to coach his younger brother, Roy, who followed in Max's footsteps on the top line, scoring 49 points in 52 games that season.

Mosienko's ankle was sufficiently healed to see him return to the Chicago lineup on December 8, only two months after suffering his injury. Although out of the lineup for 20 games that season, he played like a whirlwind toward the end of the campaign and wound up with 16 goals and nine assists for 25 points in 40 games.

When Bill broke his ankle, the question was whether his skating speed would be impacted as, at that point, he was the fastest man in the league. When he returned, Mosie was out there flying just like he was twelve years old again on the Tobans Rink in Winnipeg.

Former Detroit coach Tommy Ivan later recalled, "Bill was small and fast, incredibly fast; I'd hate to see him come to town. Chicagoans loved him. In those days, he was often the only saving grace on the last-place team."

Mosienko skated so low that even on clear days, top defencemen like Babe Pratt scarcely could see him, let alone get low enough to check him. "When he found out that he couldn't reach me," Mosienko told writer Scott Young once, "he used to punch me when I went by."

Despite Bill and his teammates' best efforts, the Black Hawks never made it out of the NHL cellar that year. As for Toronto, their Bentley-boosted lineup won another Stanley Cup in the spring of 1948, the second of three in a row, and one of four they'd win in five years in the 1940s.

Interestingly, Chicago led the NHL in both goals for and against that season, meaning that even though they lost Max, it didn't really change much on the stat-sheet. They still scored goals in bunches and had their usual holes at defence.

Mosienko was determined that his Black Hawks would be able to climb their way out of the league basement the following season. However, when he returned to Winnipeg, he suddenly had a new venture to attend to that would start to take up his summers.

When Bill began to embark on his professional hockey career as a young whippersnapper, I'm sure that he seldom ever thought of bowling. He certainly never thought that he would one day own a bowling alley. But that's precisely what happened, and for the rest of his life, bowling became a major part of Bill Mosienko.

After the war ended, Mosienko was looking for something to invest money in. His mentor Joe Cooper pushed the idea of a bowling alley in 1946.

In 1947, the alley was constructed at the corner of Main Street and Redwood Avenue in Winnipeg's North End.

Bill sold everything, including his house and his car, to help finance his share of the bowling alley. Bill and Wanda moved back in with Bill's mom for the time being at 1198 Selkirk Avenue.

"Back then, it was tough to borrow money from the bank, so when Dad started the business, he had to sell everything he owned," recalled Brian Mosienko. "They built the alley from scratch. And they probably had contractors do it, but knowing them, Joe and Bill did a fair bit of it themselves."

Joe and Bill both split the costs for the construction of the alley equally. All in all, it cost them around $75,000 to get the place up and running.

Joe Cooper's brother, John, was the architect of the building, and he did a lot of work on it getting it up to par.

Joe Cooper and Bill working on their bowling alley COURTESY MOSIENKO FAMILY

Mosie the bowler! COURTESY MOSIENKO FAMILY

"The caretaker that used to be at the alley told me that when they first built it, they dug that hole in the ground with the help of horses, digging it out with ploughs and stuff," said Bill Mosienko Jr. "It was supposed to be one of the most modern buildings around at the time. It's kind of silly, but on the roof, there's a brick ledge that goes all around, and the roof was supposed to be able to hold water to keep the building cool in the summer. It's silly because that leads to leaky roofs, and you don't want to get water on your bowling lanes, or they'll warp. Thankfully that idea never came to fruition, and they never put water on the roof."

Reg Abbott had a three-game stint with the Montreal Canadiens in 1952-53. A fellow Winnipegger, he recalls how "My Dad was the

Winnipeg-based manager for the Brunswick-Balke Company (bowling alley and billiard-table maker). He worked with Mosienko and Joe Cooper to set up their location back in the day. I don't recall Dad ever mentioning it at the time—it was quite a bit later that I learned that the Mosienko/Cooper 'thing' was one of Dad's projects for Brunswick Balke."

The Cooper-Mosienko Lanes officially opened on April 19, 1948, after Joe and Bill had returned to Winnipeg for the summer. During this time, Bill and Wanda lived with Wanda's parents, Babcia and Jadju, who helped with baby Bill Jr. and played an essential role in the development of all of their grandchildren.

An ad to showcase the opening read that, "Joe Cooper and Bill Mosienko of NHL hockey fame, invite you to drop around and enjoy a game of bowling in their luxurious and most modern bowling plant in Winnipeg. Ten alleys now ready for you, and ten more alleys ready soon!"

When the alley opened, it was considered a state-of-the-art place for bowling in North America.

The ad promotes that, "Our ventilating and exhaust fans always ensure a clean, fresh atmosphere in our alleys. Our alley has fully modern lighting, comfortable seating, ample parking space, Brunswick-Balke's latest equipment, modern ladies powder room, and checking facilities."

When it opened, there was no such thing as pinsetters yet. They used "pinboys," who would replace the pins after each throw. Where you put the pins in on the far end of the alley, there was a lever that the pinboy would step on, and the pins would all come up and then you'd put the bowling pins on these things that were sticking up.

"I was 15 when the bowling alley opened," recalled Norm Shanas, a former national five-pin bowling champion. "I remember I was walking home from school, and I passed the bowling alley because it just opened. I didn't know what a bowling alley was, but I walked in, and Joe Cooper was there because Bill was still away playing hockey. But Joe offered me a job setting pins and I took it. I set pins for three years and then I started really bowling and got serious into it. Joe was by all accounts a pretty tough guy from his hockey days. And Billy, well I've never met a nicer man in my life than him. There was never a bad word out of his mouth, and I really enjoyed working for him."

Only one person perhaps was more excited than Bill with the opening of the alleys, and that was his partner, Joe Cooper.

"You know, when I was a kid, I always dreamed that someday I might own a bowling alley like this, and now that dream has come true," Joe Cooper said at the time of opening.

Born with the last name Krupiak, Cooper was the baby of a family of seven. As mentioned previously, his hard-working immigrant parents were dead set against him playing hockey growing up, with the result he used to have to hide his skates from them. Joe's father was a carpenter by trade, and Joe went to work with a hammer and saw during his summer holidays. Along came the Depression years, and with work of any kind practically non-existent, Joe did what a lot of other young Winnipeggers did—he turned to hockey as a means of earning a living.

Cooper went on to enjoy an eleven-season NHL career as a sturdy defenceman in the 1930s and 1940s with the New York Rangers and Chicago Black Hawks. He scored 96 points in 420 NHL games and added 442 penalty minutes.

In his best years, Cooper never could have matched salaries with some of the more-publicized NHL stars, but he was always a careful man with a dollar. The carefree spenders may have kidded Joe about it and asserted that he still had the first dollar he ever earned in hockey, but Joe had the same respect for money as anyone who had known what it meant to be without it. And a kid brought up in the North End, who used to walk to and from the Amphitheatre when he played junior hockey for the Winnipeg Columbus Club, wasn't likely to adopt extravagant ways overnight.

Joe was a mighty useful defenceman over a period of years in the NHL, but it is not on record that he endeared himself to his bosses, Lester Patrick in New York and Bill Tobin in Chicago. Players who insist on being paid every cent they are worth and who are prepared to argue the matter are never too popular with the hockey magnates. And, in Joe's case, the feeling appeared to have been mutual.

When Cooper and Tobin parted ways over a $500 cut in salary, Cooper saw the writing on the wall.

"I saw my hockey days were almost over," Cooper said. "And that it was time I made plans to do something about it. Also, I made up my mind that, when I was through hockey, I wasn't going to work for somebody else."

Joe got the idea of operating a bowling alley from Alex Levinsky, another ex-Black Hawks defenceman who ran a profitable establishment in Toronto.

"I liked the idea," Cooper explained, "because I'd been in sports all my life, and I wanted to stay in the sports business. Bowling is healthful. It's one of the most popular games on the North American continent and is still growing in popularity."

Joe Cooper retired from hockey after the 1947-48 season so that he could focus solely on the bowling alley, especially while Bill was away in the winter. He lived on McPhillips Street and then later on Inkster Boulevard, both just a few minutes from the alley.

Bill would then come back from Chicago in the spring and work at the alley all summer, giving Cooper some time off from the business.

In 1950, the Cooper-Mosienko Lanes added ten more alleys in the basement to make it twenty in all. When they were expanding the basement, Bill helped out the work crews as much as he could by doing odd tasks such as hauling up pails of mud from the basement.

A young Bill Mosienko Jr. recalls helping his dad out at the bowling alley from about as early as he can remember:

> When the full 20 alleys were complete, 10 Pin bowling was downstairs and 5 Pin (which was more popular in Canada) was on the main floor. They went to automated pinsetters in the mid-1960s because you couldn't rely on pinboys coming in every day as it was a bustling alley. I was about five years old, and one of the pinboys couldn't come in, so I did it. My dad was so nervous about letting me go back there because the pins fly and he didn't wanna see me get hurt. But when the pinboy finally arrived, I was really

disappointed when he told me I had to back to the front of the alley because Dad didn't want me back there!

Just as I was getting old enough to work, they stopped using pinboys and had automated machines in the alleys. I would work up front on Saturdays helping Dad out. He'd play in one of the leagues, and I'd watch the counter and go back and fix any jams in the machines. I worked there from age twelve to university, so a lot of hours spent there!

Originally, they had pinball machines and pool tables in there and things like that. And then they got rid of all of it, and it became straight bowling. I remember working there and selling a box of twenty cigarettes for 52 cents and 56 cents for twenty-five. So everyone smoked in there, and you couldn't see the alleys because of the haze! Large drinks were 10 cents, and when it went up to 12 cents, I was cursing because making change became more difficult to figure out as we didn't have the cash registers they have today.

The final word on the Pony Line goes to long-time Black Hawks public address announcer Harvey Wittenberg who got into hockey as a young-ster by watching the three Prairie boys frolic on the ice:

I've been attending Black Hawks games since 1946, and I've seen plenty of great players and great lines. The thing that makes a line great—more than just a collection of talented skaters—is chemistry. You could have three All-Stars together, and if they don't complement each other, it probably won't add up to much.

But that is why I think the 'Pony Line' was so special. They didn't have the longevity of some other great lines in Blackhawks history—they only played together for two seasons between 1945 and 1947—but the combination of Doug Bentley, his younger brother Max, and Bill Mosienko was more than the sum of its parts.

Though small, left wing Doug was a grinder and was the type of player who could dig in the corners when needed but could also score. Doug completed the first-ever Black Hawks playoff hat trick in 1944, and then he repeated the effort two nights later for good measure. More than 50 years after he played, he's still ranked twelfth all-time in franchise history for both assists and points scored.

Centre Max was the playmaker of the group and, in my opinion, the best all-around player. He was a tremendous stickhandler, and he performed with a lot of flair. Originally the property of the Montreal Canadiens, he was dropped by the Habs because of a heart condition they said would prevent him from playing in the NHL. But like his brother, he became a steal when he made it to Chicago in 1940. By the time he left to fight in World War II after the 1942-43 season, he was the Black Hawks' team leader in assists, and he regained the title the season he returned.

Right winger Mosienko, meanwhile, had joined the Black Hawks full-time while Max was in the war and Doug was away from the team, and he'd become a spectacular talent in his own right. Mosie had great vision, and he was amazingly fast; he scooted around the ice. Years later, he came back to play in an old-timer's game at Chicago Stadium—he was close to 60 by then—and he still had a hop.

It's well-known that chemistry matters in hockey, but watching the Pony Line is how I first learned that lesson. Max and Doug Bentley had great chemistry but adding Mosienko really made all three great. None of them were better than when they were part of the line.

There is no doubt in my mind that all three of them could still play today, and they'd be All-Stars. The game has changed, the speed of the game has changed, but the talent is still there. A truly great hockey player can play at any time.

By the late 1950s, the Black Hawks had the start of a Stanley Cup team—Bobby Hull, Stan Mikita, Glenn Hall, and Pierre

Pilote included. It's easy to overlook the Pony Line because they never brought a championship to Chicago, and most people today never saw them. I was very young, but even then I appreciated what they could do.

Though they may all be best remembered for what they did as individuals, for many like me, the Pony Line will always be remembered together, as one unit. They played an important part in the history of the Black Hawks, not just by being the best, but by giving the city and Black Hawks fans someone to cheer for even if the team was not winning. Many great players have worn the Indian Head since, but few have been as exciting while doing so.

DELISLE

The flowers lined up along the side of the highway quickly makes you realize that you're in the heart of Saskatchewan. That's what I thought to myself the last few hours of my drive to Delisle from Winnipeg in the heat of a July summer.

I pass another prairie field that a farmer is tending to in a tractor, and I quickly think of the Bentley brothers that ran a farm many years ago in these parts.

Looking back on things, I had no clue that writing Bill Mosienko's biography would lead me to the small town of Delisle, Saskatchewan—population 1,000. But when I first gave Max Bentley's son, Lynn, a call to chat about his father's time on the Pony Line, it turned into an invitation to come stay at his place and give the town a visit if I was ever out that way.

Well, a month or so passed, and then I thought about it and realized I had a couple of free days coming up on my calendar. So with that, I called up Lynn, and we made something happen to come visit Delisle. A COVID-19 outbreak in the town's surrounding area delayed the trip a week, but I did get there in the end, driving nine hours early one morning from Winnipeg.

Coming to Delisle, I prepared to soak the town in for as long as I was there. I needed to include the Bentley story in this book to give readers the full scope of just how incredible the Pony Line was.

I pulled up to Lynn and his wife Gloria's home on Main Street in Delisle at about 1:30 p.m. on a balmy afternoon and knocked on the door.

Lynn Bentley in front of the sign showcasing his family
in Delisle, Saskatchewan.   COURTESY TY DILELLO

A very in-shape seventy-eight-year-old Lynn Bentley answered the door. And I immediately noticed how good he looked for his age and thought that this man could pass for fifty-five.

"It's a pleasure to meet you, Lynn."

"Call me 'Spinner' pal. That's what everyone calls me around here."

Lynn picked up the 'Spinner' nickname as a youngster on the hockey rink, and it has stuck for his entire life.

He brought me down to the guest bedroom, where I dropped off my stuff. The guest bedroom also serves as the landing spot for his dad's hockey memorabilia. Two trays and one Stanley Cup bowl for the Cup wins in 1948, 1949, and 1951 sat proudly in a china cabinet with a ton of other mementos, including Max's 200th NHL goal puck.

"Some pretty neat stuff in there, eh."

"No kidding. This is incredible," I said in awe of my surroundings.

After a quick chat, we hopped in Spinner's golf cart and drove a block from his place to the town's golf course to get a round in. The course sits behind the original log house that his grandpa Bill Bentley first settled at.

The weather could not have been more perfect for golf.

After the first hole, in which we both bogeyed, we noticed a man cutting the grass in a riding mower approaching us.

"That's Jack Miller's son," Spinner relayed to me. Jack Miller was another player from Delisle that played briefly with the Bentleys in Chicago during the 1940s.

"Barney! This young man right here is writing a book about Bill Mosienko and drove all the way from Winnipeg this morning," boasted Spinner to Brian (Barney) Miller. "He's writing a chapter about the boys as they all played on the Pony Line together."

"Your father was the nicest guy," Brian relayed. "It's funny, but my daughter told this story a few weeks ago how she was in the ice cream parlour here in town as a child at the same time that Max happened to be getting ice cream as well. Max said to the clerk, 'give that young girl one too,' and paid for it. She thought it was so cool that a celebrity bought her an ice cream!"

"That's the way he was," Spinner replied. "He'd go to the bar, and when someone new would walk in, he'd say, 'bring him a beer.'"

We all had a chuckle and then carried on to the next hole.

After teeing off, Spinner told me, "Dad was the type of guy that he'd give you the shirt off his back. No questions asked."

Not surprisingly in the slightest, Spinner is the same way.

After a few hours of some pars and some bogeys for the both of us, we wrapped up a wonderful afternoon of golf with a glass of wine at the clubhouse.

"Let's go back to the house and have a bullshit."

Outside on his patio, Spinner relayed the Bentley family's history in Delisle and how the boys got into hockey as youngsters.

The Bentley clan originally hails from Yorkshire, England, where William (Bill) Bentley Sr. was born on August 15, 1873, one of a family of six. The family emigrated in 1882 and settled at Pembina, North Dakota, just across the Manitoba border.

Though Bill played little or no hockey, he was a blistering fast speedskater. He competed on numerous occasions with the world-famous speedskater, Norval Baptie, who was at one time a mate of Bill's in Pembina.

Everybody used to laugh at him and kid him about his skating exploits, particularly his claim that he had once beaten Baptie, who was probably the greatest speed skater of his time and later a top figure skater. It's a claim that Bill clung onto throughout his life.

"Go ahead and laugh," Bentley senior would say with a shrug of his shoulders, "but if you ever get the chance, just ask Baptie. We grew up together, and I raced him a lot, and I beat him once. After that, he quit speedskating and became a figure skater."

The family was always skeptical that Bill had skated with Baptie until one year when Doug came across a picture of Baptie in an old Chicago Stadium program. He brought it home, covered Baptie's name and asked his dad to identify the photo. Bill did.

With that said, it's no surprise that Max and Doug turned out to be two of the fastest skaters in the National Hockey League.

When Bill was twenty, he married Mathilda Wagner, who was seventeen. Bill had a livery barn in the town of Pembina, which at the time boasted twenty-two saloons and a fort.

Bill later recalled this anecdote about Pembina to *Maclean's* magazine in 1948:

> There are 22 saloons, see? All right, we get prohibition. In no time, 150 speakeasies spring up in the town. All the young guys like myself want to get out of that kind of a town. All right, before we pull out of there, the soldiers get sore about somethin', I can't even remember what, and they burned that fort down one night; yessir, burned it right down. All right, we chartered a 33-freight

car train, and the railway threw in a sleeper. We load our cattle and horses and furniture onto that train, and we come out here to Saskatchewan. This is 1903.

The Bentleys were among the first families to settle in the Delisle area. It was actually a tossup between Delisle and Bentley on which they were going to name the town after. The record shows that the family that came to the area shortly before the Bentleys was a woman with the last name Delisle, or the town could have very easily been known today as 'Bentley.'

Bill and Mathilda had six boys and seven girls together. Another child died as a baby, so fourteen in total. They were all spread out quite a bit, with Max being the youngest (born in 1920) and Doug, the third youngest (born in 1916).

The senior Bentley provided Delisle, a town of fewer than five hundred people, with a covered hockey arena as early as 1917. It wasn't a palatial rink, naturally. It was of wooden construction, and barn-like, but it was protection from the icy blasts of prairie winter, and the townspeople who flocked into it to see the hockey games sure appreciated it.

"The Boss," as he was known as in Delisle, was quite a man in his heyday. He had been in farming, real estate, the clothing business, general merchandise, owned and raced harness horses and thoroughbreds. He had served Delisle as mayor for fifteen years and as postmaster. He taught all his kids how to skate when they were all around three or four years old on a small sheet of ice in their home's backyard and then coached his sons as they played hockey in their youth. He envisioned all six of his sons being big-league hockey stars one day.

"I used to go down to my grandpa's store all the time," Spinner recalled. "They're going to tear it down soon even though it's a hundred years old. After school, I remember how I'd walk to his shop—he sold insurance, land, was in the real estate business, and he was in the clothing business also, selling all kinds of old clothes for farming."

Doug started to skate when he was four years old, in the enclosed rink. A few years later, Max started as well. Doug and Max trailed after their older brothers Jack and Roy to teach them the game, but up in Delisle, they learned the game for the most part by playing on frozen roads using frozen horse turds as pucks.

Max and Doug would also spend hours shooting a tennis ball back and forth on their house's veranda. Doug would shoot and Max would play goalie, and then they'd switch. After that, they'd try to stickhandle around each other.

Being the youngest, Max was sent to the barn every day to milk the cows, and that became his regular job. Milking those cows, he would say, is how his wrists got so strong. He had as hard a shot as some of the guys that slapped it with merely a wrist shot. That's also where his strong dangling came from, and he'd be the first to tell you that.

Max and Doug attended school throughout their youth in Delisle, but they never did well there. They were always too focused on hockey.

After a wonderful chicken dinner with Spinner and Gloria, we retired to the basement where Spinner keeps his dad's hockey memorabilia. I thought how it was like being in a mini hockey museum—to me anyway.

Our conversation from before dinner picked up where we left off as we sat down for a few hours chatting, while I thumbed my way through Max's hockey scrapbooks. Over a half-century later the scrapbooks are still in immaculate condition. Incredible.

Going through some old team photos, I learned that Doug played hockey in the school league until he was fifteen when he joined the Delisle Tigers. He was there for two years before going to the Saskatoon Wesleys and then to the Regina Victorias when he was eighteen. That year, he tried out for the Toronto Maple Leafs but was turned down. After that, Doug spent three years with the Moose Jaw Millers, and when he was twenty-two, he went to the Drumheller Miners to play with his older brothers.

Max began playing midget hockey when Doug was with the Moose Jaw team. He first played hockey outside of Delisle in 1936-37 when he played intermediate just down the highway with the Rosetown Red Wings. He led the league in scoring that year.

The brothers got together in 1938-39 with the Drumheller Miners of the Alberta Senior league. In fact, five of the six Bentley brothers played on that team: Roy, Scoop, Reg, Doug, Max. Max played two years with the Drumheller Miners and led the league in scoring the first year and tied with Doug for second the other year.

Before that season, Max had gone with Doug to a Boston Bruins training camp in September of 1938 in Hershey, Pennsylvania. When they arrived, the Bruins told Max that some mistakes were made and that he actually belonged to the Montreal Canadiens. Doug tried out, but Boston figured he was too small. The Bruins then arranged the brothers' transportation home so they could stop off in Montreal.

The pair arrived in Montreal with Max played out and rundown. "Habs manager Cecil Hart took one look at me and called a heart specialist," Max later recalled to *The Star Weekly*. "After an examination, the specialist said I had a bad heart and should never play again. 'Forget the game—go home and take it easy.'"

Max quickly decided that if he was going to die, he was going to die with his skates on. So he joined his brothers in Drumheller that year and promptly won the league scoring title.

"Dad had a heart problem, but it wasn't anything significant," Spinner said. "Why they made it out as bad as it was—it wasn't that severe. That was why Montreal and other teams didn't want anything to do with him."

It was Harry Scott, a Western sportswriter, who recommended Doug Bentley to the Black Hawks for a tryout. Coach Paul Thompson had heard a great deal about the Bentleys, but he had also heard that they were too small for pro hockey and that Doug had been passed up by Toronto, New York, and Boston.

Whenever hockey men talked about the Bentleys and how good they were, someone invariably closed out the discussion by saying: "Little guys like that wouldn't stand up in the NHL. One hard check, and they'd be out for the season. Why even bother with risks like that?"

But Paul Thompson was beginning to wonder. There had been and still were a lot of great players who were not big men but who had still managed to star in the toughest of NHL competition. The Hawks had a pretty good example in their own Mush March. And the NHL record books were dotted with the names of great little guys who had made good—Aurele Joliat, King Clancy, Joe Primeau and so on down the list.

As he mentally toyed with his problem, the oddity that struck Paul Thompson was that the little fellows who made good usually were not far from being superstars. Maybe, he mused, too much stress was being placed on big, strong, tough players. Perhaps a fellow like this Doug Bentley might be a superstar, too, if he had the chance.

Finally, Paul sat down and wrote a letter to Doug, asking him to report to Chicago's training camp in the iron-range town of Hibbing, Minnesota, the following October.

It was one of a great many letters he sent out at the close of the 1938-39 National Hockey League season, and with good reason. The Hawks had finished a sorrowful last place and urgently needed a transfusion of new blood.

Paul Thompson's hunch that Doug Bentley might fit into Chicago's rebuilding program proved to be one of the greatest things that could have happened to hockey in the Windy City. It also helped pave the way for other smaller stars like Bill Mosienko and Max Bentley to join the Hawks as well in the coming years.

Doug accepted Paul's invitation to attend the 1939-40 training camp with no great enthusiasm because his previous tryouts with big-league clubs hadn't gone well at all. Nevertheless, the Hawks were not going to dismiss him as lightly as had the Bruins. This was Doug's "make or break" chance, he knew, and he wasn't going to muff the opportunity if it were humanly possible.

"If they send me home this time," he told Max at the time, "I'll forget all about pro hockey. But if I click, I'll make sure you get a chance."

"Don't worry about me," Max grinned. "I'm the guy with the bad heart, remember? Good luck, Doug. Show 'em how."

When Doug reported to Hibbing, Paul Thompson welcomed him warmly, which was a pleasant surprise. He also introduced him to the club president, Bill Tobin, who managed the Chicago hockey interests for Major Frederic McLaughlin, the Manor House coffee baron.

Tobin courteously shook hands with Doug and wished him luck. Later Tobin said to Thompson: "Is he one of our new prospects?"

Thompson nodded.

Tobin shook his head. "I didn't know things were that tough," he sighed. "What did you say his name was?"

"Doug Bentley," Paul replied.

"Doug Bentley, eh?" Tobin mused. "He's the first walking ghost I've ever seen."

Tobin had to return to Chicago that day on business, so he missed the Hawks' early workouts. But a few days later, he received a wire from Thompson suggesting that he hurry back and take a look at his "walking ghost."

"He's not a walking ghost; he's a skating ghost," Thompson added. "The kid's terrific."

Tobin stared at the telegram unbelievingly.

"This," he murmured, "is something I must see."

No more than a couple of looks were needed to convince Tobin that despite his lack of weight and anything else that might be wrong with him, the skeleton-like Doug Bentley possessed the makings of a big-league hockey player. He watched him with growing admiration as the training activities continued. Then one day, Tobin called Doug into his office. They sat and chatted for a while, and finally, Tobin said: "Paul thinks you can make good in the NHL, Doug, and I think so, too. We're ready to sign you—that is, if you're interested."

Doug grinned. "I sure am, Mr. Tobin," he said.

They talked over terms, agreed on a salary, and Tobin produced a contract. There was a minor league clause in the contract, which meant that if Doug wasn't considered good enough to stay up with the Hawks, he could be farmed out to one of Chicago's minor-league affiliates at a minor league salary.

But it was a clause that was never exercised. Once he became a Hawk, Doug Bentley was a Hawk to stay for the rest of his career.

Six rookies made their National Hockey League debuts with the Black Hawks when the 1939-40 season got underway—George Allen, Ab DeMarco, Phil Hergesheimer, Des Smith, Les Cunningham, and Doug Bentley.

Doug skated on a line with Bill Thoms and Mush March that first year. And it wasn't long before all of Chicago was singing the praises of diminutive Doug. His dazzling speed, whip-like shots, and the dancing way he evaded the lunges of bigger, stronger opponents, the dash and determination that he put into his efforts, captivated Windy City fans.

Bill Tobin was so pleased that he called Doug into his office. He noticed that Bentley looked rather nervous, almost scared.

"What's wrong, Doug?" Tobin asked.

Doug looked at him rather glumly. "I thought I was doing pretty good, Mr. Tobin." he said. "You're not going to send me to the minors, are you?"

Tobin burst into laughter.

"By all means, no," he said. "I called you in here to congratulate you on the way you've been playing. In fact, I'm so tickled, I'm going to give you a bonus."

"Gee, Mr. Tobin," he said. "That's wonderful, and I really appreciate it. But if you think I'm good, you should see my brother Max. He's twice as good as I am."

Tobin looked at him in amazement. At that time, he didn't know that Doug had a brother. Nor did he know about the fabulous Bentley family of Delisle.

"Is that so?" he said. "Well, in that case, maybe we'd better grab him, too."

Doug beamed. "You won't go wrong, Mr. Tobin. Wait till you see Max—he's terrific!"

The fact that Doug had finally made the grade in pro hockey seemed to excite Max to new heights. He had switched his hockey allegiance from Drumheller to Saskatoon, and all through that 1939-40 season, he was one of the top stars of the Saskatoon Quakers as they battled for the Saskatchewan Senior League title.

Forgotten now were all worries about his heart. Max was like a kid again, and he was winning more acclaim as the season progressed. He was scoring frequently, but he hardly seemed interested in his own record. Whenever he picked up a Saskatoon newspaper, the first thing he looked for was Doug's name in the sports section. Stories that Doug had taken Chicago—and the NHL—by storm with his dazzling play brought to Max's face a grin that stretched almost from ear to ear.

"I knew he could do it," he would tell anyone within earshot. "He's really great!"

Letters from Doug added to Max's renewed enthusiasm for hockey. Doug's descriptions of life with a pro hockey team revived Max's dreams of someday reaching the big leagues too:

"It's a pretty tough league, and I sometimes feel like a maggot among all these big guys, but I've been doing all right. One thing you have to do all the time is to keep your head up," Doug wrote in a letter to Max. "I scored the winning goal in New York, and Mr. Tobin was so pleased he called me in and gave me a bonus, so I told him about you, and he seemed interested. Keep your fingers crossed."

The fact that Doug hadn't forgotten his promise to get him a tryout with the Hawks pleased Max and made him concentrate more on improving his technique.

"Maybe the Hawks will call me any day now," he thought. "I'd better be ready."

But the Hawks didn't call him. Then, in January, Max picked up a paper and read that Doug had been injured in a game with the Toronto Maple Leafs. Rugged Bucko McDonald had bounced him hard, and Doug had suffered a shoulder separation. The story read: "Bentley, a strong candidate for the Calder Trophy as the year's top rookie, will be lost to the Hawks for at least three weeks."

Max put down the paper, and there was a hollow feeling in his stomach.

Fortunately, when Doug returned to the team in March, he was able to pick up almost right where he left off, starring in game after game as Chicago battled to a playoff spot.

It wasn't an easy chore, though, as injuries started to add up.

"We won't have anyone left if this keeps up," coach Paul Thompson moaned one day in the dressing room.

Doug, stripping off his equipment, looked at Thompson and said, "Why don't you get my brother Max to help us out for a few games."

Thompson just laughed.

Doug scowled. "Okay," he said. "If you're not interested, then maybe I can convince Mr. Tobin."

"He'll throw you out of his office if you mention Max again."

But Doug was determined. Later that day, he wandered into Tobin's office. Tobin and Joe Farrell, the veteran Chicago publicity director, were playing rummy and verbally jousting with each other.

"Hello Doug," Tobin said and went right on playing. So did Farrell. Doug stood there silently for several minutes. Then just as he was going to speak, Farrell said, "Why don't you sign my brother Max, Mr. Tobin."

Doug flushed. Old Joe was quite a joker. But this was one time that Doug was intent on a decisive answer.

"That's what I'm here for," Doug said. "Look, Mr. Tobin. We're really up against it, and we can use a guy like Max. Honest, he's far better than me."

Tobin looked up at him and shook his hand.

"I know how you feel about Max," he said, "but Max is too small, Doug. I've had my scouts report on him, and they all say the same thing. Montreal let him go because he has a bad heart. We can't take a chance on a player like that."

Doug replied angrily: "Bad heart! There's nothing wrong with his heart. He was terrific last year. He scored five more goals than I did—and he's still scoring 'em. Won't you give him a chance, Mr. Tobin?"

Tobin, a trifle embarrassed, shook his head.

"I'm sorry, Doug."

Doug stared at him, then turned quickly and went out the door. It slammed behind him with emphasis.

Farrell looked at Tobin. "Why don't we get this Max down here, just to look at him," he queried. "To tell you the truth, Bill, he fascinates me. I'm curious to see what he looks like."

Tobin grinned wryly. "So am I," he said.

Max Bentley was sitting on top of the world. In the final game of the Saskatchewan League schedule, he had scored five goals to win the scoring championship, a feat which in itself was cause for considerable jubilation.

But there was another reason for high spirits—and that was a telegram from Chicago. He had read it a thousand times, and he knew it word for word.

"WOULD YOU LIKE TO JOIN US IN DETROIT FOR TRY-OUT STOP SUGGEST YOU TRAVEL BY PLANE REGARDS BILL TOBIN"

Doug came through. Max was so nervous and excited that he could hardly sit still as the plane winged its way toward Detroit. It was his first time on a plane, too, and airsickness hit him quickly. By the time he reached Detroit, Max wouldn't have cared if the aircraft had plunged to the earth, he was so sick.

When he stepped off the plane, Doug, Bill Tobin, and Johnny Gottselig were there to meet him. Doug introduced him to Tobin, and Bill just stared.

Max looked so pale, so thin, so small, so sick, and so bewildered that Tobin almost swooned on the spot. He had waited a long time to see Max, but he had never pictured Doug's "fabulous" brother looking like this!

"Phew!" he murmured to Thompson later, "and I thought Doug looked like a walking ghost when I first saw him! That Max is the sickest looking kid I ever saw!"

And Max stayed sick. He came down with the flu and was unable to play the final two league games that Chicago had with Detroit. But the trip wasn't a waste of time. Max stayed with the Hawks and, as a spectator, got his first glimpse of Stanley Cup playoff competition. And he found out, too, that pro hockey players played the game with all the will-to-win that kids invariably display and reacted to victory or defeat the same way.

In this case, it was defeat. The Hawks met the Toronto Maple Leafs and were eliminated in two straight games by 3-2 and 2-1 scores. The goal that decided the series was knocked into Chicago's net by one of their own players, big Jack Portland, who had been a member of the Boston Bruins when Doug and Max had tried out with them at Hershey.

Max had never seen anyone as heartbroken as Portland. The big defenceman cried bitterly in the dressing room after the game and for the next day or two, locked himself in his room and wouldn't talk to anyone.

Max was slated to return to the Saskatoon Quakers senior team for the 1940-41 season, but when the Quakers asked him to take a cut in salary, he rebelled. The dispute over terms resulted in the breaking of Max's contract with Saskatoon and made him free to sign with any club.

The Quakers management later repented their action, but by this time, "Boss" Bentley and the Hawks had stepped into picture. "You won't play for Saskatoon again," his dad told Max, "no matter what they offer you."

The Hawks, in the meantime, had invited Max to their training camp in Hibbing, Minnesota. And while the Hawks brass was impressed with Max at its training camp, they wanted to send him to the minors to start the year for conditioning. And so, Max skated on a line with Winnipeggers Bill Mosienko and Paul Platz with the Providence Reds. After only nine games in Providence of the AHL and five games with the Kansas City Americans (AHA), where he scored ten points in five games, Max was called up to the Black Hawks for good.

While Max and Doug were excelling together with the Black Hawks in the early 1940s, a third Bentley brother also made his way to the National Hockey League.

Desperate for help in 1942-43 when players were enlisting in World War II, Chicago grabbed Reg Bentley from Delisle to help boost the team. And for the first time in hockey history, an all-brother line skated in the NHL when Max, Doug and Reg played a few games together on the same forward line. It created quite the story in the press.

Reg had some issues once he got to Chicago as he was a drinker and a gambler. He also became good friends in Chicago with Al Capone's little brother Matty. Basically, wherever the party was, Reg was there.

"Chicago called him up a few times, but he just couldn't behave himself," Spinner recalled. "He was out all-night pissing around, so they'd send him down. They'd then call him up again, and he'd do the same thing."

Reg scored one goal and two assists in eleven games with the Black Hawks in 1942-43. After that season, he never played in the NHL again.

The following year, Max received a call to the Canadian Army and made the trip from Delisle to Calgary, where he was stationed at the A-16 Canadian Infantry Training Centre, Currie Barracks. He played baseball and hockey for army teams in Alberta, and his two years with the Currie Army resulted in two Western Service Hockey Championships.

Sadly, Max lost two years of his prime because of the war, as he was just heating up when he enlisted. In 1942-43, he had scored 70 points in 47 games.

Doug didn't enlist, but his NHL career was also halted because of the war. After playing an exhibition game with Chicago in Canada prior to the 1944–45 season, Canadian officials refused to allow him to return to the United States. He was given permission by military authorities to return to his family farm for the duration of the war, and that winter, Doug worked a wartime grain elevator job. Determined to stay in condition for the day he could rejoin the Black Hawks, Doug would get up every day at 5 a.m. and work out in the local rink before going to work. In the evenings, he played with the local team, pulling no punches and ignoring the possibility of injury.

When the Bentley brothers returned to Chicago after World War II ended in time for the 1945-46 season, they were paired on Chicago's top line with Bill Mosienko. In Jack Batten's book *The Leafs in Autumn*, Max Bentley recalls his time with the Pony Line:

> We had so much fun playing together. In my heart, those two were the best I ever saw, the fastest. They had different styles you know. Like, when we were coming up to the other team's blueline, Mosie liked me to pass him the puck before he hit the defence and he'd carry it around them. With Doug, he wanted me to dump the puck between the two defencemen and he'd swoop around and pick it up. We used to talk about ideas like that—Mosie was very conscientious for talking—and I had to keep all ideas in my head. But I always knew those two were the best and I'd be all right.

When asked if the Pony Line's small size made them victims for the league's heavy body-checkers, Max said,

That's where the speed comes in. We had to keep moving fast all the time. We had to have our legs in shape. It was hard in Chicago because there was never any ice to practice on. The Black Hawks had nice teams in those days, but most of our guys couldn't get in that good condition. We'd be ahead at the end of the first period or the second period, then we'd fade out of the picture and lose. The only guys who were okay for condition were me and Doug and Mosie. That's because we played at least half of every game by ourselves.

In 1945, Mosienko had tried to get a three-way salary parlay for the Pony Line, but it fell through.

"I told Max and Doug we should bargain as a line at contract time," Mosienko said to *The Hockey News*. "All or nothing. This was years before Sandy Koufax and Don Drysdale did it with the Dodgers. But Doug, well, Doug and Max just wanted to play hockey. I don't think they cared much what they got paid."

Playing on the Pony Line, Max led the NHL in scoring for two straight seasons in 1945-46 and 1946-47.

"I won the scoring championship in 1947 on the last day of the schedule," Max told Stan Fischler in the 1980s. "I beat out Rocket Richard. We played New York that night, and he played in Boston. They were giving reports back and forth as the game progressed. I was a point ahead of him, and then he scored two points. But in the last period, I scored two points, and he didn't get any, so I beat the Rocket by a point. That was some thrill."

As big of a superstar as Max was throughout his career, it should be noted that Max was also a major hypochondriac. Joe Farrell, former publicity director of the Black Hawks, once said that "If they named a new disease tomorrow, Max would catch it by nightfall. At times he might complain about not feeling too well, but then he'd go out and play a tremendous game. He was a tremendous competitor."

One of my best friends in hockey, ninety-one-year-old Bob Chrystal, played for the New York Rangers from 1953 to 1955 and was a teammate of Max and Doug as they played their final NHL season in New York in 1953-54. Bob knew of Max's hypochondriac tendencies then and recalled this story with a chuckle as he reminisces, "Bev Bentley was our spare goalie that year. He came up to keep his cousin, the Hall of Famer Max Bentley, happy and babysit because he was homesick and wanted to go home. We used to be at the Grand Central Station going to Montreal or Toronto, and we'd all make bets on whether Max was feeling good enough to make the trip or not. If he walked in holding his neck, we knew he wasn't going to go. He joined the Rangers at the tail end of his career, but he was still a hell of a hockey player. He basically just played on the point for powerplays. He'd feed the puck to Camille Henry, who would tip them in. Camille went on to win the Calder Trophy that year strictly on his points total alone."

"He was also paranoid," Spinner added. "He was always bothered by something all the time. As mom said, 'on days that he wasn't feeling good, look out.' The boys were all pretty good, but being the youngest in the family might have had something to do with it. But he worked the hardest, and that's why he ended up being as good as he was."

Going through Max's scrapbooks, I found a ton of clippings relating to the big trade when Max was dealt from Chicago to the Toronto Maple Leafs in 1947. In Batten's book, Bentley describes the deal:

> I didn't have to go to Toronto if I didn't want. Mr. Tobin called me and Doug into his office for a talk this one day. I'd heard rumours about a trade, but I never dreamed it'd be me. Mr. Tobin said it was up to myself whether I went or not. He said it'd help Chicago a lot, getting five top players like that. So I thought, well, I'll go. One person was very disappointed when he learned about the trade—my dad. He heard it on the radio. He wanted me and Doug to stay together. Maybe I should've phoned him right away so he wouldn't have heard it first on the radio. The trade broke his heart. He felt better when we won three Cups in four years, but he never got over that Doug and I were apart.

"Smythe said he wanted Doug, too, but maybe he was too old. He was thirty-one, and I was twenty-seven. I did hear that Bill Tobin wanted ten players if Doug was included in the trade."

As noted above, the trade worked out very well for Max as he won three Stanley Cups with the Leafs in 1948, 1949 and 1951.

After the Leafs won the Cup in 1948, Bill Tobin came to Max in the dressing room, put his arm around him and said, "That deal was the biggest mistake in my life. People came just to see your line play."

Max never won the scoring title again after leaving Chicago, although he came close once or twice. In 1950-51, he finished third in league scoring after only Gordie Howe and Maurice Richard.

Doug played in Chicago until 1951-52. At that time, he decided to return home and play for the Saskatoon Quakers of the WHL. Max and Doug reunited in 1953-54 when they spent their final NHL season together with the New York Rangers.

Doug finished with 543 points in 565 games over 13 NHL seasons and was inducted to the Hockey Hall of Fame in 1964. He was named to four NHL All-Star Teams in his career and was the NHL's scoring leader in points and goals in 1942-43 and again in goals in 1943-44. It should be noted that the Art Ross Trophy was not awarded until 1947-48, while the Maurice "Rocket" Richard Trophy wasn't handed out until 1998-99.

Max scored with 544 points in 645 NHL games over twelve NHL seasons and was inducted into the Hockey Hall of Fame in 1966. He was the NHL's scoring champion for two straight seasons (1945-46 and 1946-47) and won the Hart Trophy as the league's most valuable player in 1945-46. He also won a Lady Byng Trophy in 1942-43. Max skated in four NHL All-Star Games and was twice named to a post-season All-Star team.

In 2017, Max was named one of the NHL's 100 greatest players of all time by the NHL during the league's hundredth-anniversary celebrations.

The Bentley brothers both enjoyed playing in Chicago a great deal but were, of course, disappointed that the team couldn't have had more success in the years that they were there.

"The trouble with playing in Chicago was we could never get enough ice time," Max said to Stan Fischler. "The Stadium was always booked up with events, and we'd go four or five days at a stretch without ice. To play good hockey, you've got to be in condition."

That night I slept in Spinner's guest bedroom in the basement. Yes, the one with all of Max Bentley's hockey memorabilia. In one of the coolest experiences I'll likely ever have as a hockey historian, I got to sleep with the Stanley Cup. Literally.

Historically, one must win the Stanley Cup to earn a night with it. I know that I'm never going to win a Stanley Cup as a player—I've accepted that. With that said, I wasn't going to let this once in a lifetime opportunity pass me by.

I slept like a baby that night as Max's 1948 Stanley Cup bowl sat proudly on the nightstand next to me. When I woke up in the morning, the shiny silver bowl was the first thing that caught my eye. I tried to savour the moment as long as possible until I finally got out of bed.

After a quick breakfast, Spinner took me around town to check out the various houses that the boys lived at and the buildings that were once connected to the Bentley clan. First, however, we stopped at the cemetery in Delisle, where Max and Doug are interned.

We both paid our respects as Spinner took me around the cemetery and showed me where each Bentley family member is buried. When we got to Max's grave, I noticed a Toronto Maple Leafs mini-stick and an old-looking hockey puck sitting atop the headstone.

Spinner looked at me and proudly said, "Those were put there in 1984 after the funeral, and after all these years, they haven't moved and are surprisingly still in pretty good shape."

Afterwards, Spinner showed me the sights around town. I have to say that I was shocked and disappointed to see that Delisle's arena wasn't even named after the Bentleys. And besides the one sign in town that was recently put up, there's nothing that celebrates that the famous Bentley brothers hailed from Delisle. It's a damn shame.

Over lunch back at the house, I asked Spinner about his own hockey career as he was a very talented player in his own right. I also asked him what it was like being the son of Max Bentley and trying to make it as a hockey player. Everywhere he played from the time he started playing organized hockey, people must have watched him play and pointed out: "That's Max Bentley's son." I can't even imagine what that must have been like and the pressure he must have faced to succeed in the sport.

"My dad wasn't around that much. He always seemed to be busy when I was going to the rink. My mom would be there once in a while, but dad didn't seem to have time to come to the rink as much as he should have."

On the times when Max and Doug were around, they were always telling Spinner what he was doing wrong, without much encouragement. That kind of stuff can play a significant role on a young hockey player. Lord only knows how big a shoe it was to fill being the great Max Bentley's son and trying to find his way in the hockey world.

After Lynn played three years of junior hockey for the Saskatoon Quakers of the SJHL, a semi-pro league in California started up in 1962. This was a few years after Max and Doug had hung up the skates, but they were brought back to play for one more season. Max was forty-two that winter and became player-coach of the Burbank Stars. Lynn, twenty, played centre, and his cousin Bev, thirty, was the team's goaltender. Doug, forty-six, was player-coach for another team in the league, the Long Beach Gulls. The two teams had quite a rivalry, but the Burbank Stars won the league championship in the end.

"Dad played on the powerplay with us and could still handle the puck amazingly well at forty-two years old."

Despite Max only really playing on the power play in Burbank, he still put up 33 points on the season. Lynn had 85 points, which was good for fifth in the league scoring. That year, he was even called up a couple of times to the Los Angeles Blades of the WHL.

Spinner later attended a couple of Chicago Black Hawks training camps out east.

"I could have made it to the NHL probably," Spinner said with a tinge of regret in his voice. "Chicago offered me a minor league contract the last time I went to their training camp and offered me $5,000. Instead, I thought I'd come back to Delisle and see what's going to happen."

Spinner went out to Trail, British Columbia, that season to play senior hockey. Early into the year, he suffered a nasty leg injury and was in a cast for a couple of months. He returned to Delisle and farmed with his dad and settled in playing senior hockey with the local boys in town.

If he could go back in time, he says he'd like to give making the NHL another shot.

"I probably would. I'd probably give 'er both barrels."

In the afternoon, Spinner treated me to another round of golf at the beautiful Valleyview Golf Course in Delisle. Again, the weather was perfect for golf.

Between holes, I'd pick his brain about what Max and Doug got up to in Delisle after they had retired from hockey. I was very impressed with how Max picked up curling and played lead with three of his buddies for a run to the provincial senior final one year. He also helped make the ice at the Delisle Curling Club for a number of years.

Spinner then talked of his long days working on the farm for Max and Doug in his youth.

"Doug was the boss of the family. He took charge and didn't like to do much work. He liked going around, making sure everyone was working, and then I don't know what he did when he went back to the house! He was a good guy of course, and never gave me any trouble. But I did a lot of work for him at the farm. I'd work all day for Doug working my butt off, and he'd give me $5 instead of the $20 bill that I'd expect!"

By this time, the Bentley brothers couldn't seem to work together on the farm, and so they split up. Rightfully so, perhaps, as they were by all accounts not the greatest of farmers to begin with. The boys were usually too focused on hockey in the winter and baseball in the summer to care much for farming.

"They were bad farmers, plain and simple," Spinner said while holding back laughter. "When the other farmers around them had forty bushels of crop, they'd have twenty."

"Max and Doug should have started a sporting goods store or something along those lines so they could use their name and the fact that they were two of the greatest hockey players on the planet. But instead, they did their farming or ran the frozen locker plant in town that they owned. They could have done anything with the money they had. But they weren't businessmen; they were just happy-go-lucky guys living in small-town Saskatchewan."

Doug passed away from cancer in 1972, shortly after the famous Summit Series between Canada and the Soviet Union. But he did get to watch all of the Summit Series games.

"Ah, those Russians," said Doug in 1972. "They pass like Max and I used to. We were too small to shoot it in the corner and then try to dig it out. We'd get killed if we went into the corners. So we had to pass and stickhandle."

Max lived long enough to see a young Wayne Gretzky make his mark in the National Hockey League. Towards the end of his life, he was compared to Wayne Gretzky quite a bit in the newspapers of the 1980s.

"Max Bentley was every bit as good as Wayne Gretzky," said hockey historian Stan Fischler. "Anyone who saw him will tell you that."

"I did play like him," Max told *The Hockey News*. "I carried the puck a lot. The difference is that Gretzky carries it from the redline in while I took it from behind my net. I used to wind up on the powerplay behind my net. My idea was to try to set up somebody. I'd beat two or three guys and then make a pass."

Max died in 1984 at age sixty-three. Both brothers passed away too young.

When Max passed away, Bill Mosienko said to the *Saskatoon Star-Phoenix*, "We didn't play all that long together, but we were just like brothers. It was a sad day when we broke up when Max was traded to Toronto. He was never too forward. He would never take the floor. But he always liked to laugh, and he sure enjoyed people."

After another spectacular round of golf, I said goodbye to Spinner and Gloria and departed from the town of Delisle for my nine-hour drive back to Winnipeg.

On the drive home, I thought of the great time I had and how I accomplished my goal of soaking in the town of Delisle during my visit. Spinner and Gloria took me into their home and treated me like I was their grandson. They are such wonderful people, and I can't say enough good things about them.

The whole Bentley family is very proud of what Max and Doug did in hockey.

Talking with both of Bill Mosienko's sons, they both told me how their father loved the Bentley brothers and that they all stayed good friends throughout their lives. Spinner had the exact same sentiments to pass on about Mosie.

"Dad and Doug both talked so highly of Billy," Spinner recalled. "Dad said Billy and Doug were the two fastest skaters in the league at that time, and that they were hard guys to keep up to."

Of all the years they played in Chicago, the Ponies never won a Stanley Cup in the Windy City, which was disappointing. Chicago Stadium was packed to the rafters every night despite the Black Hawks being not that great of a team. But Max and Doug both said it was unreal to play there.

"Dad said that the saddest thing in hockey was that Doug and Bill never got to win a Stanley Cup. It was a damn shame they couldn't have been on a winner."

Spinner has some regrets when it comes to his own hockey career. He wishes that he took the sport more seriously so that he could have had a shot at making the NHL.

But on the other hand, Spinner has made a great life for himself and his family in Delisle and wouldn't give it up for the world. His wife, Gloria, and their three kids are all lovely people and were a pleasure getting to know.

"At seventy-eight years old, I do everything in my power to stay healthy. I'm out walking and riding my bike every day. I ride a few miles every day and walk a few miles every morning. If you don't have health, you don't have much in life."

The final word on this chapter goes to Max Bentley, who said shortly before he passed away in 1984 that, "A lot of things changed when I was traded from Chicago to Toronto in 1947. I made more money than I would have in Chicago. I got to play for wonderful teams—Toronto had a terrific defence in those days—and with some nice lines, but I never got to play with a line as good as the one with Doug and Mosienko in Chicago. I often wonder what kind of records our line would have set if we'd stayed together."

THE RECORD

Unfortunately for Mosienko, the dark days would only continue for the Black Hawks over the next couple of seasons.

Prior to the start of the 1948-49 campaign, Bill Tobin folded and finally made his deal with the Rangers. Wanting to upgrade their goaltending, Chicago traded Emile Francis and Alex Kaleta to New York for Sugar Jim Henry. A few weeks later, after the Black Hawks started the season by losing their first four games, they traded George Gee and Bud Poile to Detroit for Jim Conacher, Bep Guidolin and Doug McCaig.

The trade would initially pay off, as the Black Hawks would post a 14-9-2 record in the next twenty-five games. However, they slumped again, winning only seven of their remaining twenty-one games and would miss the playoffs for the third straight season, finishing in fifth place, seven points behind the Toronto Maple Leafs for the final playoff spot.

In a midseason game with Detroit that season, Bill suffered thirteen stitches above his eye after Gordie Howe caught him with a high stick. "That was Gordie Howe's autograph," laughs Brian Mosienko. "A game or two later, Bill caught Gordie with his head down and gave him a hip check at center ice, which put him on his head. Gordie never touched my dad after that as there was now mutual respect."

The highlight of the season came on November 27 when Mosienko exploded for four goals and one assist in a 5-3 victory over the Detroit Red Wings. It marked the one and only time in Bill's NHL career that he scored four goals in a single game.

Photo of Bill for a Chicago program   COURTESY MOSIENKO FAMILY

Offensively in 1948-49, the Hawks were led by Roy Conacher, who would win the Art Ross Trophy as he led the NHL with 68 points, scoring a team-high 26 goals. Doug Bentley would finish just behind Conacher, with 66 points, including an NHL high 43 assists. Mosienko put up 42 points in 60 games.

Howie Meeker was the last surviving member of the Toronto Maple Leafs Stanley Cup team from 1947. He also won the Calder Trophy that season and went on to win four Stanley Cups (1947, 1948, 1949, 1951) with Toronto before retiring in 1954 and going on to an illustrious broadcasting career as a colour commentator with Hockey Night in Canada. He was inducted into the Hockey Hall of Fame as a broad-caster in 1998.

"Mosie! Golly gee that man could sure motor, he could skate!" recalled Howie Meeker. "Thank god he was small. He and I ran into each other a number of times, and we both ended up laughing about it. We both enjoyed the pressure we were putting on each other, and everything came out all right. He won some games, and we won some games."

Sadly, Meeker passed away at the age of ninety-seven, just a few months after I chatted with him from his home in Qualicum Beach, British Columbia.

The NHL had a bit of a new look when the players returned for the 1949-50 season. First off, the league decided to increase the number of games played from 60 to 70 games. Each team played every other team four-teen times. Also, goaltenders would no longer have to face a penalty shot if they took a major penalty. A teammate could now serve the sentence in the penalty box.

Finally, the NHL decided to have teams paint their arena's ice surface white. This was done by adding white paint to the water before freezing. Previously, the ice surface was just frozen water on concrete, which made a dull grey or black ice type of colour. By "whitening" the ice surface, it made seeing and following the puck much easier, especially on the rela-tively new medium of television.

The Hawks held training camp that year in North Bay, Ontario. From there, they started a nine-game exhibition tour against its farm club Kansas City and various senior teams across Ontario and Quebec.

Chicago then bought Frank Brimsek from Boston for cash prior to the start of the season. Known as "Mr. Zero" throughout his career, the future Hall of Famer Brimsek requested a trade from Boston to Chicago in order to be closer to his home in Eveleth, Minnesota. And so that he could help out with the new blueprint business that his brother in Chicago had started. Brimsek would play in all seventy games for the Hawks that season before retiring from hockey.

Mosienko headed to Toronto from training camp, where he took part in the 1949 NHL All-Star Game at Maple Leaf Gardens with his Chicago teammates Roy Conacher, Doug Bentley, and Bob Goldham. On October 10, 1949, the All-Stars defeated the defending Stanley Cup champs Toronto Maple Leafs by a 3-1 score.

When the season started, Chicago again was susceptible to inconsistent play, and it showed as they'd win some games and then lose a whole bunch.

During a few days break in the season in January of 1950, Mosienko won a speed-skating contest of NHL players held at the Montreal Forum for the benefit of the family of a former junior coach that had passed away. Some 8,281 spectators paid in a net of $7,688.32, which was turned over to his widow and their children.

One of the main events on the program was a puck-carrying speed race among NHL skaters (note they carried the puck as opposed to All-Star skills competitions today). The contestants skated up to the puck at the centre-ice red-line and circled the ice once, going behind the nets and finishing at the red line, and each of the contestants had two tries. Mosienko negotiated the distance in 14.8 seconds in each trial. Max McNabb of Detroit was second with a time of 15 seconds flat. Tony Leswick of the Rangers and Floyd Curry of Montreal both circled the rink in 15.4 seconds on their second attempt.

No one was surprised when Bill breezily beat the speedsters sent by the five other clubs to win an inscribed wristwatch.

"He sure wore that watch out, so he must have been very proud for receiving it!" exclaimed Brian Mosienko.

Mosienko's time that night was rated as the best-ever for the distance. A short while later, a poll of sportswriters voted him the fastest skater in hockey.

"He loved skating," recalled Bill Jr. "He was a speedskater as a kid. He would even jump barrels on skates as a kid. He told me that he had tried everything to improve his skating, so it's no wonder he was known for his quickness on the ice."

The Chicago Black Hawks 1949-50 season can be summed up in one story. After the Red Wings clobbered Chicago 9-2 on February 8, reporter Lew Walter tried to interview Chicago coach Charlie Conacher. Conacher exploded in anger, criticized Walter's past stories and punched Walter, knocking him down to the floor. Walter announced that he would seek a warrant for Conacher's arrest. NHL president Clarence Campbell took a dim view of Conacher's actions and fined him $200. Conacher then phoned Walter and apologized, saying he regretted what had taken place.

In a 1957 issue of *Maclean's,* Charlie Conacher recalled:

> Easily the most frustrating experience in hockey is to coach a losing club, "You try everything you can think of to make the change that will spell the difference between victory and defeat— juggle the forward lines, switch the tactics, cajole your players, praise them or snarl—and all you can do once the game starts is sit at the end of the bench, or, in some NHL rinks, pace restlessly behind it, and watch helplessly. Not many fans realize that the dif ference between a first-place club and a last-place club is only two or three players. The rest of the players are so evenly matched that those changes would make all the difference. Coaches of losing clubs can't digest their food properly, and their mood is usually dark. One-goal defeats night after night drives them up the walls, which is where I figuratively spent most of my time during my two and a half years with the Hawks. Crazy things happen.
>
> One night in Montreal, Bill Durnan, the Canadiens' goal- keeper, stopped a shot as the Black Hawks drove for a goal. He spotted Maurice Richard up past his own blueline, and he fired the puck up to him. Richard actually was away out of position; he wasn't backchecking. But when he got the puck, he had a clear path to our goal, and he combined with Elmer Lach to score. The official scorer rightly gave goalkeeper Durnan an assist because he'd made the play possible. It isn't twice in five years that a goalkeeper will get an assist, but it happened against the Black Hawks, and it made me sick. Losing coaches have short tempers. I became one of the few NHL hockey coaches—if not the only

one—who ever punched a hockey writer. He was Lew Walter, a Detroit newspaperman who wrote that three of my players were well up in the scoring because they were picking up phony assists from a lenient Chicago official scorer. A couple of nights later, we went into Detroit and got badly beaten. In that game, I figured the referee, Bill Chadwick, had overlooked a number of infractions by Detroit players, and I was steaming. When Walter, the newspaperman, came into our dressing room after the game, I didn't want to talk to him, and I told him to get out. 'No so-and-so coach is going to tell me to get out,' Walter said, only he didn't say so-and-so. I knocked him down. He was going to sue for assault, and Clarence Campbell, the league president, was going to fine me, but nothing came of it, probably because a couple of days later, back in Chicago, our fine old publicity man, Joe Farrell, told me I was gaining nothing going around slugging writers. I looked at Joe's white hair and figured he was probably right, so I followed his suggestion and wired an apology to Walter.

Vic Stasiuk joined the Black Hawks as a rookie that season. He later went on to succeed with Detroit and Chicago for many years and even coached in the NHL after his own playing career ended in 1966. At ninety-one years old, Stasiuk is pretty deaf nowadays. Although I had to yell over the phone for him to hear my questions, he was quite pleased when he found out that someone was calling to chat about Billy Mosienko.

"Mosie was the best small player in the game, I think," recalled Vic Stasiuk. "I don't know anyone smaller that had such success. I came up to Chicago in 1949 and started to play on his team, and he was just an excellent player. A strong forward on the attack, he was always on the top line of the team and one of Chicago's top scorers for many years."

Despite the extra games added to the season, the Black Hawks would only win one more game than the previous campaign and finish in last place in the NHL with 54 points, 13 behind the New York Rangers for the final playoff spot, missing the playoffs for the fourth straight season.

Mosienko managed to stay relatively healthy all season, scoring 46 points in 69 games. However, another big shake-up came to Chicago shortly after, as in the offseason, Charlie Conacher resigned as head coach and was replaced with Ebbie Goodfellow.

Conacher later recalled,

> Tobin and I began not seeing eye to eye when he wanted to sell Metro Prystai to Detroit, but there were other incidents. I talked Connie Smythe of Toronto into letting me buy any three players he owned who were playing in the minor leagues. This was about a month before the 1949-50 season ended, and Smythe agreed to let me take my three for ten thousand dollars each. I scouted the American Hockey League for two weeks and then named the three: Tod Sloan, Fleming Mackell, and Harry Taylor. When I got back to Chicago, Tobin told me that if Smythe had agreed to sell those three players that there must be something wrong with them. I told him there was nothing wrong with them, that I'd scouted them. Tobin refused to listen, and the moment he vetoed that deal was the moment I decided I'd be through as soon as the season ended. Incidentally, two weeks later, Sloan and Mackell played so well in the AHL playoffs that the Leafs called them both up and they stayed up ever since, going on to great careers. That was my own farewell to the NHL.

Ralph Condon was born in Summerside, Prince Edward Island, in 1933. His family moved to the North End of Winnipeg in the late 1940s, and one of the first places he went to in the city was the nearby Tobans Rink.

Because Mosienko and Shero played for the lowly Black Hawks and Rangers, their teams usually didn't make the playoffs, which meant some years they'd be back in Winnipeg before the ice had melted in the spring. Condon described his time at Tobans to me:

> When I came to the city, I moved right in with the guys that played at Tobans. The first time I met Fred Shero and Bill Mosienko, I

walked into Tobans, and they were sitting there. I told them where I was from, and Mosie said, 'Oh, you guys play hockey in the Maritimes?' I said, 'I sure do!'

I can remember one night at Tobans there was Mosienko, Shero, Nick Mickoski, Aggie Kukulowicz, and Terry Sawchuk came over from Elmwood to play goal.

There would be twenty kids at the Tobans Rink to play, and we'd have all the kids in the middle. Shero would pick his team, and Mosienko would pick his team. They'd drop the puck, and away you go. Whoever got the damn puck, you learned how to stickhandle. It was all kids from the ages of 7-16, and that's how you learned how to play—none of this sitting on the bench, you played the whole time.

When we played at Tobans, we used to get a 45-gallon drum from the CPR and cut the bottom out and throw wood in there to keep warm with a fire. Another thing we'd do is to put a poker inside the drum, red hot, and burn our names on the stake with the poker.

Condon recalls being chums with Mosienko and Fred Shero as they were all living in close proximity to each other.

Mosie and Shero were ten years older than me. When Shero played for the Rangers, he'd come home, and he mentored us because we were teenagers and he was playing in the NHL. Mosie was already married and had a business at the time, so he didn't have much time to spend with the teenagers.

Mosie had a different demeanour to us teenagers. Shero was more down to our age, but Mosie would tell us to smarten up. When we'd play outside in the wintertime, older people would tell us to shovel the bloody ice, and then we could go on it. We'd shovel and flood it as there was no such thing as Zambonis then.

But Mosie was a very soft-spoken gentleman. He played with a straight-blade wooden Northland pro stick. He had a brother named Jimmy that didn't make the pros, but he played for the Dauphin Kings and hung around Tobans. Jimmy was so strong that he once took a silver dollar and bent the goddamn thing. I saw it with my own two eyes!

In those days, nobody had a car in 1950, but the hockey players did. Shero had a brand-new Pontiac, and we'd get a ride around with him to watch Terry Sawchuk play baseball out in Transcona.

The legendary Manitoba hockey names that Condon can recall hanging out at Tobans at one point or another is quite endless.

Mosie, Shero, and Aggie hung around at Tobans lots. Ab McDonald would come over from Weston to play with us. Bill Juzda too once in a while, and Terry Sawchuk.

Sawchuk was a loner and wouldn't associate with us guys. Once in a while, he would come over to Tobans, but you couldn't score on him. He was too good. He'd maybe play for twenty minutes, and then he'd bugger off. He wouldn't associate with us too much because he was from a different area of town.

A lot of good players at Tobans could have played pro but didn't end up playing. If you got a job in those days, you stuck with it and didn't bother trying out for teams.

Condon wound up playing a couple games of junior with the Winnipeg Barons and has stayed involved in hockey throughout his life. In his late eighties now, Condon lives on his own in the St. James area of Winnipeg, where he is still as big a hockey fanatic as when he was a wide-eyed youngster stepping onto the Tobans Rink for the first time.

During the summer of 1950, the Detroit Red Wings made a big trade to pave the way for young Terry Sawchuk to take the goaltending reins from Harry Lumley. It was the biggest trade in NHL history at the time, as Chicago sent Jim Henry, Gaye Stewart, Bob Goldham, and Metro Prystai to Detroit for Harry Lumley, Jack Stewart, Al Dewsbury, Don Morrison, and Pete Babando.

Things were looking up for Chicago as Ebbie Goodfellow was now in as coach, and he quickly named the newly acquired defender Black Jack Stewart team captain.

Harry Lumley was to take over for Frank Brimsek as the latter had recently retired from the sport to return to his hometown of Eveleth in northern Minnesota. Lumley had just come off winning the Stanley Cup with Detroit a few months prior to the trade, so the Chicago brass was thrilled to have a goaltender of Lumley's calibre playing for them.

A letter to Bill's residence in Winnipeg dated September 5, 1950, from Bill Tobin of the Black Hawks reads,

> *Dear Bill,*
> *In reply to yours of September 2, I will agree to the amount of the contract as suggested in your letter. I feel sure, Bill, that with the change of coaches, you will go much better. With regard to being a few days late in reporting, if you report on Sunday, September 17, that will be satisfactory. Note you will arrange your own transportation. Looking forward to seeing you and with kindest regards.*
>
> *Yours very truly,*
> *Bill Tobin.*

A few weeks later, the *Chicago Tribune* reported at training camp that, "Doug Bentley and Billy Mosienko will be centred by either Pete Babando or Jim Conacher this season. Babando, who was a 20-goal man in his first season with Boston, weighs around 200 pounds and would be an adequate protector for the lighter Bentley and Mosienko."

Before the season got underway, Mosienko, Doug Bentley, and Black Jack Stewart skated at the 1950 NHL All-Star Game in Detroit. Ted Lindsay of the Red Wings scored the first hat trick in an All-Star Game, as the Red Wings cruised to a 7–1 win over the league All-Stars.

Pete Babando ended up centring Mosie and Doug when the season started, and the trio was hot to start the year, scoring at a rapid pace. After Bill scored three points against Montreal one night, he gave credit for his successful career to his past coaches who helped him have his start in professional hockey. "Bun Cook at Providence, Johnny Gottselig at Kansas City and of course Paul Thompson at Chicago were the men that got me to click, and if they hadn't taught me the tricks that I know today, I'd probably still be sneaking into practices back in Winnipeg."

Chicago started the season off playing excellent hockey, as they went a solid 7-3-2 in their opening twelve games. The Black Hawks then fell into a slump. After twenty-seven games, they had an 11-10-6 record and were clinging onto a playoff spot.

In December, Chicago dealt Bert Olmstead and Vic Stasiuk to Detroit for Steve Black and Lee Fogolin Sr. In hindsight, it was an awful trade for the Hawks as Olmstead and Stasiuk would both go on to have long and successful careers in the National Hockey League, while Black and Fogolin Sr. didn't pan out the way the club had hoped.

In this same season, Bill experienced a personal tragedy that certainly didn't help matters. His beloved mother, Natalia, passed away on December 13, 1950, at the age of seventy.

Bill was in shambles with the loss. He immediately took a train back home to Winnipeg for the funeral and would miss five games before returning to the Black Hawks lineup.

"I remember my grandma being at my aunt Alice's place in the living room lying in a hospital bed there," Bill Jr. recalls. "My aunt had been a nurse at one point, so she was taking care of her. That's my only real recollection of her."

Chicago ran into injury problems soon after Bill returned to the team as team captain Jack Stewart ruptured a disc in his back, ending his season after only twenty-six games, while Gus Bodnar and Bill Gadsby would also run into severe injuries.

The Black Hawks would go on to a pitiful 2-37-4 record in their last forty-three games, finishing in last place for the second consecutive season. The 36 points the Hawks earned was the lowest total since 1944-45 when the team earned 33; however, they had played twenty fewer games that season.

Bill finished with 21 goals and 15 assists for 36 points in 65 games.

Not great. But in his defence, Bill was playing with a heavy heart for the second part of the season after his mother's death.

Also, new coach Ebbie Goodfellow didn't really do a whole lot to motivate his troops, and Bill wondered if maybe the more spirited Charlie Conacher would decide to come back.

"My dad a lot of the time told me that coaches had no idea how to coach back then," said Brian Mosienko. "They'd pat Bill on the shoulder and say, 'Go Bill, go give 'er hell.' That's all some coaches did, and it was pretty pathetic."

One of the perks of being a hockey celebrity was that you ended up becoming a spokesman to help promote various products. During the 1950-51 season, Bill agreed to be the face for a brand of milk in Chicago. For doing so, he received a small cheque for $52 and a free quart of milk delivered each day for the year.

"At one time, you could not receive any more money from endorsements, so we got free milk every day," recalled Bill Jr. "The milkman would pick up the empty bottles and leave fresh ones at your front door."

Bill would end up doing many different endorsements throughout his career. Flipping through pages of programs and newspapers, you would see that classic Bill Mosienko smile holding up whatever product he was promoting at that time.

One of his things was that he helped promote was ties. When Bill would come home at the end of the season every year, he would bring a small collection of beautiful silk ties, and he would give them out to his brothers and dear friends.

Edward Leier was a fringe NHL player at a time when there was an abundance of solid pros but only six teams in the big league. The ninety-three-year-old Leier, who now resides in South Surrey, British Columbia, was more than happy to share his hockey story with me when I called him up.

Breaking into the pros was hard, as Leier found out. But still, he scored two goals and one assist with the Chicago Black Hawks in the sixteen NHL games he played spread out over two seasons in the early 1950s.

The 5'11", 175-pound centerman was originally born in Poland before coming across the Atlantic Ocean as a baby. His family eventually made their way to Winnipeg and settled in East Kildonan. A childhood friend of the great Terry Sawchuk, the pair played together growing up in both baseball and hockey before later going up against one another in the National Hockey League. An added bonus is that Eddie scored one of his two career NHL goals against Sawchuk.

Of his time playing with Mosienko, Leier says,

> My first NHL game was on January 18, 1950, against the Red Wings, and I was centring a line with two future Hall of Famers Bill Mosienko and Roy Conacher. And I got an assist that night. I always joke—I say I hit Billy Mosienko in the rear end, and he put the puck into the net, and that's kind of what happened—I assisted on his goal.
>
> I remember the three quickest goals, of course. But that was after my time in Chicago. If anybody could do it, it was him. He was a very great skater. I just remember Mosie as being a very nice and likeable guy. A veteran, but not a long-time veteran. I was a rookie coming up, and he treated me very well with us both coming from Winnipeg, that kind of thing.
>
> He treated me like I was a long-time member of the team when I had just been a rookie that was called up. He was a very nice guy and a heck of a player. He had a lot of talent with his great legs, and his ability to skate and carry the puck was unbelievable. Just a really good player that you had to admire.
>
> I didn't spend a lot of time with Mosie because I was just a young fellow coming up for a shot on the team. I was there for parts of two years in Chicago, and then they traded me after that, but I had a taste of what it was like in the dressing room of a National Hockey League team. That's all you can ever ask for in hockey.

On August 20, 1951, the Black Hawks were involved in the largest cash deal at the time, as they gave the Detroit Red Wings $75,000 in exchange for Jim McFadden, George Gee, Jimmy Peters, Clare Martin, Clare Raglan, and Max McNab. The key piece of the deal being Jimmy McFadden, the 1948 Calder Trophy winner and 1950 Stanley Cup champ with Detroit, who was supposed to bolster the Hawks scoring.

Sadly, Bill's long-time friend and linemate, Doug Bentley, would be leaving the team permanently. Doug had been a victim of injuries as of late and didn't know if he could keep up in the NHL anymore. A pulled groin muscle limited him to forty-four games in 1950-51. He played only eight games of the 1951-52 NHL season before the Black Hawks allowed him to return to Saskatchewan to play for the Saskatoon Quakers in the Western League.

Things continued to get worse from there as Chicago only won three of their opening thirteen games to start the season.

Some good news happened on November 24 against the Detroit Red Wings at the Detroit Olympia when Black Hawks captain Black Jack Stewart made his return to the team after missing nearly a year of action due to a back injury. The Black Hawks defeated the mighty Red Wings 6-2 in his return.

The following night in Chicago, goaltender Harry Lumley suffered a minor knee injury mid-game. Team trainer Moe Roberts, who had first played in the NHL in 1925-26 with the Boston Bruins, and had not played in the league since 1933-34 with the New York Americans, was an emergency third-period replacement in goal for Chicago. The forty-five-year-old Roberts stopped every shot he faced in the third period despite the Hawks falling 5-2 that night.

That night, Roberts became the oldest player to play in an NHL game, a record he held until it was broken by Gordie Howe in 1979, and also passed by Chris Chelios. He remains the oldest goaltender to play in an NHL game.

Although the Hawks were off to another losing season, personally, Mosienko was having a great season and was playing like he was ten years younger. He had shaken off the effects of the head injury suffered by Gordie Howe's stick during an exhibition game and was scoring a ton of points.

Bill receiving his 200th NHL goal puck from Hall of Famer Babe Dye
COURTESY MOSIENKO FAMILY

During the 1951-52 campaign, Mosienko rolled into the NHL's life-time two hundred-goal club on January 17, 1952, at Chicago Stadium. By an odd coincidence, he scored that magic two hundredth against Sugar Jim Henry, who also was in the nets on a February night of 1942 when he got his first NHL goal while Henry was with the New York Rangers.

Bill recalled to *The Hockey News* that, "I got two goals and an assist that night. But I never dreamed I'd get as many as 200 before I was through. Guess my biggest thrill was two or three years ago when I got four goals and one assist in a 5-4 victory over Detroit. I've had the hat trick three, four times…but four's the most I ever got in one game."

Bill's two hundredth, incidentally, came with only 1:33 to go in the third period against Boston. He went into the contest in a deep, discouraging slump. He had gone eight straight games without a point and then, at 1:34 of the first, soloed in for his 199th goal.

Then, late in the game, he finished a rush into the Boston net with Number 200, but later, he confessed, "I didn't even see the light wink on, so I skated around the nets and whacked the puck in again to be sure. Guess it went in the first time at that."

Mosienko became the twenty-first player in league history to score two hundred goals and the fourth Chicago player to hit the mark after Babe Dye, Roy Conacher, and Doug Bentley. And the second to break two hundred that season, after his buddy Max Bentley did so for Toronto. Bill was also the first Winnipegger and Manitoban to reach two hundred.

The game that night ended in a 6-6 tie, and afterwards, Babe Dye presented Bill with an award to commemorate his big accomplishment.

Bill Tobin has always had high praise for Mosienko and said after Bill scored his two hundredth goal, "He's one of the finest players we've ever had. Never any salary difficulties, never any worries about his physical condition. He is just about the cleanest-living fellow in the game."

Three days before the final game of another poor season that would see the Black Hawks miss the postseason for the sixth consecutive year, Mosienko found himself in Toronto visiting a friend.

"That night, we were thumbing through the NHL record book," he remembered later. "I remarked how nice it would be to have my name in there with some of the hockey greats."

Ironically, it would be just a few nights later that Mosienko would do something so out-of-this-world that even younger generations of hockey fans today know his name because of it.

The night in question was March 23, 1952. The Chicago Black Hawks and New York Rangers met at Madison Square Garden for the final game of the season for both clubs. It was a seemingly meaningless game for both sides as neither team would be making the playoffs.

Still, Bill was motivated to play his heart out and finish the season on a winning note. In the dressing room before the game, he told his troops, "We've had another disastrous season. Let's try hard to win our final game."

Team captain Black Jack Stewart missed the last part of the season

Bill scoring on Rangers netminder Lorne Anderson during his famous three goals in 21 seconds record on March 23, 1952.   COURTESY MOSIENKO FAMILY

due to injury, so Mosienko was wearing the captain's "C" on his sweater that night in place of Stewart.

On the other side of the rink, spare goalie Lorne Anderson was being used for the Blueshirts instead of incumbent Chuck Rayner.

The stage was set at Madison Square Garden with about four thousand Rangers fans in the crowd, many of whom were disguised by dressing up as seats.

After forty minutes of play, most of the other Chicago players had not shown much effort. Both the game and the season were coming to an end, and the Black Hawks had been trailing by a wide margin. It was 6-2 for the Rangers after two periods.

The outcome did not appear to be in doubt—but Mosienko never gave up.

Six minutes into the final period, Chicago centreman Gus Bodnar picked up a loose puck at center ice and fed it Mosienko's way near the Rangers blueline.

"When Bodnar got me the puck, I took off and went in around Hy Buller," Mosienko told Stan Fischler in *Hockey's 100*. "That left me one on one with the goalie. I got off a low wrist shot along the ice, and it went in on the right side."

"Chicago goal by Bill Mosienko, assisted by Gus Bodnar. Time: 6:09," said the public address announcer.

The goal was Mosienko's twenty-nineth of the season, and not knowing if he'd score thirty, Bill picked the puck out of the net and tossed it to his coach Eddie Goodfellow.

"I just said to hold this, that I want it for a souvenir," Bill later recalled.

Just seconds later, Bodnar got control of the puck off the faceoff and once again spotted Mosienko at the Rangers blueline. Despite falling backwards a bit in grabbing the pass, Mosienko took the puck and skated through Hy Buller once again. In an almost exact replay of his previous goal, he slapped the puck flat along the ice past Lorne Anderson and into the right side of the cage.

Time: 6:20.

"I had him all to myself," smiled Mosienko. "I figured since I'd been able to beat him on the right side, his glove hand, I'd try it again. So, just like the first time, I slid the puck along the ice. I don't think Anderson was ready for the quick shot, and it got by him.

"I'm sure Anderson was expecting high shots. Twice before during the game, he had stopped high ones, and I thought that he'd fall for the low shot. He did—a lucky thing for me."

Mosienko skated into the goalmouth, picked up the puck and took it back to the Chicago bench. "I dug that puck out because it was my thirtieth goal of the season," said Mosienko. "I guess some of the fans thought it was pretty funny when I got the puck. A bunch of them hooted and laughed while Anderson gave me a look as I grabbed the puck. I gave the puck to our coach and told him, 'Forget the other puck, this is the one I want.'"

Black Hawks coach Ebbie Goodfellow motioned for Mosienko's line to stay on the ice, and, just as the fans finished cheering in appreciation of Mosienko's two quick goals, the referee dropped the puck. Again, Bodnar won the draw, but this time he dished the puck to left winger George Gee, who then relayed it to Mosienko at the Rangers blueline, his usual spot.

"George saw me cutting over the blueline and laid a perfect pass on my stick," recalled Mosienko. "Buller was waiting for me, but like the first two times, I cut around him and went in on Anderson. He'd been burned twice on the right side. This time, he moved to the right, figuring I'd try it again. Instead, I pulled him out of the net to the left and then put one over him right into the top right-hand corner. I remember Anderson had a few choice words for me!"

Time: 6:30.

For a moment, the entire crowd was dead quiet. Finally, when Mosienko skated to his team's bench, the stunned crowd rose as one and burst into great applause. "I wasn't quite sure what to do," said Mosienko, "until one of our forwards, Jimmy Peters, told me to get the puck. 'That's a record, Mosie,' he kept yelling."

Bill had just scored a natural hat-trick in a mere twenty-one seconds. It smashed the previous NHL record of three goals in 1 minute, 52 seconds, set by Detroit's Carl Liscombe in 1938.

It's an NHL record that still stands to this day and will most likely never be broken.

"It happened so quickly I never realized it was a record," said Mosienko. "I was just thinking of the hat-trick. It's unbelievable when I look back at it, it was so quick, so spontaneous. I was always pretty well on the go. This way, I was able to freewheel a little more, and that night it certainly paid off."

A little-known fact is that less than a minute after scoring the third goal, Mosienko had a glorious opportunity to score a fourth.

"About forty-five seconds after this had happened, I had a break-in on Anderson and pulled him out of the net. And I slipped the puck right across the open net, but it slid through the goal crease and missed the far goal post by about two inches! I can still see that puck travelling just past the goal post."

At this point, coach Goodfellow summoned Mosienko to the bench, yelling, "Bill, get off the ice. You're in a slump!"

The scoring flurry rattled Lorne Anderson and the Rangers. Before the game ended, the Black Hawks added two more goals to their total to complete a remarkable comeback. The final score was 7-6 in Chicago's favour. For poor Anderson, it would mark the last time that he was ever spotted inside an NHL arena.

"I couldn't believe it," recalled centerman Gus Bodnar, who assisted on all three goals. "Mosie was a super skater and one of the best guys who could cut in on the net from the right side. He was the type of individual who never stood still. He was always circling, always in motion. And as soon as you threw the puck over to the right side, he was gone."

After the game and in his team's dressing room, Bill posed for the iconic photo of him holding up the three pucks he scored with. He swiped the pucks from the net after each goal because scoring his 29th, 30th, and 31st goal of the season was a huge deal at the time. This was in an era where you were considered an elite player if you scored twenty goals in a season.

Today, the three pucks and Bill's stick from that game are proudly displayed in Toronto at the Hockey Hall of Fame.

Speaking with reporters after the game, Mosie quipped about his record, "I was so dazed that I hardly realized what had happened. You can say I caught lightning in a beer bottle."

"We were thumbing through the NHL record book a few days ago, and I remarked how nice it would be to have my name in there with some of the hockey greats. But I just figured it would never happen—and then it did, forty-eight hours later."

In the next day's edition of the *New York Times*, a writer defended the beleaguered Rangers netminder, suggesting that "Anderson might have stopped Mosienko on the Hawk star's first shot, an open thrust from the center alley, but the second and third shots were neatly executed and could have fooled any goalie in the league."

Bill was always a constant headache to Rangers netminders. At the time, Rocket Richard was the only sniper ahead of Bill Mosienko for career goals against New York.

"That record will never be broken. Never," said teammate Bill Gadsby years later. "It was just fantastic; it was damn near the same play off the faceoff each one. He could really skate and could fly out there. Bill scored those three goals, and I mean, it was unbelievable just to watch it!"

The iconic shot of Bill holding up the three pucks from his historic night.
COURTESY MOSIENKO FAMILY

That night was Bill's fifth and final NHL hat-trick of his career. There was a man in Toronto with a hat store who would give NHL players a free fedora hat if they scored a hat-trick. Bill was actually in an ad for the business with three other players since he scored so many. After his big night, Mosienko met up with him a few days later in Toronto to collect his fifth and final fedora.

The legend of that night has never died. Over the years, *Hockey Night in Canada* broadcaster Harry Neale used to refer to Mosie's feat when a team had a three-goal lead late in the third period, saying something like, "I think it's safe, I don't see any sign of Billy Mosienko in the building."

Bill at a Toronto hat shop, being fitted for a free hat after scoring a hat-trick.   COURTESY MOSIENKO FAMILY

Bill finished the 1951-52 campaign with thirty-one goals, his second-best single-season goal total, and second in the NHL that season. And while Bill finished seventh in league scoring with 53 points, the Black Hawks finished last, 16 points behind fifth-place New York. Yet March 23, 1952, will always be regarded as the high point of a dreadful season for Chicago and the pinnacle of Bill Mosienko's career.

Now in his thirties and a veteran of the sport, people began to wonder if Mosienko was thinking about retirement. After all, besides Max Bentley, he was the only Chicago player from his rookie 1941-42 season that was still actively playing in the National Hockey League.

However, Mosienko quickly told *The Hockey News* after the season that he had plenty of good hockey left in him and that he wasn't planning on retiring from the game anytime soon.

By this point, Bill had had his fair share of injuries over a long playing career—ranging from a fractured ankle in the 1947 All-Star Game to such other incapacitating mishaps such as wrenched knee tendons, torn cartilages, a shoulder separation, and various sprained ankles.

"He also broke his nose a bunch," recalled Bill Jr. "There's a picture we have with tape over his nose. He broke it numerous times and had to go back to Chicago during one offseason to have it operated on."

At the end of the season, Mosienko was invited to go with Chicago against the Montreal Canadiens on a European Tour of exhibition games but turned it down, citing he'd rather spend more time at home with his family. "We play a full 70-game schedule, and I think that's enough," Bill told *The Hockey News*. It would be a great experience, and those that do make the tour should really enjoy it, but I think my family would rather have me around for that additional six or seven weeks."

On that special night, Bill caught lightning in a bottle. In doing so, he became a hockey legend.

Mosienko had etched his name in the lore of hockey greatness just as he was entering the twilight of his career. However, Bill wanted one more thing in the game before hanging up his skates.

The Stanley Cup.

GAME SEVEN

Fred Hucul was one of Mosienko's teammates in the early 1950s. A defenceman from Tuberose, Saskatchewan, Hucul made his NHL debut with Chicago in 1950-51 and spent the next four seasons as a Black Hawk. He then played in the WHL for a long time before returning to the NHL in 1967-68 when the league grew to twelve teams with the expansion St. Louis Blues.

Hucul claims that he's the player with the biggest gap between NHL games in league history—fourteen years. And he's probably right.

Hucul retired from hockey in 1969 and is now living in Tucson, Arizona with his wife. I called up the now eighty-nine-year-old. He had trouble remembering things at first, but with his wife's assistance, he was able to string some thoughts together.

Hucul had two assists on the night of Bill's historic March 23, 1952 game. Sadly, he's the only player from that game on either side that is still alive today.

"I was there that night on the bench when Mosie scored three goals in twenty-one seconds. Boy, he could sure fly. To be there at that time was a big thrill in my life," recalled Hucul.

Helped by his wife to spark his memory, Hucul was able to remember some of the times he spent hanging out with Mosienko in Chicago.

> I remember Mosienko being with us at the old Midwest Hotel in Chicago, the hotel we stayed at that our team's owner also owned. His wife Wanda was staying at home with the kids, I guess, but

Mosie was there with me and the Bentleys as we all lived at the hotel. We'd all bunk in there together, those that were single or if their wives weren't there.

Mosie played cards all the time with Doug Bentley. The guys used to always play cards after practice with a cold beer back at the hotel. They'd all gather in one room to kill time as the hotel wasn't the greatest area to be in in Chicago. My car was even stolen overnight one time there.

In 1951-52, Mosienko was one of the team's oldest players, while Hucul was the youngest. Hucul recalled how Bill mentored him and showed him what to takes to play at the NHL level.

Mosie was one of the older guys, and I was the young guy. They were all getting up there, and I was pretty much the only young guy. Rags Raglan was the closest to me, and he was twenty-three, while I was nineteen.

I went to training camp with the Black Hawks quite a bit because I played junior in Moose Jaw, which was a Chicago-sponsored team in those days. So I'd always see the pros once a year when I was real young at those camps. They took Guyle Fielder and myself, and a couple of guys from the east like Pete Conacher, and we all attended Chicago's main training camp.

We'd have drills at training camp where they'd put Mosie at the blueline and us in the corner. The coach would blow the whistle and told us to catch him. We couldn't catch Mosie with a lasso. He had a real motor and could change gears too and was really quite something on the wing.

Mosie was a little guy but was good in the corners. He was tough, and you had to be in those days to play. But he could really go and had a terrific right-handed shot, a damn good one and very accurate with it. He liked to put it right on the outside post and could tuck it in there if the goalie didn't make sure it was closed off. He could really fire it.

His wife then grabbed the phone from Fred and said, "Bill was a very nice fellow. He made us feel welcome in a new city when we first came to Chicago and helped make it a positive experience."

Fred was happy to hear that someone was finally writing a book about Mosienko. He told me, "Bill was a good guy to be around, just a great guy and good family man. What else could you want in a teammate?"

In the off-season heading into the 1952-53 campaign, the Black Hawks and Toronto Maple Leafs completed a trade which sent Harry Lumley to Toronto for Al Rollins, Cal Gardner, Ray Hannigan, and Gus Mortson. Chicago also fired head coach Ebbie Goodfellow and replaced him with Sid Abel, who would act as player-coach. Soon afterwards, Abel would name defenceman Bill Gadsby the new team captain.

Chicago also saw a change in ownership, as Arthur Wirtz and James D. Norris took over the now struggling and near-bankrupt franchise.

During most Bill's time in Chicago, the Mosienkos lived in a large brownstone apartment on the second floor at 3638 W. Flournoy Street.

Bill's wife, Wanda, told a local newspaper: "Naturally, the atmosphere's a little better in the house when we win. Billy often can't get to sleep at all on nights when we lose. Win or lose, though, if he does sleep, he replays the whole game in his sleep. Billy gets kind of grouchy in a losing streak, but it's nothing serious."

Wanda would attend all the Hawks home games unless their sons Bill Jr. or Brian were ill.

Bill Jr. recalled,

> Another resident's oldest kid would babysit us when our parents were away at games.
>
> Dad often brought us small gifts when he returned from road trips. One of our favourites, though, was playing cards. Can you imagine ten decks of cards tossed into the air as we ran through the apartment in Chicago? Maybe that's why Dad took up dice; he could never find a full deck of cards.
>
> We were alone with Mom a lot when he was on road trips and whatnot. I only remember going into the old Chicago Stadium

once for a game as a little kid, and the only thing I remember about it was walking in through the back of the stands. I went to school up to Grade 3 in Chicago, and I was eight when Dad stopped playing there.

Mosienko explained his game-day eating routine for *The Hockey News*:

I get up pretty early, and for breakfast at 8:30, I'll have juice, toast and coffee. Around 11:30, I'll have some soft-boiled eggs, a fruit cocktail, toast, and cereal. My big meal—sometimes a steak, sometimes roast, but anyway heavy—comes about 6:30 p.m., or an hour or so after the game.

On night games, I'll eat heavy at three in the afternoon. It has been a little difficult to get adjusted to this change of routine, particularly because of our children. When we play a night game, we can have a babysitter, put them to bed, and my wife can go to the Stadium.

I do get up earlier on the morning of an afternoon game, and there is some readjustment of the youngsters' feeding schedules. However, as long as the crowds are turning out, I'm all for it.

Bill's 1952-53 season was just getting underway when on November 4, his estranged father, Daniel, passed away at the age of seventy-two. Since Mosienko was in Chicago already for the season, paired with the fact that he wasn't close with his father anymore, Bill didn't make it back to Winnipeg for the small funeral service that was held.

Although reeling a bit from the loss of his father, it didn't seem to affect his play as Mosienko was flying night in and night out and playing like his old self.

In late March of 1953, the *Canadian Press* did a series on outstanding players and teams in the NHL. Selections were made in a poll done by sportswriters and sportscasters across all the NHL cities. Bill Mosienko was still named "Fastest Skater" in the NHL even though he was now getting up there in age. "The high-flying Mosienko is 31 years old and already a 12-year veteran. Mosienko showed his heels to a field of seven nominated by the experts. He polled 17 votes, 14 more than veteran Milt

Schmidt of Boston, and 15 up on Fleming Mackell, also of the Bruins, Eddie Kullman and Wally Hergesheimer, New York Rangers, and Marcel Pronovost of the Wings."

The word was out that Mosie could still fly, and that age was just a number.

Pete Conacher is the son of the legendary Toronto Maple Leafs winger of the 1930s, Charlie Conacher, who was also known as "The Big Bomber." Pete had a pretty darn good career himself as he enjoyed a thirteen-year career as a professional hockey player and six years in the NHL playing for the Chicago Black Hawks, New York Rangers and Toronto Maple Leafs. When it was all said and done, Pete had played 229 NHL regular-season games and scored 47 goals and 39 assists for 86 points. I called him up at his home in Toronto to talk about Mosienko:

> My first year in Chicago (1952), it was my first pro camp, and Mosienko came into training camp late, and I just was amazed with how he was a hockey player. Mosie was skating better than anybody, and he came in late, I could never get over that. He also wore different Winnipeg Planters skates than everyone else who was wearing Tackaberry's.
>
> I played on a line that year with Mosie and Gus Bodnar for a while anyway before Chicago sent me down. He was a real gentleman and had a great career in the NHL. He was a great teammate, a friendly guy that never caused any problems. He just went out there and did his job night in and night out, and that made him a king in my eyes as far as I was concerned.
>
> They always talk about his three goals in twenty-one seconds, which happened the season before I joined the Black Hawks. I don't know if this story's true or not, but I heard he was playing on a line with Bodnar and George Gee that night. Bodnar never got out of the faceoff circle and the center ice area for all of the three goals. What I heard is that coach Eddie Goodfellow pulled the line off, and Mosie asked why. Eddie said something like, 'Oh, I thought you were tired.'

My dad had coached Bill in Chicago before I got there, and I used to ask Mosie how he liked playing for my dad. He always said it was okay, but I'm not sure exactly what the real feeling was. Bep Guidolin loved playing for him, and Mosie was a different style player than him. I'm not sure what kind of coach my dad was, but I'm sure he was hard to play for because they weren't winning in those years, and that would have been upsetting for my dad.

We wrapped up our phone call, then to my surprise, Pete called me back ten minutes later because he remembered one more story about Bill:

I was playing my last year of junior hockey for the Galt Black Hawks in 1951-52. My uncle Roy Conacher was retiring from Chicago, and they called me up in late November for my first NHL game when I was nineteen. I played in Guelph on the Friday night and went to Chicago to play Saturday night against Toronto. Coach Eddie Goodfellow put me on a line centring Jimmy McFadden and Bill Mosienko. I remember chasing a Leafs player who had the puck around the back of the Leaf net. The puck dribbled in front of the net and onto McFadden's stick, and he drilled it in for a goal. We ended up winning the game 1-0. But what's funny is when they announced the goal, it was 'Goal by McFadden. Assisted by Mosienko and Conacher.' And neither one of us touched the puck, and I know that for sure. I thought this must be a pretty good league; I can get points without even touching the puck! Years later, I thought about it, and I realized that Chicago was giving me a break because I was a junior coming up, and they wanted to give me an assist, and they gave Mosie one too. Things were a little different back then, I guess, with how things are run in the National Hockey League.

I was sent back to junior after two games because you could only play a couple of games in the NHL as an amateur. But it was quite an experience, and playing my first game against Toronto, my hometown and my dad's team. Playing on a line with McFadden, who won the Calder Trophy at twenty-seven and Mosienko, who was a name that everyone knew and a future Hall of Famer. I hadn't been at training camp with Mosie prior to that or anything, so it was quite the night for me just being on the ice with them.

"I thought you might enjoy that story," Pete said before we ended our phone call.

I sure did.

The Black Hawks started the 1952-53 season off strong, sitting with a 10-5-3 record after their first eighteen games. However, the club would fall into a slump and went 2-7-5 in their next fourteen games to fall to .500. Chicago would continue to hover around the .500 for the rest of the season, battling with the Toronto Maple Leafs and Boston Bruins for the final playoff spot.

Going into the final weekend of the season, Chicago would earn big wins against the Detroit Red Wings and New York Rangers to clinch the fourth and final playoff spot and advance to the playoffs for the first time since 1946. The Hawks finished with club records in wins with 27 and points with 69.

Sid Abel's presence coaching and his play on the ice certainly played a significant role in getting Chicago to the playoffs for the first time in seven years. Al Rollins' strong play in goal was also a major factor in the team's newfound success, while Mosienko finished the regular season with 37 points in 65 games.

Chicago would face the second-place Montreal Canadiens in a best-of-seven semifinal series. The Canadiens finished the year with a 28-23-19 record, earning 75 points.

Game 1 at the Montreal Forum took place on the evening of March 24. Chicago scored the first goal in the best-of-seven series at 13:34 of the second period when Gerry (Doc) Couture rifled in Sid Finney's rebound. Gerry McNeil, the Canadiens netminder, fell flat on his back in stopping Finney's drive, and Couture quickly scooped up the rebound and scored.

The lead didn't last long. Bernie "Boom Boom" Geoffrion pushed in Paul Meger's pass from behind the Chicago net at 14:15, a little more than a minute later, to even the count. Meger had drawn Rollins to the side and almost to the rear of his net before passing to the waiting Geoffrion.

Veteran Habs defenceman Butch Bouchard scored early in the third period to break the deadlock when he slapped in a shot from the blueline.

The tally had been set up, however, by defenceman Tom Johnson's dash from one side of the rink to the other. Johnson then circled the Chicago net with the puck and shot on goalie Al Rollins. The puck bounced off the netminder's stick and slid out to Bouchard. Bouchard whacked it in the fashion of a golfer, and Rollins never had a chance to stop it.

The goal broke up one of the fiercest checking games seen in the Forum in years.

A few minutes later, Maurice Richard skated in on Rollins and crashed into him. Richard, Rollins, and the puck all wound up in the net, but the goal judge and referee both agreed that Richard had not taken a shot but merely crashed through the crease.

Then with two minutes left in the game, Paul Meger took a pass from Bernie Geoffrion at centre ice and sailed in alone for a shot at Rollins. He fired away, and the goal judge flashed the light for a score. The Chicago players swarmed the officials protesting that Meger's shot had hit the post. Led by coach Sid Abel, who made one of his rare appearances as player, the Hawks kept up their protests for ten minutes but to no avail. Bouchard's goal would hold-up as the game-winner as the Canadiens took Game 1 by a 3-1 score.

A couple of nights later, the clubs met up again at the Forum for Game 2. The Hawks were determined to get back in the series with a win as their engines were going full blast from puck drop.

A sizzling shot from the Hawks' Jim McFadden whistled into the Canadiens net after only 2:35 minutes of play. Floyd Curry scored at the 5:17 mark to tie the game when he converted Dollard St. Laurent's perfectly placed pass from the Chicago blueline.

The deadlock didn't last for long as George Gee got in front of Gerry McNeil in time to convert Bill Mosienko's pass out at 5:29—twelve seconds after the Canadiens goal—and the Hawks were in front. McFadden then scored again, this time from the blueline to make it 3-1 Hawks at the intermission.

The Hawks' two-goal lead quickly evaporated as Dickie Moore, Bernie Geoffrion, and Dick Gamble scored in the space of seven minutes during the middle frame to give Montreal a 4-3 edge.

Moore deflected in Tom Johnson's slapshot. Geoffrion sizzled Elmer Lach's pass home on a screened shot, and Gamble was at the side of Rollins' net in time to tip in defenceman Jim MacPherson's scorcher from the sideboards.

Also, in the second period, Paul Meger from the Habs was rushed to the hospital after he was whacked solidly by the heel of Jimmy Peters' stick. After the game, word from the hospital was that Meger had a "damaged right eye" and would be confined there for at least forty-eight hours.

Al Rollins made a dozen sensational saves to keep his team in it as he stopped 39 shots on the night. However, Chicago couldn't get anything going in the third period, and they lost 4-3.

"I'm downright disappointed," player-coach Sid Abel shouted across the Chicago dressing room to his team after they had blown a two-goal lead and lost.

Every player on the club, heads hung low, heard him.

"I'm plain disgusted," Abel continued. "After the first period, I thought it would be a walkaway for us."

The *Montreal Gazette* reported in the next day's paper that, "It was the most free-wheeling game seen in the Forum this year as both clubs spread out like relay runners. The Canadiens again outskated the Hawks and were more effective at the goalmouth than they appeared in Game 1."

If Chicago was going to get back into the series, they would need to be able to skate with Montreal for a full sixty minutes—something they had failed to do in the first two games.

The series moved to Chicago Stadium for Game 3 and Game 4 and the Hawks hoped that their home crowd would spark the troops.

Fans began lining up outside the massive Chicago Stadium doors on W. Madison Street a good eight hours before game time. They had purchased their tickets a couple of days earlier but were now primarily interested in getting to the unreserved seats they had used all season before someone else could.

Once the stadium gates were thrown open at 7 p.m., the balcony stalwarts bounced up the stairs to the top tier at breakneck speed for those all-important regular spots. As soon as they could, they then took to their favourite pre-game pastime, and within half an hour, the rink was littered with hundreds of paper airplanes.

By the time the teams had made their way to the ice for Game 3, the fans had become tired of such preliminary activities and were growing impatient for the opening faceoff. They cheered the Hawks loudly and singled out several Canadiens with assorted boos and jeers. Treated with even less respect were the referee and linesmen.

The first period was only five minutes old when Chicago's crowd displayed their first real belligerence. A four-player tangle along the boards to the left of the Montreal cage was a harmless enough scuffle until someone tossed a lit cigarette down Tom Johnson's neck.

While the Habs rearguard hopped around like a jackrabbit on skates, teammate Butch Bouchard stormed over and pointed an accusing finger at the spectator he thought had committed the offence. This action brought on a double-barrelled counterattack from virtually the entire crowd.

The behaviour of the Chicago crowd was ruthless, to say the least. Another fan pelted Johnson in the head with an egg, while a turnip narrowly missed Elmer Lach. Other things thrown on the ice included coins, playing cards, peanuts, bolts, hats, shoes, paper darts, cigars, cigarettes, torn-up newspapers—even a toupee! At one point, toilet-paper streamers trailed behind a few players.

Chicago Stadium was truly a madhouse that evening.

While Bouchard attempted to reprimand the alleged culprit, he was subjected to the most abusive of verbal assaults. The explosive onlookers also gestured with their fists and waved handkerchiefs in sassy retort. Things might have gone further had officials and ushers not stepped into quiet hostilities.

Chicago enthusiasts found numerous other chances to let out their special brand of criticism. They bellowed bitterly late in the first period when Vic Lynn's goal was disallowed. The play was called back when the linesmen blew his whistle, erroneously thinking that the puck had gone into the seats instead of the net.

Boom Boom Geoffrion tallied for the Canadiens in the second period to open the scoring. He came down the side of the rink and, at centre ice, skated behind Rags Raglan, took a pass from Doug Harvey, and beat Rollins with a shot from ten feet out.

The Hawks appeared outclassed until the last seven minutes of the game. Then they turned it on.

With two minutes left in the third period, a scramble broke out in front of the Habs net. Bill Mosienko grabbed a pass from Al Dewsbury and slapped a four-foot backhand into the Montreal net to force overtime.

The Stadium rafters then shook and rumbled to the most thunderous ovation heard during a hockey game in Chicago in many years. People screamed, danced, hugged each other in as wild an exhibition of mass hysteria as reporters and players had ever seen.

"I thought they were going nuts," Mosienko said after the game. "To hear that noise and see those people was undoubtedly the biggest thrill I have ever experienced in hockey."

TV sportscaster Joe Wilson remarked, "I've often wondered if the building might collapse if the racket ever got loud enough. Boy, I thought this was the time!"

That night, the final heroics belonged to Al Dewsbury, who brought the Hawks to victory after five minutes and eighteen seconds of overtime with a forty-foot blockbuster. Habs goalie Gerry McNeil had the puck under his arm but didn't know it, and when he looked to see where it was, it dropped back into the net.

The intensity of the jubilation from the crowd was somewhat less than when Mosie scored, however, for the physical need for such a spontaneous reaction had not yet been restored to many of the watchers.

Dewsbury, nevertheless, was accorded the satisfying honour of being the top offensive skater of the night. In addition to tallying the decisive goal, he had set up the play for Mosie's tying goal.

It was the Hawks' first playoff win since 1944 and their first win in the last eleven playoff games with the Canadiens.

But more importantly, they were back in the series.

"We finally got the breaks," commented Sid Abel, in subdued contentment after the game. "But why did Mosienko have to wait so long for that goal?" he grinned.

"Rollins saved us," he continued. "I thought we were goners in the first three minutes of that overtime. But he stopped three shots that were labelled, and when you stop shots by these guys, you're playing."

The shots Abel cited were fired by none other than Elmer Lach and Maurice Richard.

"I thought Richard had us when he came out from behind the goal with the puck," Abel said. "He made that long, sweeping motion, and Rollins stopped him. Last year, when I was with Detroit, he made four of the those same saves on us in overtime."

Abel said that this series had taught him to make no special defence for the Richard-Lach-Bert Olmstead line.

"We tried to have Vic Lynn on Richard," he said, "but in the first two games, we couldn't keep shifting lines fast enough, and we held them pretty well. So now we just play them as they come."

"It works out all right. Lynn is best on Richard, but Sid Finney can't hold Lach any better than somebody else."

Habs coach Dick Irvin complained about the Hawks fans' poor behavior and said that the debris they threw on the ice cost the Canadiens when Mosienko scored to tie the game.

"We had possession, and then one of our fellows fell and lost the puck, and then the other guy tripped and fell on the same thing. They both tripped on stuff thrown on the ice by the spectators."

Two nights later, the teams met once again in Chicago for Game 4.

Chicago squared the series with a 3-1 win before 16,487 fans on Vic Lynn's first goal of the season with less than eight minutes left in the game.

It was a come-from-behind triumph for the Hawks. Bert Olmstead, a former Hawk, put the Canadiens ahead midway through the first period, and with Montreal forcing the play regularly, it appeared the margin might stand up.

But Mosienko stayed hot and scored for the second straight game, less than three minutes after the second period got underway. Bill Gadsby was the playmaker in setting up this one. He swooped down the north side of the rink carrying the puck into the Canadiens zone, and passed out to Mosienko in front of the net. Gadsby threw a pass from the left lane on Mosienko's stick, and the veteran sniper turned and blasted a ten-footer head-on past McNeil.

The *Montreal Star* reported after the game, "When Mosienko starts for a target, let everyone beware because he is one of the great right-wing players next to Richard and Howe in the league. He is a twist and twirl guy, and he can score from right or left-wing, and he showed his versatility by shooting on a backhand shot last night."

Then the game became rough and fast, with both teams going at top speed in an attempt to break the deadlock.

Vic Lynn, who didn't score all season for Chicago, eventually broke it in the third period. After a faceoff near the Montreal cage, he picked up the puck near the blueline and, with one sweep of his stick, lifted it waist-high through a mass of players on the route to the net. Habs goalie Gerry McNeil saw the puck too late, and it dropped into the net behind him as he vainly lifted his stick to attempt a save.

Jimmy McFadden scored the Hawks insurance marker in the last few seconds of the game with the Habs goalie pulled.

Rollins was the star of the game, turning away twenty-five shots, most of them spectacular. Once, he stopped what appeared to be a certain goal when Dollard St. Laurent broke between the Hawk defencemen for a breakaway.

Al Rollins worked so hard that he lost seven pounds in the game. "I weighed 177 pounds before the game and 170 afterwards," he quipped. "I usually lose five pounds a game."

Sid Abel credited a change in strategy for his team's amazing comeback in the series. After coming from behind each time to win two games in the Stadium and tie the series, Abel's Hawks were now headed for Montreal, determined to move out in front of the Canadiens in Game 5.

"We tried defensive hockey before in Montreal, and it fizzled," Sid said before leaving for Montreal. "So we switched to offensive play at home and won. We'll keep carrying the play to the Canadiens the rest of the way."

"We got the breaks up there; they got them down here," snapped Habs coach Dick Irvin. "It's as simple as that. We'll win at home Thursday, and then when we come back here Saturday, it's all over. We can even afford to lose here Saturday and get them at home for that seventh game."

Hawks player-coach Sid Abel had nearly as rosy an attitude.

"That was the big one," he told the *Montreal Gazette*. "We sure stopped all that talk of theirs about 'four straight.'"

Both coaches praised the play of Al Rollins. And the Hawks had words of exultant praise for Mosienko, who, for the second straight game, hit the goal that brought them into a tie and made victory possible.

However, Irvin complained morosely that the Black Hawks' first goal by Mosienko to tie the score in the second period should never have been allowed.

"George Gee was ten feet offside," Irvin barked. "He never came out across the blueline, and the puck came out and went back in. All our players thought there'd be the whistle, and that's how Mosienko got the puck all alone."

As the old saying goes in hockey, your job is to play hard until you hear a whistle.

"He's full of baloney," Abel shot back. "Gee stood just across the line, and Bill Gadsby passed the puck in. It hit one of their player's skates and went over to Mosie."

Vic Lynn, who came to the team in mid-season from Cleveland, was the toast of his teammates on the train ride to Montreal as he scored the game-winner for the Hawks. It was also his first goal since joining the club. Lynn had scored two nights before, but the goal was called back.

"I waited a long time for this, but it couldn't have come at a better time," the perspiring Lynn laughed to reporters.

The packed crowd in Chicago Stadium surely played a role in the Hawks' victories at home.

Two banners hung around Chicago Stadium in Game 4 read as follows: "Go-Go Hawks" and "Richard's Crying Towel." The latter was a huge white banner that resembled a towel in appearance. "Go-Go Hawks" is the battle cry of many Chicago fans. It was adopted from the previous season's White Sox when the slogan was "Go-Go Sox."

"Those big crowds really spur you on," Mosienko said. "When you know that they are right behind you all the time, it gives you an added incentive to dig just a little harder."

Back at the Montreal Forum for Game 5, the Hawks seemed to carry over the momentum from the previous two games as they struck quickly, scoring three goals in the first period as Canadiens netminder Gerry McNeil appeared shaky. First, Fred Hucul scored on a looping drive from outside the Habs blueline after just four minutes of play. The puck made a fluke bounce and darted past the confused McNeil.

Mosienko, who the *Montreal Gazette* called "a speedball that has been a standout for the Hawks since the series began," made it 2-0 at 6:59 when he picked up George Gee's rebound and rifled it past McNeil, who appeared to make no attempt to save it.

Five minutes later, Mosienko carried McNeil and defenceman Butch Bouchard wide of the net and left the puck sitting at the crease for Gus Bodnar to poke home to extend the Hawks lead to 3-0.

The Canadiens tried to switch their strategy to back-alley shenanigans after they got down 3-0 in the first period.

With six inches advantage in height and fifty extra pounds in weight, Bud MacPherson smashed Mosienko into the end boards. When Mosie came up punching, MacPherson countered with the boldness of a pop sparring with a junior. They traded punches and had a decent scrap.

It was one of the few times in Mosienko's career in which he received a fighting major.

Maurice Richard scored five minutes into the second period when Elmer Lach put a pass on his stick five feet out from Al Rollins, who had robbed the Rocket with brilliant saves in the first period.

Later in the game, Dickie Moore forgot about chasing the puck and instead took a full two-handed swipe at Jimmy McFadden. And then Rocket Richard got revenge on Vic Lynn, who was frustrating the Rocket all game, and shoved him into the Montreal bench.

The game had a disorderly ending to it, with Sid Abel's hands accusing the Canadiens of deliberately trying to maim one of his players. Shortly after, 14,426 Habs fans showered the Forum ice with everything from peanuts to Homburg hats.

The big story on the night was Al Rollins continuing to stand on his head for Chicago as they would go on to win 4-2. Chicago had won Game 5 and now had two chances to punch their first ticket to the Cup final since 1944.

Talking to journalists after the game, Rocket Richard gave full credit to Al Rollins for the tremendous job he was doing in goal. "The man is 75 percent better than he was in Toronto. I dig in on him, and he is like an octopus—all hands and feet and body and so many of all of it, it seems," Richard said.

Al Rollins played such a good series that one veteran Montreal writer was moved to mention him in the same sentence with George Hainsworth and Bill Durnan.

Chicago would now have a chance to win the series at home, and the Hawks were convinced that they were on the verge of an upset.

Coach Abel was beaming "We have a hotter attack, a stiffer defence and a goaltender no club in this league can match," he said.

Montreal reporter Elmer Ferguson noted that Rollins' performance was so stellar that it earned applause from the Forum fans and then repeated the belief that hot goaltending can steal a series.

While Chicago appeared to have all the momentum, the series was far from over as Habs coach Dick Irvin had a big trick up his sleeve for Game 6.

Irvin waited until the last minute but then announced before the game that McNeil had asked to be relieved "for the good of the team" in favour of a rookie call-up by the name of Jacques Plante. McNeil had felt largely responsible for Montreal's three successive defeats after winning the first two games of the series.

Irvin had apparently given Plante the nod late that afternoon at the Hotel LaSalle. Afterwards, the young replacement would admit that he was so nervous that he had trouble doing up his skates before the game.

As it turns out, it was the Chicago team who were the shaky ones when the puck was dropped.

Bernie Geoffrion scored in the first period as the Canadiens took a 1-0 lead. Maurice Richard got an unassisted goal early in the second period, and Ken Mosdell wound up scoring later in the same frame to make it 3-0 Montreal after two periods.

Geoffrion's goal came off a pass from Dickie Moore, who picked up the loose puck after Mosienko had missed a pass. Geoffrion fired his patented slap shot from fifteen feet out, and after Rollins stopped the initial shot, he slapped in the rebound into the corner of the net.

Richard's goal, his second of the series, came at 3:23. He lofted the puck against the backboards, then raced in to puck it up and poke it in off Rollins' skate.

Calum MacKay and Lorne Davis carried the puck in, and Mosdell tipped it past Rollins for the third goal at 16:50.

One side of Mosienko's face became badly bruised during the second frame as a result of a puck he stopped with his face. Teammate Gus Bodnar's pass deflected and hit him accidentally.

The Hawks couldn't muster any offence in the final period as Jacques Plante shutout the Hawks 3-0 to force a Game 7. Plante faced a considerably lighter workload as he only stopped twenty-three shots to Rollins' thirty-eight. But the rookie operated well under pressure when Mosie and the Hawks were buzzing on the powerplay on two occasions.

After the game, Dick Irvin quickly announced that he would stick with Plante for the final contest.

Although he admitted he was nervous for a few minutes early in the first period, that all changed when Jimmy McFadden swept in on the Montreal goal and let go of a hotshot that Plante gloved neatly.

"I relaxed after that," Plante said. "I just happened to pick the right corner to cover when the shot came in, and I stopped it."

Irvin also thought that save might have been the turning point.

"Plante might have saved the game with that first save," he said. "We picked up confidence."

The Hawks, however, were reserving opinions on the rookie netminder. "We don't know how yet how good that young goalie is. We had only two or three real good shots on him all night," said Sid Abel. "He made a great save on McFadden and again on George Gee. Another time Gus Bodnar had a chance and hit the post. Otherwise, we weren't digging through. That's the worst game we've played all year."

Mosienko's stance on how great the crowd was earlier in the series quickly changed after Game 6. The Stadium attendants had to make seven appearances during the game, clearing debris off the ice. Bill blamed the fans that tossed the carload of junk upon the Stadium ice during the game as aiding and abetting the Canadiens cause.

"We might have pulled that came out of the fire, had not fans in the upper balconies tossed all of that stuff on the ice," Mosienko, the usually quiet, soft-spoken gent said in obvious anger. "The crowd was doing just what Montreal players wanted. They were ahead, so every delay helped their cause. Every time we got a break and started a drive, it seemed like a bundle of paper, an egg, and once, a sack full of charcoal was spilled upon the ice. Time was called, and we were thwarted, not the Canadiens."

Mosienko explained that he believes fans have a mistaken idea when they toss such junk upon the ice. "Maybe they think they are harming the opposing team," he explained. "An egg did hit Tom Johnson on the forehead. Another did clog the skates of goalie Jacques Plante. But each time, it stopped play—and that was what the Canadiens wanted. They wanted to check us from working up scoring drives."

Mosienko also pointed out that every time fans tossed pennies upon the ice, it only deterred the Hawks' chances of winning. "I skated over pennies several times, and it seemed this would happen just when I was in position to put on a scoring rush," he pointed out. "Each time I had to go off the ice and have my skates re-sharpened."

You can tell that Mosienko was feeling the pressure of trying to win the Stanley Cup. In his mind, he must have thought that this was his last chance at it, and he was going to do everything in his power to win.

The Hawks and Canadiens met up at Montreal Forum on the evening of April 7 to decide this series once and for all in Game 7.

Boom Boom Geoffrion opened the scoring for Montreal in the game's opening two minutes. It was a typical Geoffrion goal: a wicked shot that did not give lanky Al Rollins time to flex a single muscle.

It stayed 1-0 after the first period.

The pride of Winnipeg, Bill Mosienko—who was unquestionably Chicago's best forward of the playoffs—tied the game at 14:15 of the second period. Mosie carried the puck into Montreal territory, passed to Gus Mortson, who passed it right back, and fired it into the Montreal cage for his fourth goal of the series.

It marked the third time in the playoffs that Bill had pulled the Hawks from behind.

Bill was hoping to build off the tying goal and carry his troops to victory, but sadly it wasn't meant to be. Another Winnipegger by the name of Eddie "Spider" Mazur, a twenty-three-year-old rookie for the Canadiens that was inserted on the first line with Elmer Lach and Rocket Richard, became the hero of the series.

The tie lasted just eighty-eight seconds before Eddie Mazur picked up a loose puck in the Chicago end, moved quickly, and rifled a sizzler at the net. It ricocheted in off of Gus Mortson's skate.

Rocket Richard's third goal of the series at 4:51 of the third period completely disorganized the Black Hawks, who had not been able to muster an effective attack all night. It came on a pass from Mazur after Rollins had stopped at least five Habs shots in a few seconds.

Mazur scored his second goal and the cleanest of the night at 13:55 of the final frame when he and Elmer Lach sailed in alone. Lach put the pass right on Mazur's stick, and the big rookie roared around the Chicago defence and fired a shot on which Rollins had no chance whatsoever.

For the second straight game, rookie netminder Jacques Plante had held the fort down in goal. The Canadiens won 4-1 to win the series and advance to the Stanley Cup Finals.

Mazur's two goals stole some glory from Maurice Richard, who scored the fiftieth goal of his playoff career as the Canadiens completely overpowered the Hawks in this decisive game.

In the Habs dressing room after the game, coach Dick Irvin walked up to Mazur and, with a smile and a handshake, said, "An old Winnipegger, eh?"

Then turning to the crowd in the room, Irvin said, "Wasn't that guy terrific? He sure can move for a big fellow. Did you see how he wheeled around Bill Gadsby for that fourth goal?"

Irvin then told reporters, "It was a nice game to win and a good, clean series. I thought all seven games were good. Actually, the best two were in Chicago, and the Hawks won both of them. I think our gamble of putting in four fresh players made the difference."

Hawks coach Sid Abel hustled into the Canadiens room to congratulate Irvin and the team. He shook hands with each Montreal player.

"Hope you go all the way, boys," said Abel. Then, as he was leaving, he called out to Irvin, "Give 'em hell, Dick."

The Hawks were able to leave with their head held high. They at least had the consolation of winning three playoff games after losing ten in a row in the playoffs to Montreal over the years.

Back in their dressing room, the Hawk players quietly took off their uniforms for the last time that season.

Al Rollins, who played outstanding in goal for Chicago, stoically told the press, "Canadiens certainly played well. It was a good series, but it is all over now."

Comments by Elmer Lach and most others suggested that the truly outstanding netminder of the series was Al Rollins, who made a point of shaking hands with both Plante and McNeil at the end of the game. Rollins made 41 saves in Game 7 to Plante's 33.

Jim Norris, the wealthy owner of the Chicago team, kept close to his players that season. He was in the team's dressing room after every game and travelled to all their road games. After Game 7, he gave each player their $500 bonus for reaching the league semifinals. Had the Hawks won the series, they would have received $1,000, while if they'd won the Stanley Cup, each player would have taken home a $2,500 bonus.

The Hockey News editor Ken McKenzie noted that Al Rollins and Bill Mosienko were the star players for Chicago in the series:

> Rollins' terrific goaltending had broken the hearts of Montreal players throughout the series. His play during the fifth game was as great an exhibition of goalkeeping as we've ever had the pleasure to watch. He repeatedly robbed Canadiens players of sure goals while Wee Willie Mosienko ignited the spark for the rest of the Chicago players. Mosie, one of the league's veterans, was playing

the finest hockey he's displayed in years. Billy was constantly a headache to goalie Gerry McNeil, and it was Mosie's tying goal in the third period in Game 3 that sent the game to overtime and ultimately a win for Chicago that started to turn the series around for them.

A deeper dive into this series shows that Irvin's gamble of benching four of his regulars—Paul Meger, Dick Gamble, Paul Masnick and Gerry McNeil—and replacing them with minor league call-ups Calum Mackay, Lorne Davis, Eddie Mazur, and Jacques Plante was the difference.

The question going into Game 6 was whether Irvin would stand pat with a team that had lost three straight games, or if he would gamble with minor leaguers.

"A desperate situation calls for desperate measures," Irvin later said to the *Montreal Gazette*. "If I take a chance and lose, I'm going to be second-guessed to death, but what of it? It's now or never. I've had a feeling ever since the World Series last fall that the Dodgers would have won if Dressen had benched Gil Hodges. What was the point in keeping Hodges in the lineup? He was in a slump, and everybody knew it. He wasn't doing the team any good. Casey Stengel didn't hesitate to make changes all season long, did he? He wouldn't hesitate if he were in my position right now."

Mosienko was asked by the *Chicago Tribune* what his plans were for the offseason. As always, he'd be returning to Winnipeg, where he had his bowling operation with Joe Cooper. "We operate twenty bowling alleys in Winnipeg. Joe handles the business in the winter while I'm playing hockey," said Mosienko. "After every season, I rush back to help. As a result, I've never seen a Major League Baseball game. Maybe this time I can stay over and see the Cubs and Sox in action. That would be a thrill."

Mosienko was, in fact, able to take in a Chicago Cubs game before heading back to Winnipeg. Something he had never been able to do before because his Hawks had never played that late in spring before.

Through it all, Bill sadly realized that this would likely be his last real chance to win a Stanley Cup, and it had slipped him by.

Ed Sandford was one heck of a hockey player. Born in 1928, Ed grew up in the Toronto area and played junior hockey with the St. Michael's Majors. He led his club to the Memorial Cup playoffs in back-to-back years (1946 and 1947). In 1947, Sandford exploded for 67 points in only 27 games. In the playoffs that year, he put up 52 points in nine OHA (Ontario Hockey Association) playoffs and ten Memorial Cup games, leading St. Michael's to their third Memorial Cup championships. Ed was awarded the Red Tilson Trophy as the OHA's most valuable player for his prolific scoring that year.

Sandford was quickly signed by the Boston Bruins and inserted right into their lineup in the 1947-48 season. He was one of the more reliable players for the Bruins in those days and played in the NHL All-Star Game for five straight seasons starting in 1951. During his last season in Boston, he was named team captain following the departure of long-time Bruins star forward Milt Schmidt.

Sandford retired in the late 1950s with 251 points in 503 career games. In 2001, the Society for International Hockey Research (SIHR), in efforts with the Hockey Hall of Fame and *The Hockey News*, produced a list of Conn Smythe Trophy winners if the award had been handed out prior to 1965 when it was first presented. It was determined that Sandford's performance in the 1953 playoffs, where he scored eight goals in eleven games, would have been good enough to win the Conn Smythe that year had the award, given to the most valuable player for their team in the playoffs, been given out back then.

After he retired, Ed stayed with the Bruins by taking on various off-ice duties. These included being a goal judge, official scorer, and eventually becoming the off-ice officials' supervisor for the Bruins. Later in life, Sandford got into the sport of curling and played for decades. Sandford is ninety-two years old now and is one of the few players still around that got to play against Mosienko in the NHL. Standford recalled:

Mosie could skate like the dickens. You'd turn around and try to get him, and he'd be gone in a flash. He was an awfully good hockey player and a very good skater. I played against him, but I had to work hard to stay with him. He was on a top line with the Bentleys, and they could move the puck very well. If the Chicago Blackhawks had better defence and a little better goaltending in those years, then they could have been a contender because they had the offensive firepower. But as I remember, they just lacked the defence and goaltending, so they never got too far in the playoffs.

In the early 1950s, Mosienko built a house for himself and his family at 889 Cathedral Avenue in the North End of Winnipeg. It's the home that he and Wanda would live in for the remainder of their lives.

"Dad pretty much built the house on Cathedral by himself and the help of his family and contractors," said Bill Jr. "We have a movie of him and the brothers working on the roof, shirts off in the hot sun. I think my dad's house, in the 50s, the cost was $5,000. It was a beautiful house, but it was only two bedrooms and an office. They weren't expecting any more kids, and then my sister Wendy was born, and the office became her little bedroom. We were pretty lucky as kids and pretty fortunate."

The Mosienko family had a bit of a scare in 1953 when two-year-old Brian was diagnosed with polio in his legs.

"He was walking and then one day he wasn't," recalled Bill Jr. "Our parents took him to the hospital and they wouldn't let mom come in. They took Brian at the door, stripped his clothes off, handed them to mom, and for a week she didn't know if her son was alive or dead. It was right at the peak of polio and lots of kids had it, so the hospitals were full at the time. Thankfully, our family knew a doctor that was able to track down how Brian was doing as he was in isolation for a while. He's had many operations on his legs since then, but he managed to get through it."

It was during the 1953-54 season that Bill began to have some serious thoughts about quitting the game of hockey so he could spend more

Father time! Bill with Brian, Wendy and Bill Jr. COURTESY MOSIENKO FAMILY

time working his bowling business, in addition to being around his family more.

Bill could see the writing was on the wall with the Hawks when they dealt his pal Gus Bodnar to Boston on February 16, 1954, for Jerry Toppazzini.

"I've been thinking about quitting for quite some time," Mosienko told the *Winnipeg Tribune*. "I may do so at the end of this season. Of course, you never know."

The Black Hawks were looking to build on their newfound success from the previous season; however, the club would open the year with a record of 0-7-1 to quickly fall into last place in the NHL standings. As would be the case for most of the past decade, wins would be few and far between for the club, as they won consecutive games only three times throughout the season and finished dead last with a 12-51-7 record, earning 31 points. The twelve wins was Chicago's fewest since the 1938-39 season, while the 31 points was their lowest total since the 1928-29 season.

Mosienko finished the year with 34 points in 65 games. One bright spot for Chicago was that their goaltender Al Rollins was awarded the Hart Trophy as the league's most valuable player at the end of the year, even though he only won 12 games and lost 47 that season. That should show just how vital Rollins was to that Chicago team night in and night out.

When the season concluded, Mosienko announced that he would be retiring from hockey to focus on his bowling business back home in Winnipeg:

"I don't feel tired; I feel like I could go on for a couple more years. I love hockey, and it's been good to me. So have the Hawks and Mr. Tobin. But I feel I should devote more of my time to my business at home. I have a twenty-lane bowling alley there."

Bill's long-time Chicago Black Hawks organization held a special "night" for him towards the end of the season with a generous supply of gifts for him and his family. The fans treated it as a "goodbye ceremony," and many were in tears to see Mosie go.

Bill also received a letter from the NHL's president Clarence Campbell congratulating him on his long and illustrious career:

> Dear Bill,
>
> It has come to my attention that the hockey fans of Chicago are planning to stage a 'Night' for you on March 19, in recognition of the many years of enjoyment they have received during your long career as a member of the Chicago Black Hawks.
>
> During that career, you have established a very enviable record as a skilful player and as a fine representative of professional hockey.
>
> The recognition which is being tendered to you on this occasion is well merited, and I hope that the occasion will be one which will give you cause to remember with pleasure and satisfaction.
>
> As one of your admirers, I hope that this does not indicate the termination of your career as a player, for the experience of all clubs in the National Hockey League in recent years has indicated that older players may not be able to stand the strain of playing the complete, long schedule but they are invaluable nevertheless in providing experience in tough competition.
>
> With kindest personal regards, I am, Yours very sincerely,
> Clarence Campbell.

It was a busy off-season for Chicago in the summer of 1954, as Tommy Ivan replaced Bill Tobin as general manager of the club. Ivan had previously been the Detroit Red Wings head coach from 1947 to 1954, winning three Stanley Cups with the team. Ivan soon hired Frank Eddolls to be his head coach, as Sid Abel was let go after the 1953-54 season. Eddolls had previously been a player-coach of the Buffalo Bisons of the AHL. One of Ivan's first moves as the team's general manager was to build a farm system, as the Black Hawks were the only team in the NHL without one.

An SOS from the Black Hawks one night in October reached Mosienko back in Winnipeg. The Hawks were desperately in need of their speedster for one more season.

They wanted him to reconsider his retirement.

Mosienko was enjoying his time back home in Winnipeg. However, when the Hawks wanted him back in the fall, he changed his mind. "I figured our business in Winnipeg needed more attention, so I quit," said Mosienko, "but when Chicago called me, I figured that if I could help them, I should."

It was a difficult decision for Mosie. He had announced in January of 1954 and had emphasized his intention of leaving the rinks of the National Hockey League forever, except perhaps as a spectator if he happened to be visiting in the neighbourhood of a franchise.

He was sincere about his plans at the time, but he had a mental reservation of sorts when he decided it was time to put away the tools of a trade that had been good to him.

Mosienko told *Blueline Magazine*:

> I guess it really wasn't too tough for me to reconsider after I had talked it over with my wife and with Joe Cooper, my partner in the bowling business. You see, I had decided to quit only because our bowling establishment had been getting larger—twenty alleys now where we started with ten. I had been away from it during the hockey season for the past six, seven years.
>
> I thought I should devote more time to it, in fairness to Joe. But I never once had the notion I was through as a player. I felt then—and feel now—that I had a couple of seasons of good

hockey left. After all, I've always been in good physical shape, and it does seem that little fellows like myself don't really age physically like big men. We don't put on excess weight, for one thing.

After getting that urgent telephone plea from Chicago, Mosienko discussed it with his wife and Cooper and, within a matter of hours, was on his way back to the NHL.

During the 1954-55 season, the Hawks were involved in a couple of trades. Metro Prystai was required by Chicago in November from Detroit for Lorne Davis. The Hawks then acquired Nick Mickoski, Allan Stanley and Rich Lamoureux from New York for Pete Conacher and Bill Gadsby. The Litzenberger trade paid off immediately, as he was awarded the Calder Memorial Trophy for the best rookie in the league at the conclusion of the season.

Mosienko managed to score 27 points in 64 appearances as he missed a few games due to injury. An errant puck struck Mosie in the face during one practice, inflicting a cut on his left eyelid, which took thirteen stitches to close. He missed some time in the lineup as it healed.

Once again, it would be another long season in Chicago. The team only won consecutive games twice throughout the season and had numerous losing streaks. The Hawks finished the year with a 13-40-17 record, earning 43 points, which represented a 12-point increase over the previous season; however, the club finished in last place in the league for the second year in a row.

After the season, Mosienko refused to respond to a ridiculously low contract offer from the Hawks. It was a sad way for the Black Hawks to end their relationship with one of the greatest players ever to don a Black Hawks sweater. But alas, Mosienko retired from hockey for the second time during the summer of 1955.

Over fourteen seasons in the National Hockey League, Mosienko had endured his fair share of injuries. After Mosienko announced his retirement from hockey for the second time, *The Hockey News* asked him to go through some of his most painful experiences in the league:

Mosie is still smiling after breaking his nose for the
1000th time!   COURTESY MOSIENKO FAMILY

Early on, Jack Shewchuk of Boston pushed me into the boards,
and I twisted my left ankle. I've missed quite a bit of playing time
since then, too, with various injuries. In 1945-46, Bill Moe of the
Rangers checked me, and I got torn ligaments in my knee. Later
that year, Don Grosso of Detroit bumped me into the boards,
which resulted in a shoulder separation.

In the 1947 All-Star game, Jim Thomson of Toronto checked
me into the boards, my skate caught, and I had a broken ankle. I
also had a separation in my other shoulder; torn knee ligaments
four times; a fractured toe; a fractured cheekbone—but I didn't
miss any playing time—and a fractured nose three times.

Ted Lindsay and Elmer Lach were pretty handy with the stick.
Howe plays for keeps. He's been brought up that way, and he
stops at nothing to stop you. I played against Richard for many

years, and he never did anything dirty to me. I never once saw him start anything, but they were on him all the time, and he just naturally blew up.

Even worse than the injuries, nothing was more painful than losing out on a Stanley Cup. That would have made my career complete.

Mosienko had also broken his nose so many times that he needed a nose operation in Chicago where they rebroke the nose to set it. After that, he wore a leather harness to protect it for a period of time, but opposing players were trying to grab it, and so he did away with it in short order.

"Dad had his nose broken so many times he had no cartilage left, that's why his nose was kind of flat," recalled Bill Jr. "He also told me they used to pack it with long strings of gauze, and it hurt like the dickens when they pulled out the gauze. I recall pictures of him with bandages on his nose and a shield over it when he played at one point."

It's worth noting the longevity of Bill's fourteen years in the NHL as only four other players were still around in the league in 1955 from when Bill started in 1942: Harry Watson, Bob Goldham, Butch Bouchard, and Sugar Jim Henry, who were all rookies at the time, along with Bill.

Looking back on his time in the NHL, Bill said to *Blueline Magazine*, "I guess that getting to the big league finally was the greatest thrill I ever had. It had been my aim always, but I sometimes used to think I'd never make it. I had read of the stars of that time—guys like Syl Apps, Syd Howe, Milt Schmidt, Bobby Bauer, Lynn Patrick and so on—but to play against them was something else."

And funnily enough, Bill said that the hat-trick he was the proudest of when he first left the NHL, is not the three goals in twenty-one seconds, but the night against Detroit in 1948 when he lit the lamp for four goals and an assist.

After all his years in hockey, he only has one mild gripe with the game, and that's the fact that he only won one Lady Byng Trophy:

That Detroit team has always played harder against me than any other team in the league. They seemed to be trying to goad me into penalties to help Red Kelly get the sportsmanship award. I honestly feel they were trying to set certain players on me to force me into rules infractions so I'd get a penalty!

Of course, when I first broke in, there were always 'policemen' to take care of me and such other small players as Doug and Max Bentley. Guys like Mariucci, Cooper, Babe Siebert and so on would make the other players stick to hockey and quit bullying. I never have had any serious fights. I just can't seem to get mad enough, and anyway, I can't fight very well. Besides, with a stick in my hand, I'd be afraid I'd do something I might always regret.

Bill left the NHL after scoring 258 goals and 282 assists for 540 points in 711 NHL games over fourteen seasons. He also scored 14 points in 22 Stanley Cup playoff games.

When he left the NHL in 1955, Mosienko ranked seventh on the all-time goals lists and ninth on the all-time points list. A legend of the sport, there was no doubt that he would be a future Hockey Hall of Fame inductee.

However, that would have to wait because—although Bill's time in the National Hockey League was ending—another door was opening before his eyes that would extend his professional hockey career.

COMING HOME

When the Winnipeg Warriors began play in the Western Hockey League (WHL) in the autumn of 1955, it marked the first time since the Winnipeg Maroons of 1928 that the city of Winnipeg had a professional hockey team.

The Warriors joined a nine-team league that consisted of the Vancouver Canucks, Victoria Cougars, New Westminster Royals, Seattle Totems, Calgary Stampeders, Saskatoon Quakers, Edmonton Flyers and St. Paul Regals. They would be playing their home games in the brand-new Winnipeg Arena, which was a state-of-the-art venue for hockey at the time. It was constructed to replace the obsolete Shea's Amphitheatre.

The men who were granted the new franchise were John Draper Perrin Sr., a wealthy mining entrepreneur, and his son, J.D. Perrin, Jr., the truly active owner. John Jr., or "Jack" as he was typically called, was both vice-president and general manager of the club.

At the time, the WHL was perhaps the second-best and certainly not worse than the third-best league in the world, behind only the National Hockey League and perhaps the American Hockey League. The league had a mix of young talent, minor league "superstars," and NHL veterans that had fallen out of the big league but were still wanting to play at a high-level.

The grand opening of Winnipeg Arena was on October 18, 1955, during the club's first game, against the Calgary Stampeders. The ceremonial faceoff, conducted by J.D. Perrin, Sr., President of the Warriors, occurred before a standing-room crowd of 9,671 fans, the largest in WHL history.

The Warriors were coached by Alf Pike, a Winnipegger who had had a solid NHL career with the New York Rangers as a sturdy winger. His time in the league was highlighted by winning the 1940 Stanley Cup.

Stocked through working agreements with the Toronto Maple Leafs and the Montreal Canadiens, the Warriors lineup had a nice mix of local talent and NHL prospects. Jack Perrin Jr. purchased veteran AHL defenceman Danny Summers to form an all-Winnipeg defence with captain Fred Shero, Mickey Keating, and Bill Burega. Bill's Game 7 nemesis Eddie "Spider" Mazur was sent home to Winnipeg by the Canadiens, as was Regina's Paul Masnick, who had played parts of five seasons with the NHL club.

Before the season began, the Maple Leafs shipped goalie Ed Chadwick to Winnipeg with young forwards Barry and Brian Cullen, Hugh Barlow, Mike Nykoluk and Winnipeg's Gary Aldcorn. The first three were line-mates on the 1954 Canadian junior champion St. Catharines TeePees, while Nykoluk and Aldcorn played for the 1955 Memorial Cup champion Toronto Marlboros.

The Warriors were immediately looking like a team that was built for a championship.

Initially, Mosienko said he didn't really consider playing hockey again after he left the NHL. Life was good in Winnipeg, working at the bowling alley and being around his family more. However, Mosienko's interest was certainly piqued when he found out the Warriors had been granted a franchise.

He was still doing the regular exercises that he always did in the off-season to stay in shape. For fifteen minutes every night, he would even make a "bicycling" motion with his legs, pumping them furiously over-head as he lay on the floor. He was always about strengthening his legs as it helped contribute to his fast skating.

With the season just getting underway, the Perrins and Alf Pike approached Bill and asked if he wanted to come out of retirement and play his last few years of pro hockey in Winnipeg in front of his family and friends.

Mosienko got the okay from his family and business partner Joe Cooper in short order and signed with the Warriors on October 21.

"My dad, being a true lover of Winnipeg, took them up on the deal. And he made more money in Winnipeg than he ever did in Chicago," said Brian Mosienko. "He always said one of his best moves was coming to the Warriors. Chicago didn't offer him a great contract, and so after playing fourteen years in the NHL, he decided that coming home was important. He could help with the bowling alley more and be around with his family all the time."

One of Bill's old teammates in Chicago, Nick Mickoski, who was also from the North End of Winnipeg, tipped off the Chicago owner that Bill was planning on resuming his pro hockey career elsewhere.

However, the Calgary Stampeders had actually bought Mosienko's rights after the previous season. They wanted Bill to play for them and not the Warriors, but Bill didn't want to play anywhere but home. A deal was made with them as well, and Bill finally joined the Warriors. The cost was around $7,000 in total fees for Mosienko's rights that the Perrins paid to both Chicago and Calgary.

Mosie wasn't all that impressed with Chicago's efforts after all he'd done for the organization and wondered why they just didn't release him so he could play at home without having to jump through so many hoops. Though, at the end of the day, Bill was just happy to be playing hockey again.

Mosienko had been skating at the Olympic Rink, loosening up and then flew to Vancouver to meet the team as they were on the road at the time of his signing.

"I hope too much isn't expected of me right away because I have only been on skates twice this season. It will take me a couple of weeks to work into condition," said Mosienko.

Bill said that with Winnipeg returning to professional hockey, he had felt that he wanted to help even before being approached to play for the Warriors.

Asked by the press if he had any preference for which line he would play on, Bill answered that he would play where the coach could use him best.

Bill and his Winnipeg Warriors squad getting in some team-bonding
at his bowling alley. (Left-to-right: Coach Alf Pike, Ed Chadwick,
Bill, Eddie Mazur, Skip Burchell) COURTESY MOSIENKO FAMILY

"I watched them play in their first game, and they didn't look too good, but I think they will go places. They have the talent and will be tough to stop when they get a few more games behind them."

With the Warriors, Bill got to become a teammate of childhood friend Fred Shero from Tobans. He also joined forces with Eddie Mazur, the fellow Winnipegger that was the hero in Game 7 of the Habs/Hawks series of 1953. They would go on to be good friends for life.

"Bill was just a beautiful skater. He wasn't very tall, but he was extremely strong," recalled Eddie Mazur years later to the *Winnipeg Free Press*. "The thing that stands out with Billy is that while being such a great hockey player, he was such a wonderful person, too. He cared about other people."

Mosienko skated on a line that season with Eddie Mazur at left wing and Skip Burchell at centre. And ever since coach Alf Pike put them together, they were the most dominant line in the league. Burchell was an excellent playmaker, and Mazur was a big guy with a scoring drive that worked well with Mosie.

Besides being a top-scoring winger, one of Mosienko's roles on the team as a veteran was to help develop some of the younger talent. One of these was Warriors rookie Barry Cullen.

Cullen led the Warriors in points that season with 72 in 67 games. Cullen would go on to play the next four seasons with the Toronto Maple Leafs before ending his time in the NHL with Detroit.

"Our paths only crossed briefly," recalled Cullen. "I was a rookie, and he was in the twilight of his career with the Warriors. I remember Bill being a real gentleman and the best skater in the league by a country mile. I was only twenty, so I would be in awe of this man who was a star in the NHL, that still skated like the wind, and at thirty-five, was the winger on the league's best line."

Gary Aldcorn was born in Shaunavon, Saskatchewan, on March 7, 1935, and moved to Winnipeg at the age of twelve. If there was a sport to be played, you can bet that Aldcorn not only played it but played it well. Hockey, baseball, basketball, track & field, lacrosse, football, and curling… you name it, he played it.

Aldcorn was also a rookie in 1955 with the Warriors before embarking on a five-year NHL career with the Toronto Maple Leafs, Detroit Red Wings and Boston Bruins.

"When I was growing up, we used to go to Baldy Northcott Sporting Goods, and Mosie's picture would be on the wall for the three goals that he had, so I grew up looking up to him as a legend of the game. And then getting to play with him with the Warriors was such a positive experience for me. Mosie was a great guy, super friendly, and a good motivator for everyone on the team. I learned a lot from him that season."

Midway into the season, Mosienko was sitting on the bench one night when teammate Cecil Hoekstra scored two goals in 21 seconds. Coach Alf Pike was ready to change lines when the usually mild-mannered Mosienko suddenly became agitated.

"Leave him on!" shouted Mosienko. "He's got a chance to break my record."

Hoekstra stayed on the ice and got another excellent scoring chance a few seconds later—but he hit the goal post.

"That told you what kind of guy Bill Mosienko was," recalled Fred Shero.

The word was out that Mosienko was still a speedster. He hadn't lost his touch in the slightest. Maple Leafs owner Conn Smythe watched a Warriors game in Winnipeg that year and was enthralled with how well Mosie played and said that he should still be playing in the NHL. "I don't run the Chicago hockey club. They've made a lot of mistakes down there. And they never should have broken up the Bentley-Mosienko line even though I profited by it," said Smythe.

Towards the end of the 1955-56 season, Mosienko was honoured prior to the start of the second period in a game at Winnipeg Arena against the Brandon Regals. He was honoured by the St. James and Brooklands Cadet Corps, sponsored by the 39th Field Regiment, RCA. Mosie was presented with the St. James Brooklands Cadet Corps Trophy, a new trophy that was awarded annually to the Winnipeg hockey player whose conduct on and off the ice paralleled the character development objectives of the cadet corps. More than fifty-five cadets of the two corps, 39th Regiment officers, and officers from the Army's Prairie Command attended the game and cheered on Mosienko.

Winnipeg Tribune reporter Vince Leah wrote that "Bill is no milquetoast character either, despite his friendly personality but having never gone around looking for trouble he has never found it."

All in all, the season was looking like a big success for Mosienko.

For young Bill Jr., he remembers being used to changing schools three times a year when his dad played for Chicago. With Bill playing at home now, it meant his kids could all live at their house year-round and not have to worry about moving during the school year anymore. It was the perfect set-up for Bill and his family.

All that talent on the Warriors team came through as they edged

Calgary by two points to win the Prairie Division. Mosienko would end the season with 45 points in 64 games.

In the playoffs, the Warriors swept Saskatoon in three straight games and then disposed of Calgary four-games-to-one to advance to the league final against the Coast Division champion Vancouver Canucks.

In Vancouver, the teams split the first four games of the best-of-seven series. Back home in Winnipeg, the Warriors won Game 5 handily by a 4-0 scoreline.

Heading into Game 6, Winnipeg was up three-games-to-two and had a chance to close out the series. Vancouver was up 2-0 after the first period, but when the game was over, the final score showed 6-3 Winnipeg.

Mosienko's goal started the avalanche of Warriors goals. Finding himself on the outside of the circle by the right boards near the Canucks goal, he spun in a familiar fashion and let the puck fly. Vancouver goalie Ray Mikulan, appearing as if he thought Mosienko was trying a pass, made his move. The puck caught the inside of his right skate and clicked into the net. No one appeared more surprised than Mosienko.

After the final horn sounded, Mosie accepted the President's Cup from league president Al Leader at centre ice.

The Winnipeg Warriors were President's Cup champs, and the biggest smile in the locker room afterwards certainly belonged to Mosie. After all, it was his first championship since he was eleven years old with his Tobans playground team.

In the dressing room, champagne flowed freely, and the Warriors celebrated joyfully.

"Took a long time, didn't it?" yelled Skip Burchell at Mosie. He was referring to championships, for in all Mosienko's years in the NHL, he never won a Cup.

"We got close one year in Chicago, but Montreal beat us in the final."

To top things off, the Mosienko family welcomed a brand-new daughter, Wendy, to the fold shortly after the President's Cup triumph.

After the game, Bill rushed to the hospital, where he was presented with his daughter. Still out of breath, he gulped, "Just what we wanted."

Bill and the team's celebration was short-lived because the season wasn't over yet. Winnipeg now had to play the Montreal Royals in a best-of-nine series for the Canadian minor pro championship.

The Edinburgh Trophy final featured the champions of the Quebec Hockey League and the Western Hockey League. All the games were held in western Canada because of the expense of travelling across the country and the travel time involved. Cross-country flights were not that common yet!

The Edinburgh Trophy finals were held after the Stanley Cup playoffs had wrapped up in order to minimize competition from television and radio broadcasts of the Stanley Cup games.

It was a best-of-nine series that was played in Calgary, Edmonton, and Winnipeg. However, the Warriors needed only six of those games to dispatch the Montreal club.

The final game saw the largest crowd in Winnipeg hockey history to that point, 10,072, witness the Warriors win the championships by a 3-1 score.

The applause for Mosienko after the Warriors won was tremendous. He was the last player to be introduced after the game.

It was a touching moment. The fans kept up a terrific yell until arena manager Stew MacPherson motioned Mosienko to say a few words. The roar continued for forty-five seconds and probably would have lasted much longer had Mosie not taken the mic.

"Chicago was never like this," said Billy, and he sounded as if he'd just sprinted around the rink a dozen times. Then he thanked the fans for their tremendous patronage and Jack Perrin and coach Alf Pike for the way they handled the club.

The fans cheered the Montreal Royals, who played hard, and for every Warriors player that was introduced. But that prolonged cheer for Mosie was the greatest.

"It will probably be remembered long after the Edinburgh trophy is forgotten," wrote the *Winnipeg Free Press*. "Bill scored a couple of goals that night, but that wasn't what caused such an ovation. He played his heart out all year and provided the fans with more excitement than any other player. It was the fans' opportunity to say 'thanks, Bill Mosienko.'"

"I've played with some great teams and some great guys," said Mosienko, "but it's hard to beat this bunch!"

Once again, champagne flowed in the dressing room. And each player on the Warriors also earned an extra $2,100 as a playoff bonus, which was more than the NHL players received for winning the Stanley Cup.

When asked where to go from here after winning the championship, Bill said, "Our spring league at the alleys is all ready to go right now, then maybe a little golf and some work around the house. I've got more family now, you know!"

The *Winnipeg Tribune* reported that "The best all-round player in the series was Bill Mosienko, primarily because of his offensive strength and consistent positional checking on defence. Eric Nesterenko was the best defensive forward, having had only three goals scored by the opposition while on the ice."

Mosienko remarked that the Warriors were a "happy family," and that the team's strong friendship and camaraderie helped the club bring home this championship.

Owner Jack Perrin said the turning point on the road to success was the day the club signed Mosienko. "Mosie has been a wonderful inspiration to every player on the team, especially the younger members," said Perrin. "He's a fine, proud hockey player who is not satisfied with mediocrity."

"When they won the Edinburgh Trophy against Montreal, the celebration party when they returned was at our home on Cathedral Avenue," recalled Bill Jr. "It was still an unfinished basement, but they partied hard late into the next day. Early on in the evening, I can still recall Pete Kapusta and another player carting a huge stereo record player down into the basement to keep the party going strong throughout the night!"

The goaltender of that championship Winnipeg Warriors team was Ed Chadwick. Born with a congenital disability called clubfoot, Chadwick's odds at a hockey career weren't likely when he was a young kid growing up in Ontario. But he persevered and went on to a strong pro career, notably his years in the late 1950s as the Toronto Maple Leafs netminder.

For the last fifty-seven years, after he retired from hockey, Chadwick has lived in beautiful Fort Erie, Ontario. He chuckles when I ask him about his time with Mosienko.

> That was a long time ago. We'll see if I can remember that far back! We started off a little slow that season and then we finally got going. Having Mosienko on our team made a big difference because he was quite a good guy and took care of some of the young guys on the team, and that built 'em up pretty good. Bill did things the right way.
>
> It was my first-year pro, and I remember we had 180 inches of snow that winter in Winnipeg, but it was nice. Things were good. I had my wife out with me, and the boys on the team got along good with one another. Some days you had problems getting your car started, but I really enjoyed it out there.
>
> I played every game, 140 games in a row for the Toronto Maple Leafs. I came close to some championships after that in the AHL, but I never won again after that year in Winnipeg.
>
> I remember Mosienko was sitting with us when we were in Calgary during the year, and he said, 'Let's go rent a car and go out to the Springs.' I came back from that trip with him, and there was a message to come see the coach. I saw the coach, and he said I'm out of here. I asked if he traded me. He said, 'No, you're going to Toronto.'

Chadwick went to Toronto and made his NHL debut playing five games while Harry Lumley was hurt. When Lumley returned to action, Chadwick came back to Winnipeg and led the Warriors to a championship.

Looking back, Chadwick has nothing but fond memories of his time on the prairies.

"Winnipeg was a great place to play. They treated you really well. I always remember when the team signed Mosie, and then he came along and got everybody going as he was a hometown boy who had all kinds of success in the NHL. He picked up the whole team, and we kept going from there. We knocked off Calgary, Vancouver, and Montreal to be Edinburgh Trophy champs. It was a good first year of professional hockey, you could say."

Today, Paul Masnick is all that's left of the 1953 Stanley Cup-winning Montreal Canadiens team. Every other member has since passed on.

At ninety years old, Paul lives quietly alone in Barrie, Ontario, in a tall apartment building overlooking Kempenfelt Bay. He doesn't own a television or a car. Instead, he enjoys listening to the radio and likes to bus around to get his groceries and visit his girlfriend. For fun, he enjoys playing penny stocks and reading various mineral magazines.

"I'm old school," said Masnick. "I guess I'm living in the past, but I still prefer to listen to the radio."

I was fortunate enough to have visited Paul while I was in Toronto at the beginning of 2020, right before the COVID-19 pandemic hit.

Masnick, who was born and raised in Regina, grew up having a fellow Ukrainian by the name of Bill Mosienko as his hockey idol. Masnick would listen to Bill on Foster Hewitt's radio broadcasts whenever the Hawks were playing Toronto.

> And then getting to play with Bill was something else. When I somehow managed to outscore him that season, I was so proud of myself.
>
> I got to play with Bill Mosienko when I joined the Winnipeg Warriors for the 1955-56 season, and that was one of the reasons I joined the Warriors was to play with a legend like Bill. It was also a great season for me personally. I remember a big game against Calgary that we needed to beat them, and we won 4-3, and I scored three goals. Coach Alf Pike used to put me on the powerplay. We won the Edinburgh trophy that year. And I remember we flew all over instead of taking the bus with Jack Perrin as our team's owner.

Masnick noted that the Warriors players each got a $2,100 bonus for winning the Edinburgh Trophy, while the Montreal Canadiens players who had won the Stanley Cup that year only received $2,000.

I then asked Paul about his 1953 Stanley Cup triumph with Montreal, and he quipped, "I'm so old I'm not even on the Stanley Cup anymore!"

At ninety years of age, Masnick credits the great shape he's in to doing everything he can over the last sixty years to live a healthy life.

"I sleep on the floor too! I feel it puts all your muscles and joints in balance. That's why I've lived so long!"

A fascinating man, I'm hoping to visit Paul again the next time I'm in southern Ontario.

In the Mosienkos new home in Winnipeg, a room was set aside to be Bill's office. And then daughter Wendy was born, which meant that the office became Wendy's tiny bedroom. Wendy was the only baby whose birth Bill was in Winnipeg for, and he scored a goal that night, too, in addition to winning a championship.

There were rumours swirling that Bill was going to retire after winning the championship. On top of that, he was suffering from a neck ailment and was wondering if he'd even be able to play.

Nonetheless, Mosienko signed on for the 1956-57 campaign during training camp.

It was during training camp that the NHL's Detroit Red Wings came to town. Detroit would go on to play an exhibition game against the Winnipeg Warriors at the beginning of every season from 1956 to 1960.

With the Warriors roster looking like a skeleton of the championship team from the spring, Detroit won handily by a 6-0 score. It was a sign of things to come that year.

When the Warriors had joined the WHL, owner Jack Perrin made a two-year deal with the Montreal Canadiens and Toronto Maple Leafs, by which the two NHL clubs agreed to provide the Warriors with fifteen players of WHL calibre while the NHL clubs would split fifty percent of the Warriors' aggregate profits. The agreement worked well in 1955-56, but the following year, Toronto and Montreal were more interested in placing players on their respective American League clubs in Rochester and Cleveland, which meant that the Warriors suffered heavily.

During the 1956-57 season, if Bill was contemplating retirement, you couldn't tell as he was really enjoying still playing hockey and being around the boys while also being around his family a ton and living at home. It was a nice balance for the ageless wonder.

"With the Warriors, Dad's pre-game ritual was broiling a T-bone steak with potatoes and vegetables for a pre-game meal at 2 or 3 p.m. as he didn't want to eat too close to game time," Bill Jr. recalled. "He would then nap for an hour or two before heading out to the rink."

"I had to be quiet when he was napping, which was tough when you're a rambunctious young lad!" added Brian Mosienko. "Mom would come in and say, 'Brian, keep it down, your dad's trying to sleep!'"

"I can remember him in those years when he would get new hockey skates. He'd put them on in the house and go around in them. He'd do some stepping in them to try and break them in before the blades were added to them."

One night that season, Bill separated his shoulder during a game in Calgary. He saw the x-rays, and everything appeared okay. But the plates also revealed that Mosie had broken a collarbone at one point, and he never knew it. A hairline fracture, as they say in the trade, and Bill traced it back to 1945-46 when he and the Hawks were battling the Montreal Canadiens in the playoffs.

"They said it was just pulled muscles or something like that when I got hurt at that time," said Mosie, "and they taped me up, and I went right back into action." It must have been a good tape job because the x-ray's revealed the break had knitted perfectly.

Bill also broke his nose for the umpteenth time that year in a game. This time, he grabbed the nose and straightened it himself. Ouch! He wore a cage after that for a few games as it healed.

Although this Warriors team was much weaker than the previous year, Bill had a great season personally, doing most of his team's scoring.

One game in New Westminster, Bill scored three goals in a 7-6 win. New Westminster Royals coach Hal Laycoe, who had to check Mosienko in the NHL, respected the speed of Winnipeg's top point-getter. "Billy is still one of the fastest hockey players on skates and has a deadly shot," Laycoe said. "I can remember when he raced the fastest man on each

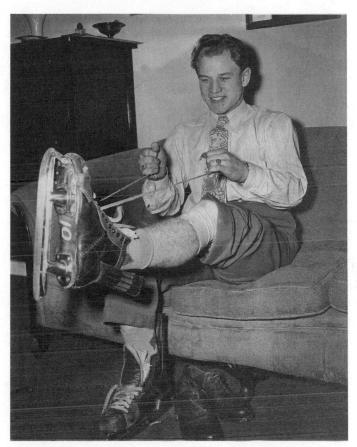

Bill trying on his custom-made skates. COURTESY MOSIENKO FAMILY

NHL club in an exhibition in Montreal and won by so much it was laughable."

Because the Warriors had affiliations with Toronto, the Maple Leafs had explored the possibility of getting Mosienko to come down to Toronto for a few games because they were dealing with injury problems throughout the year. But owner Jack Perrin quickly scoffed at that. "Would you part with Billy?" he was asked by a reporter. "Certainly not," he roared and then started reeling off half a dozen reasons why.

Bill was the leader of the Warriors and led by example. The Warriors' trainer in those years, Gordie Mackie, recalls, "These rookies would leave their laundry on the floor, and I'd tell them that I'm not your maid. I would then show them Bill's locker, and here he has everything hung up. When his game or practice ends, he comes in and hands everything up. Now you guys follow the same suit. And they usually did. Bill was a role model, plain and simple."

Unfortunately, it was a poor season for the Warriors as they finished in last place and missed the playoffs. However, Mosienko finished with 53 points in 61 games and was named to the league's All-Star team at the end of the year.

That year he was also named the first recipient of the 'Manitoba Athlete of the Year' award, which was known as the Ches McCance Trophy. At the time of the award, veteran Winnipeg sportswriter Jack Matheson called Bill "the best hockey player Winnipeg has ever turned out."

Bill returned to the Warriors for the 1957-58 WHL season, determined to get his club out of the league basement.

Jack Perrin and the Warriors greatly appreciated Bill for what he had done for not only this team but hockey in Manitoba, and so they chose to surprise him with a special honour that season.

On January 14, 1958, the Winnipeg Warriors held "Billy Mosienko Night" to honour their local hero. close to 9,000 Winnipeg hockey fans turned out at the Winnipeg Arena for that night's game and to honour Bill's extraordinary career.

Mosienko scored the Warriors two goals that night as they went down to St. Paul-Saskatoon Regals 5-2.

After the game had ended, gifts and speeches were presented to Bill and his family on the ice, while tributes came from all corners of the city and province. Alderman Walter Crawford represented the city in the absence of Mayor Stephen Juba, while Honourable Robert Bend, Minister of Health and Welfare, represented the province. Mr. Bend made Mosie a member of the Order of the Buffalo Hunt and informed him he was entitled to shoot buffalo without a license.

Others who made presentations to Billy were Hay Bryak, president of the Canadian Ukrainian Veterans, Canadian Legion; John Shaley,

Bill with Wanda and their sons Bill Jr. and Brian, with all the gifts they received on Billy Mosienko Night in 1958. COURTESY MOSIENKO FAMILY

president of Canadian Ukrainian Athletic Club (CUAC); Jack Kolt, president of the Canadian Polish Athletic Association (CPAC); Danny Summers, Warriors defenceman. And then Warriors owner Jack Perrin gave Mosie a new convertible as a gift from the fans.

The family shared in the spoils as well.

"The gifts were incredible. They presented dad with a 1958 Dodge Mayfair convertible car with a push button transmission shift. My brother and I got CCM bicycles, and my sister got a massive panda bear with a Warriors shirt on it. She was just a baby and too young to be there that night!" recalled Bill Jr. "Dad also received a golden skates plaque from Labatt's Brewery, and there were even more gifts bestowed on top of that."

The *Winnipeg Tribune* wrote,

> Yes, the fans saw all the honours and presents heaped upon their
> favourite hockey son. But when it appeared the evening was over,

and the photographers had used up their last flashbulb, the greatest thrill of the night was still to come for Mosienko that the fans didn't get to see. It was the tribute paid to him within the confines of the Warriors dressing room by his own teammates. The moment Billy walked into the dressing room with sons Brian and Bill Jr. clinging tightly to his hands, every member of the Warriors rose as one man and started singing 'For He's a Jolly Good Fellow.' It was an action as spontaneous and delightful to see as anything could be. Surprised, Mosienko just stood there, swallowing hard and fighting desperately to keep the moisture that filled his eyes from rolling down his cheeks. You knew as you watched him standing there with his two boys at his side that there had never been a prouder moment in his lifetime. Few athletes have ever been so admired by their teammates as Billy Mosienko.

It was a night that Mosie never forgot for the rest of his life.

Bill received many wires from distant points around North America, but the most humorous came from the rival Edmonton Flyers. Signed by Manager Bud Poile and Coach Tony Leswick, the wire said that Flyers were giving him a trip to Florida, on the condition he remained there until June 15 when the playoffs were done. It concluded: "Take coach Alf Pike with you."

Here are a few other examples of the esteem in which he was held elsewhere. Bill Tobin, former general manager of the Chicago Black Hawks, wired: "Mrs. Tobin, Elaine, Don and I want to be included with your hundreds of friends in remembering you on this day. You set an example that cannot be surpassed by anyone. Thank you, Bill."

From Ken Reardon of the Montreal Canadiens: "I have waved at you as you went around our defencemen more than once, and now I congratulate you on the excellence of your play in Winnipeg and of the career you had in the NHL. I'm happy the fans appreciate your worth."

Al Leader, president of the Western Hockey League, sent this message from Seattle: "Congratulations and best wishes to a great competitor who has contributed so much to our game."

Bill's old coach and friend in Chicago, Johnny Gottselig, added:

"With the hockey people of Winnipeg, I join in extending my sincere best wishes on this memorable occasion to Bill Mosienko, a fine gentleman, a wonderful father and a great hockey player. Also, a great friend and with an infinite capacity for friendship and an inspiration to the youth of America."

The team left the dressing room afterwards and headed right to Bill's home for an all-night party in the basement. The whole team and press were invited to the big party!

The next day, Dallis Beck, a sportswriter for the *Winnipeg Tribune*, wrote about Bill's big night and had some kind words for a kind man:

> My wife has a kid brother in Saskatoon who goes to see pro hockey games only when the Winnipeg Warriors are the visiting team. The prime reason for this is because a guy named Billy Mosienko plays for the Winnipeg Warriors.
>
> My wife's kid brother shook hands and chatted briefly but blissfully with Billy Mosienko two years ago in a sweaty Saskatoon Arena dressing room. He went back a year later to see the Warriors play and said hello again to Billy Mosienko. Mosie said he'd pass along the kid brother's regards to me in Winnipeg.
>
> He did, and he also stuck out his hand to renew acquaintances when the kid brother came to visit us in Winnipeg this Christmas and dropped around to the Warrior dressing room.
>
> A little home-spun, you think?
>
> Maybe so. But it's one of the ten thousand little things that make Billy Mosienko the idol of every kid brother in the country who has had the opportunity to see him play, shake his hand, or get his autograph on an old broken-down popcorn box.
>
> When they made Billy Mosienko, they made a prize.
>
> Where do you find more ability, more down-right sincerity, more unabashed humility from a great man, all of this, wrapped into a five-foot-eight, 160-pound package?
>
> The guy who said one day that 'Mosienko is the kind of man you'd like your son to grow up to be' wasn't far from wrong. It's hackneyed, but it's true.

Denis Ball, the Manitoba-based NHL scout for the New York Rangers, honoured Mosienko in that night's game program with this passage:

> His contract was sold to the new Warriors Club, and he promptly became the solid favourite with the customers as he continued to show form at the ripe old age of thirty-five that left most of the rookies gasping. Easily one of the finest skaters that local hockey ever produced, he's an effortless craftsman who still retains the old arts of stickhandling and the body swerve. Bill continues to terrify opposing defences, which remain perplexed as to where he is going. Off the ice, Bill is still the same sweet person he was when he first scribbled his name on a Board of Parks and Recreation Game Report at age ten. He has invested wisely and has a nice business of his own in partnership with another of his old Black Hawk buddies Joe Cooper. The Cooper-Mosienko Alleys are well patronized by bowling devotees largely through having the opportunity of meeting Bill on the rare occasions when he can get away from his hockey obligations. The old bogeyman of conceit, which has ruined more than one athlete's personality, fought a losing battle with Bill and quietly stole away. Bill loves everybody, and everybody loves Bill. This sturdy native son of Ukrainian parents has been a credit to his country, to his ancestry, his proud people and particularly to himself. There is no finer example anywhere for this nation's teeming legion of young athletes than this friendly, generous young man from the north side of the tracks, who gave hockey everything he had, and hockey repaid him with security, renown, and background, but it never could disturb his one crowning glory—a most wonderful self-effacing personality!

Mosienko ended up scoring 38 goals and 36 assists for 74 points in 65 games that season. He helped lead them to first place in the Prairie Division with a 39-26-5 record. In the playoffs, the Warriors fell in seven games to the Vancouver Canucks in the league semifinals. It was a bittersweet end to the year as the Warriors had had high hopes for another championship.

"This just might be the last year," grinned Bill after the Game 7 loss, "I'm finding that I always know what I want to do out there on the ice, but it's not always working out that way now."

But Mosie had one more season in him, and he was sure to give it his all one more time.

That old song "I've been everywhere, man" plays in my head when I go through Art Stratton's hockey career and look at all the cities he played in over the course of twenty seasons. The 6'1' centreman is considered one of the most respected playmakers in professional hockey, and rightfully so as he was well over a point-per-game player his entire career.

Art scored wherever he played; just look at his career stats. There was even a five-year period during the 1960s where Art was the highest-scoring player in all professional hockey. Stratton won two Les Cunningham Awards as the AHL's Most Valuable Player in 1964-65 and 1973-74 and one Calder Cup with the Buffalo Bisons in 1963. He had three AHL First Team All-Star selections (1963, 1964, 1965) and one AHL scoring championship (1965). He also had two CPHL First All-Star Team, scoring championship and MVP awards in 1966 and 1967. He also holds the AHL record for most times leading the league in assists (four), ranks sixth all-time with 555 helpers while totalling 766 points in 669 career AHL games. Not too shabby.

Art played a little bit in the National Hockey League during the early 1960s, having brief stints with the New York Rangers, Detroit Red Wings and Chicago Black Hawks. He got his break when the NHL expanded to twelve teams in 1967, and he played his one full NHL season in 1967-68, split between the Pittsburgh Penguins and Philadelphia Flyers. As I said, Art scored wherever he played, so even though he only had several brief stints in the big leagues, Stratton still scored 51 points in 96 career NHL games.

But Stratton's professional hockey career was more illustrious than his brief stints in the NHL. Starting in 1955 and playing straight until 1976, Stratton skated for the likes of the following teams: St. Catharines Teepees, Cleveland Barons, North Bay Trappers, Winnipeg Warriors, Springfield

Indians, Kitchener-Waterloo Beavers, Buffalo Bisons, Pittsburgh Hornets, St. Louis Braves, Seattle Totems, Tidewater Wings, Virginia Red Wings, Rochester Americans, Richmond Robins and Hampton Gulls. I've been everywhere, man! Maybe you see where I'm coming from now.

Stratton retired from hockey at forty and got into the cedar business back in Winnipeg. His minor league career was so impressive that he was inducted into the AHL Hall of Fame in 2015. When I spoke with Stratton, he had nothing but good things to say about his former teammate:

> I played with Mosienko on the Winnipeg Warriors in 1957-58, and he was a great guy to play with. He was a real good guy, and we had a good camaraderie. I centred a line with him on one side and Pete Kapusta on the other. When Mosie wanted the puck, he'd whistle, and I'd get it over to him."
>
> We roomed on the train a lot in those days, and we played a lot of cards to pass the time and stuff like that. It was a fun time.
>
> Mosienko assisted on my goal that was the longest overtime game in WHL history. He passed the puck from behind the net, and I actually missed my shot, and it still found its way into the net. It was at the Winnipeg Arena, and the game lasted for the equivalent of nearly two full games. What a memory that was!

Stratton later played with Mosienko on the Manitoba Jets Oldtimers team that travelled around and played in games to raise money for various charities. "I have nothing but fond memories of Bill Mosienko because he was a real good guy."

Ray Mikulan grew up in the North End and played hockey as a goaltender at Tobans in the 1940s, while Mosienko was making a name for himself in the hockey world. The two would later become teammates on the Winnipeg Warriors for two seasons.

Mikulan's dad was a cab driver, and his mom was a cook, so the family never had much money. They moved around the North End a lot in Ray's youth to houses on streets such as Aberdeen and Burrows Avenue.

"If it wasn't too windy at Tobans, you could see the puck, but the lights were high up over the ice, so it was tough to see as a goalie," recalled Ray Mikulan. "I was about fourteen playing out of Tobans, and it was a great experience there. Mosie was a great guy, hard worker and real good on and off the ice. He kept everyone going. For his size, he sure played great. It was an honour just knowing him as he was one of my idols growing up in the North End."

Mikulan played in Des Moines, Iowa, to finish his hockey career and then eventually stayed there with his wife when his career ended. Although he visited family in Winnipeg from time to time over the years, Mikulan owned and ran a bar in Polk City, Iowa, for a long time until he retired about six years ago. He's now eighty-seven and enjoying retirement.

In twenty years of pro hockey, Bill finally hit the forty-goal plateau in his final season. Mosienko led the team in points with 88 as he scored 42 goals and 46 assists in 63 games. Bill always had bonuses in his Warriors contracts for goals scored, so he certainly cashed in that season!

He also played his thousandth pro game in the team's final regular season game when the Warriors clinched the last playoff spot on the last day of the season. The Warriors defeated the Edmonton Flyers in the quarterfinals in three straight games.

Unfortunately, in the semifinals, the Warriors were on the receiving end of the sweep at the hands of the Calgary Stampeders, who eliminated them in four straight games.

With that, Bill officially retired from hockey during the summer at the age of thirty-seven. "I came to the conclusion that I'd stretched my career long enough," he said. "I've got enough bruises to remember it by."

Shortly after the announcement, the *Winnipeg Free Press* asked Bill about the personal highlights of his career.

"Well, there was my first game in Chicago Stadium," said Bill. "I think we lost 5-4 to New York, but I got two goals and two assists, and that makes a rookie feel pretty good, you know!"

He remembered the Bentleys as a genuine thrill in his career. "We played together and lived together... just like brothers," said Mosie. "It was hard to beat."

Then there were the three goals in 21 seconds record in 1951-52 against New York. "I didn't realize what was going on when I scored them," admitted Bill, "but I can always remember Jimmy Peters yelling at me every time I scored...especially on the third one. He said, 'quick, get that puck. It's a record!' I was too busy digging pucks out of the net to give it much thought at the time."

Another fond memory for Bill goes back to when he was seventeen and made the Winnipeg Monarchs. "I made the first line with Paul Platz and Bill Benson, and that was really something in my mind."

Mosie also spoke of his partnership with Joe Cooper as a high point in his career. "It was around 1946-47," he remembered, "during the summer back here at home that Joe told me he'd bought some property and was looking for a partner. I said I didn't know of anyone offhand, and first thing I knew, I was it."

He also never forgot about the night a few years prior at the Winnipeg Arena when 10,000 hometown fans gave him that fabulous standing ovation after the Warriors won the Edinburgh Trophy.

"All I ever wanted to do was to get to the top. That's all that mattered to me ever since I can remember. I guess I did, but I had the greatest help along the way that anyone could get."

Bill then reminisced about such things as his sister buying him his first pair of skates when he was six years old; about what fine people were Jim Lightfoot, Harry Neil, Joe Cooper, Paul Thompson, Johnny Gottselig, Earl Seibert, Doug and Max Bentley, Alf Pike, and so on and so on down through the years that had helped him make his way in the hockey world.

Then he summed it up with, "It was nice to be able to finish up my career at home in Winnipeg. I just wish I was five years younger."

It was a hell of a ride for Mosienko, and hockey is a greater sport because of people like him.

"You've no idea just how hard it is for me to say I'm through. After all, hockey has not only been good to me, but it's also been my life. I owe the game a lot. But I guess I'd be foolish to go against the wishes of my doctor and a host of other people who have advised me to quit. And I do have my family to think about too."

Bill was then asked to choose an all-star team of guys he played with or against during his tenure in the NHL. He gave his answers as follows: Goalie, Bill Durnan. Right defence, Earl Seibert. Left defence, Jack Stewart. Left wing, Doug Bentley. Centre, Milt Schmidt. Right wing, Gordie Howe. Coach, Dick Irvin.

As far as he was concerned, the ambidextrous Bill Durnan was in a class by himself. Mosie said old Black Jack Stewart was tops for defencemen. "Boy, he could really hit you. And Seibert was an excellent puck carrier."

After playing so many seasons in Chicago with the great Doug Bentley as his linemate, it's no surprise Mosie took him at left wing.

Mosienko gave Gordie Howe the nod over Maurice Richard for right wing because he believed the Detroit star was a better all-around player than The Rocket. However, he felt he would have had to give the rating to Richard had he been basing his judgment on goal-scoring ability alone.

Regarding his centre choice—Milt Schmidt—Billy said, "In all my years in the NHL, I don't think I ever saw another player quite so smart. At the same time, he'd take body punishment to set you up for a goal."

During Bill's career, he suffered four nose breaks, a fractured jaw, knocked out teeth, a fractured shoulder, a dislocated shoulder, a shoulder separation, a broken ankle, numerous sprains, torn ligaments in both knees and head cuts.

He must have been fortunate that injuries like that were now finally behind him!

All in all, after a twenty-year professional career with the AHL, NHL and WHL, Bill had played in 1030 games, scoring 415 goals and 453 assists for a total of 868 points. He only had a total of 138 minutes in penalties and completed some seasons without any penalty minutes.

The only thing that eluded Mosie in his career was the Stanley Cup.

"Dad always talked so highly of Billy," recalled Lynn Bentley. "He said that him and Doug were the two fastest skaters in the league at that time and that they were hard to keep up to out on the ice. They weren't big guys, but they sure could fly."

"My dad always told me that his biggest regret in hockey was not winning a Stanley Cup in Chicago when Doug and Bill were with him. That was disappointing to him."

Bill Mosienko was a superstar of the game. And with a career like the one he had, a place for him in the Hockey Hall of Fame was nearly a foregone conclusion. It was just a matter of when.

Mosienko was just getting used to the idea of missing morning practice sessions when Warriors coach Alf Pike accepted an invitation to coach the New York Rangers at the start of the 1959-60 season.

The Warriors were in a pinch and suddenly needed a head coach on short notice. Naturally, the first person that came to mind was the newly retired Billy Mosienko.

In fact, when the club held a brief phone-in where fans could give their opinion on who should coach the team, everyone wanted Mosienko, and so he took the job for the season.

Before departing for New York, Alf Pike welcomed Bill to the "Ulcer Club" for hockey coaches. And presented Bill with a glass of milk.

"I'm going to ask the players to be a little more alert, try just a little bit harder and co-operate till Mosie gets the feel of things," said owner Jack Perrin at the time of hiring Mosienko. "While the coaching of a pro hockey team and being a player are both serious callings, a coach, particularly, can't allow himself to be overpowered by an urgency to win. Rather, he's got to offer constructive leadership, winning or losing. To me, this is the secret of being a good coach."

"Morally, he's a first-class man. Winning the league or being a strong contender isn't going to be a measure of his ability. That won't be the basis on which I will judge him as a coach."

Bill's wife, Wanda, was excited at the prospect of his retirement until he took the coaching job. "I don't know when we'll get the recreation room finished, and I wanted Billy to build a toy cupboard for Wendy, but actually, I feel happy for him," said Wanda. "We were all excited over the coaching job, and I don't think Billy slept a wink last night."

As soon as he was handed the coaching reins, Mosienko took his new job very seriously. He rarely slept at night because he was constantly thinking of ways of improving his team. He started making breakout patterns in practice with his team and was one of the first coaches in professional hockey to run a "system" that all NHL teams use today.

Mosienko did the best with what he had, but unfortunately, the Warriors would miss the playoffs as they finished with a 25-42-3 record.

At the end of the season, Mosienko informed owner Jack Perrin that he would be stepping down from his coaching job. The announcement came as a surprise to no one. He was simply too pressed for time with both hockey and his year-round bowling establishment.

Friday, May 27, 1960, was the last day Mosie spent in hockey. He ended twenty years of service in the pros.

At a press conference, Mosienko said, "I gave the matter thought before I finally made up my mind to call it a day, but I feel it's in the best interest of all concerned. I've got to devote more time to my bowling alley business. Up to now, Joe Cooper has carried the load. It's time I helped out a little and gave Joe a break."

Simultaneously, Mosienko said he was beginning to feel the knocks and bumps he had taken during the many years he played professional hockey. "The doctors told me last fall that I'm okay physically, but nevertheless, my stomach keeps acting up. I guess it's the nervous tension."

"It was certainly quite an experience," Bill reflected at the press gathering. "It isn't that I wouldn't like to take another try at it, but in my situation, it wouldn't be fair to Jack Perrin. I found that a person can't do two jobs well at once."s He added, "I had to be honest with myself. Coaching demands your full time every hour of seven days a week, and to carry on wouldn't be fair either to Jack, the players, or, I guess, myself."

Apart from the fact that he considered coaching to be a full-time job, another big reason Mosienko decided to leave hockey behind him was his family. "I've neglected my children too long. When you're a hockey player or a coach, you're away from your kids far too much. First thing you know, they've grown up on you, and you haven't had time to enjoy them."

Mosie went on record that he had no regrets at having turned his hand to coaching. "I'll tell you one thing though," he said. "I found it a lot tougher than I thought it would be. When you're a player, you can relax after a game, but when you're a coach, you not only take your own troubles home but also those of your players."

"It's too bad we couldn't have done better, but it wasn't for the lack of trying. The players worked hard and tried to win for me. For that I am truly grateful."

When asked what he thought was wrong with the Warriors the last season, Mosienko said, "We needed more strength at centre ice and lacked experience on defence." Of the younger players on the team, Mosie felt defenceman Gary Bergman had an excellent chance to make it to the National Hockey League. "He can be a really good player providing he wants to be," said Mosie. "His shot is not strong, but practice will improve it. If Gary wants to work hard, he'll get to the top."

Mosie was right as Bergman went on to have a stellar NHL career of over 800 games with the Detroit Red Wings. His career was highlighted with a pivotal role on Team Canada during the 1972 Summit Series against the Soviet Union.

The consensus with most hockey pundits was that Mosie was simply too nice to be a good coach.

"In temperament, he is vastly opposite to his predecessor, Alf Pike. Pike could be loud, almost flamboyant, infinitely painstaking, a whip-cracker, frightfully impatient with incompetence. Bill's cardinal virtue is his modesty. He tries so hard to be humble it is almost painful. He'll fall over backward trying to avoid hurting people," noted legendary *Winnipeg Tribune* writer Vince Leah.

"I played with Mosienko some but not a lot," recalled Warriors teammate Laurie Langrell. "I was more on the junior team beneath them, the Winnipeg Braves. When the Warriors had some injured guys, they called players up from the Braves like myself as Jack Perrin owned both the Warriors and the Braves."

"Mosie was well-liked as he was a hell of a nice guy. I remember he tried coaching the club, but at the end of the day, he was just too nice a guy to be a good coach!"

Mosienko could have likely coached for longer than one season, if not for the ever-growing antics of his business partner Joe Cooper.

"My dad could have been an outstanding coach if Joe didn't have that jealousy streak settling in. He could have let him just go and coach and say, 'don't worry about the business, I'll handle it.' But he didn't. Cooper was foul-mouthed and would be swearing lots in front of ladies. He just didn't have that proper etiquette to be a good businessperson, and so Bill needed to be around the bowling more."

This was the beginning of when Bill and Joe's relationship deteriorated. And it would only get worse from there.

The Winnipeg Warriors franchise would also deteriorate in short order, lasting only one more season. After six years, Warriors owner Jack Perrin asked for a leave of absence from the WHL in 1961 due to financial reasons. However, the Warriors never returned to the league, and so pro hockey in Winnipeg was abandoned until the Winnipeg Jets joined the World Hockey Association (WHA) in 1972.

POST-HOCKEY LIFE

With Bill stepping away from coaching, he could now fully invest his time into the bowling alley. It was probably a good thing, too, as his partner Joe Cooper was becoming increasingly more challenging to work with.

Mosienko instantly joined a regular men's league and the 'Sunday nighters' league. He also always tried to show up on each league's opening days to help promote bowling and would attend all the banquets that were held. He was willing to do everything he could to help promote the game of bowling in Winnipeg.

Bill would get kids would work at the alley as pinboys. They were paid three cents a string (game), but the big perk was that they were allowed to bowl for free at the end of the night.

"My father was a very humble man," said Bill Jr. "When he was running things, you wouldn't have known he'd been a hockey player. Customers used to come through the doors all the time asking, 'Where's the hockey stuff?'"

Every summer, the bowling alley closed for a short period, and that's when the real work started. Bill, Joe Cooper, and custodian Stan Edwards would take that time to refurnish the alleys. Barrels of fine sawdust were hauled out. And then, after sanding the ball marks from the maple alley, came the five or six coats of lacquer.

The smell was awful," recalled Bill Jr. "The high you could get if you stayed in the building all day was phenomenal but quite unhealthy. Hourlong headaches ensued!"

Billy at his bowling lanes.   COURTESY MOSIENKO FAMILY

Bill would also bring the new pins home and, with his sander machine, would round them off so the patrons would get better scores at his alleys.

Dennis Barchuk was a strong bowler in his day that was brought up at Mosie's bowling alley. He also worked with Bill for a long time.

I worked for Bill at the bowling alley for about twenty-two years. Bill was such a nice guy. If you did something wrong, he would never yell at any of the staff, but instead, talk to them in a calm voice and give people second or third chances without hesitation.

He was quite a mentor to me because he got me off the streets when I was a teen. My mom grew up with Bill around the same time in the North End, so she got him involved with me to start bowling when he started the YBC (Youth Bowl Canada) program in the early 1960s. I would do odd jobs around the bowling alley for him, and it got me off the streets a bit and away from getting into trouble with the guys I knew that hung around Eddy's Pool Hall on Selkirk Avenue! He would tell me not to listen to my friends and that I knew right from wrong, and if they don't like what I do, then they're not your friends. Those guys ended up respecting me for not going along with them. And it was all thanks to Bill.

Since the bowling alley has always been in the rough and tumble North End neighbourhood, it certainly had its fair share of break-ins over the years.

"One time, an employee staged a robbery. Dad and I figured it out—the culprit was our employee," said Brian Mosienko. "And finally, after some deliberation, he confessed. Dad always believing in people, didn't fire his ass, but gave him another chance! I was totally flabbergasted he didn't let him go. That's Dad's love for his fellow humans right there."

As noted earlier, Bill and Joe's relationship was really starting to go downhill. Expenses were coming out that weren't legitimate when Bill was playing and coaching the Warriors, and it all came back to Joe.

Cooper was drinking too much and taking lots of pills. He was getting very paranoid that people were taking advantage of him and accused Bill of taking money from the company when in reality, it was Joe taking the money out.

"My dad sold his house, and we lived with my mom's parents for a time as he was trying to hustle up enough money not to go too deeply into debt," said Brian Mosienko. "When Dad was playing hockey, he let Joe draw a salary similar to his hockey salary. Of course, it wasn't like today's enormous salaries, but it was definitely much, much better than a normal wage."

"Joe was foul-mouthed in front of customers. His family never was much involved in the lanes like my brother and myself. His wife did bowl at one time. But there were some discrepancies in the books when Dad played hockey. It bothered Dad, but he never questioned Joe much about it and just kind of let it go. He never wanted to bring hardships on situations or create animosity, which is why what happened to him and Joe's relationship was traumatic for him. Joe kind of leaves a bad taste with me because he cheated Dad and never respected him."

Cooper became so paranoid that he couldn't even face Bill at the bowling lanes anymore.

"My dad had put so much into the business that he wasn't going to let it go downhill," added Bill Jr. "He just couldn't take Joe anymore. And Joe couldn't even face my dad—that's how paranoid he was. The caretaker would have to go outside to the restaurant next door on a pay-phone to call Bill at home and say, 'Billy, you can come now. Joe's here.'"

That's the only way that Bill was able to confront him in person. There were also many times that Joe would fire the caretaker for no reason, and Bill would have to rehire him the next day.

The charade went on for a while until Bill eventually bought out Cooper from the business in the late 1960s.

Bill had built a bowling alley and an A&W out in Selkirk and was renting them out but had to sell those businesses to help pay Joe off. He also had to borrow other money too.

It was quite the traumatic experience for Bill because Joe had been his friend and mentor. After all, it was Cooper who first discovered Bill as a pro hockey talent and recommended him to the Black Hawks brass.

After Cooper was bought out, Bill never saw or heard from Joe too much anymore.

"It's really a shame because they were such great friends at one point," said Bill Jr. "Cooper had built a new house out in East Kildonan. And my dad used to go out and help Joe with him there because family and friends would come and help you out. That's just what you did."

Sadly, Joe Cooper and his wife Oksana perished tragically in a car accident while driving back from a vacation in Florida on April 3, 1979. Joe was sixty-four. The accident occurred near Tifton, Georgia, on the first day of their drive back. According to reports, their car went out of control, flipped over a bridge, and fell forty feet to railway tracks below. Death was instantaneous.

Despite being very busy at the bowling alley, Bill always managed to find time to sneak away for some golf. He usually shot in the low 80s. Wanda used to get mad that he was always golfing.

"Dad would usually golf once a week with Joe Krol (an ex-NHLer) and also good friend Michael Petty (meat market tycoon)," said Brian Mosienko. "If they needed a fourth, I was always invited, and they were all long-time members at Elmhurst Golf & Country Club. But most time's Bill Juzda would be the fourth."

Bill would often go to the bowling alley in the morning and then hit the links in the afternoon during the summer months. It's safe to say that golf became another passion of his once he was away from hockey. He even scored a hole-in-one once at Elmhurst!

But the bowling alley was still number one for Mosienko.

Bill's son, Brian, started working full time at the bowling alley with him in 1974. It allowed for Bill to be able to hand off some of the responsibilities of his establishment.

"I was the luckiest guy in the world to do that with my dad. Once I got the hang of it, he would go in the winters to Phoenix or wherever because he loved to golf, and I would run the alleys when he was gone."

When Bill turned sixty-five in the 1980s, he told the *Winnipeg Sun*, "We opened April 19, 1948, and it's been good to me ever since. We've had marvellous relationships with our patrons over the years, and I'm really grateful to them. Some leagues have been here from Day One. As far as I'm concerned, we still run the best Golden Age Program for seniors in the city."

It was around this time that Brian started running the alley, and Bill would add in his two cents when it was needed. When Bill got older, he would go away for ten weeks in the winter, but as soon as he got home, he'd be back at the bowling alley visiting with the bowlers. "But I could never get him to do any work!" laughed Brian Mosienko.

By the time the 2000s rolled around, Brian Mosienko still owned the alleys. However, the bowling business was really changing with the times. Back in the day, during the winter months, it was always one of the things you could do for leisure and entertainment. But when video games and gyms became popular, bowling suddenly became something that was put on the backburner.

In the last ten years that the bowling alley was under Brian's ownership, he has spent over $300,000 on computer scoring, synthetic lanes, glow bowling, remodelling, and the bar installation.

> It was really a cool place where a group of friends could get together once a week and also make new acquaintances. It was a way for families to get out of the house and do something. Some senior bowlers came every morning! Many of my senior friends today do coffee or breakfast at different restaurants, but why not go bowling instead? Get a little exercise to boot!
>
> Most of the leagues probably have dwindled to a few bowlers from what it was a few decades ago. It's sad, but the area really dictates the customers. Bowlers came from every part of the city, and they loved the atmosphere we created. Unfortunately, customers became scared to come to the North End as it's now a big crime area. I saw the writing on the wall and was fortunate to sell the business, although it really troubled me for a long time to sell it because I know my dad had put a lot of blood, sweat, and tears into it.

Brian Mosienko sold the bowling alley in 2007 as the area the establishment was located was becoming more and more of a rough neighbourhood. He is currently enjoying his retirement in sunny Phoenix, Arizona.

The most striking thing today about the Billy Mosienko Lanes is the wonderful mural of Mosienko holding up the three pucks on the side of the building.

In the late 1990s, Brian was doing some renovations to the bowling alley's interior and beside the lanes, he had a blank wall. He decided to put up a mural of his dad shooting a puck at some bowling pins.

"I had such a fantastic response to the mural that when the city called and offered to pay for half of a mural outside, I said yes right away. Deal!" recalled Brian Mosienko.

The updated mural that went up in 2016 on the sidewall
of Billy Mosienko Lanes. COURTESY JEN MOSIENKO

Brian called up an old schoolmate turned artist, Al Senkiw, to paint the iconic mural outside of Billy Mosienko Lanes. It was completed in 1998.

A few years ago, the original mural was starting to become outdated and needed to be redone as the paint was beginning to chip away.

Ironically enough, it just so happened that there was an artist in the family that was up for the job.

Bill's granddaughter-in-law, Jennifer Mosienko, painted the new mural in 2016 that is currently on display outside the bowling alley. Jennifer was also gracious enough to paint the beautiful portrait of Mosienko on this book's front cover!

Billy Mosienko Lanes has withstood the test of time (albeit under new ownership) with more than seventy years of catering to the bowling public at the same Main Street and Redwood location. In addition to the mural, the large bowling pin sign out front has become a historic landmark in North Winnipeg.

John Wiens has worked at BMO Nesbitt Burns for the past thirty years. At the beginning of his career in the 1980s, he was Bill's broker. "Bill did a fair amount of business with me, buying investments or doing US dollar conversions as he went down to the States every winter. But he was a guy that didn't like doing things over the telephone. So he'd call me up and say, 'John, I'm coming downtown, but I'm not coming up to your office. So when I'm downstairs, you come down, and we'll sit in the car, and we'll talk about what we wanna do.' So he'd stop his big brown Cadillac at Portage and Main, and he didn't care if he was stopping traffic or not. He'd put his flashers on, I'd get in the car, we'd have our quick discussion, and then we'd shake hands, and I'd be on my way. My point is with him, he was that kind of guy; when he did his business, he wanted to be looking at you face to face. You didn't have to take him out to a fancy restaurant; he just wanted to know who he was dealing with."

Bob Chrystal is ninety-one years old these days. He doesn't get around too easily anymore, but he and his wife still live in their St. James home that they've owned for nearly sixty years.

"Ol' Billy Mosienko," said Chrystal with a chuckle. "That man could play hockey."

Chrystal, who grew up in the West End of Winnipeg, was the star defenceman on the 1948-49 Brandon Wheat Kings team that lost out to the Montreal Royals in the only eight-game Memorial Cup final ever played. He went on to play pro hockey, and in the 1953 Calder Cup (AHL) final, Chrystal scored the Cup-winning goal in overtime. That goal propelled Bob to the NHL, where he spent the next two seasons patrolling the New York Rangers blueline.

After his two years in New York, Chrystal was blackballed from the league by coach Phil Watson of the New York Rangers, who single-handedly cut his NHL career short. All in all, Chrystal played in 132 regular-season games for the New York Rangers between 1953 and 1955. He scored 11 goals and 14 assists for 25 points.

Chrystal would continue playing professional hockey in western Canada for another four seasons before hanging up the skates in 1959.

He spent his final pro season as a teammate of Mosienko's with their hometown Winnipeg Warriors.

Today, Chrystal is among the last remaining players from early 1950s NHL hockey.

"Mosie was playing for Chicago when I was with the New York Rangers," recalled Bob Chrystal, "and I can remember the instructions I got the first time I played against him. I was told not to let him get behind me when I was playing defence. So, lo and behold, the puck came off the boards, got behind me, and he was gone, and I was far behind chasing him. Lesson learned."

"I wouldn't say we were the greatest of friends to begin with because you had to play him hard to stop him. And, of course, it was only natural that he didn't care for that. When I really got to know him and become a good friend of his, it was my last year of pro when we were teammates on the Winnipeg Warriors. We shook hands and put our differences aside."

Bill and Bob would remain good friends in Winnipeg over the years, long after they were retired from hockey.

> He was a prince of a guy. Had he played a different position than trying to score a goal in front of the net, we would have been fine, I'm sure, during our careers. But I just didn't know him yet. We didn't start out as friends through hockey because you respected him as a hockey player, and you had to bother him to try and get him off his game.
>
> Funny thing is we played in a March of Dimes games playing against one another for charity. Schmockey Night or whatever, so anyways, we were going into the corner together, and I told him, 'Watch yourself, Billy, I'm gonna take you into the boards.' So, I just got him into the boards, and then boom, the rink came down with boos. The ref made a big thing of giving me a penalty, but I got out after one minute for good behaviour, and the crowd didn't like that either. But it was all fun and games! We had a great time playing in those charity games together.

In 1965, Mosienko was inducted into the fabled Hockey Hall of Fame. Only five years out of hockey, Bill was just forty-three years old when he received the call. He went into the Hall that year with nine others, including Clint Benedict, Syd Howe, Marty Barry, and Red Horner.

Mosienko's first inkling that he had a chance of being elected came when Jimmy Dunn, then commissioner of the MJHL and a member of the Hall's selection committee, told him that he had put Mosie's name up for consideration.

Bill was notified of his appointment to the Hall by hearing it one day on the radio. He received official confirmation from the Hall later that same night that he was going in.

"It's quite a thrill, a real honour," Mosie bubbled after receiving the news. "It still hasn't sunk home. Actually, I never dreamed it would happen so soon."

"I was really taken by surprise. Doug Bentley told me that I would never know how great the feeling of being elected was until it happened. Sure enough, I know now, and it really is a nice feeling."

Doug Bentley had been inducted the year prior. And coincidentally, the other member of the Pony Line, Max Bentley, was inducted the year after Mosie. Bill attended his induction ceremony.

Chicago Black Hawks owner Bill Wirtz sent a telegram to Bill congratulating him on the induction.

When it was time to go to Toronto for the induction ceremony, only Bill went. For some strange reason, women weren't invited to go to these ceremonies in those years or else Wanda certainly would have attended too.

Over the years, Mosienko has been inducted into many other Hall of Fames as well.

He was inducted as an inaugural member of the Manitoba Sports Hall of Fame in 1980. He was also an inaugural inductee of the Manitoba Hockey Hall of Fame in 1985.

Bill Mosienko's 1980 Manitoba Sports Hall of Fame speech was as follows: "In the many years that I've spent in hockey, I've had many wonderful memories. One of them being to come back home to Winnipeg to finish my professional hockey career. I enjoyed those five seasons

HOCKEY HALL OF FAME

CANADIAN NATIONAL EXHIBITION

TORONTO 2B, ONTARIO

June 14, 1965

Mr. William Mosienko
889 Cathedral Ave
Winnipeg 14, Manitoba

Dear Bill--
        As you have no doubt already heard vis Press,
Radio or TV, you were elected to the Hockey Hall of Fame,
Canadian National Exhibition, T ronto, as an Honoured Member
at a meeting of the Selection Committee held at M ntreal on
June 7th, 1965.

        As Secretary of the Hockey Hall of Fame Committee I am
now advising you officialy of this honor bestowed on yoursel and
offer not only the congratulations of the Committee itself,
but myself as Secretary, and also an Honoured Member.

        I wrote to Mr. James Dunn to get your home address
so this letter could be sent to you direct.

        Mr. Dunn has replied and said he talked with you and
outlined what we would require from you for the Hockey Hall of
Fame panels and book.

        First off I would like a good head picture of yourself,
and from this a Head Drawing will be made by our special artist
and naturally the better the original the better the drawing
hence I would ask this be given some thought.   The drawing will
be the head only, so it can be either a photographer's picture
or if that is not available, then a picture of a hockey head.
Actually what I want is something that those who see the drawing
will immediately know it is you.   This can be returned untouched
so it can be returned if you need same.

        Then I want a full length picture of yourself in a
Chicago uniform, as this also goes on the panel display along
with the he ad drawing.

        For information on yourself I would like your full and
proper name and nickname, the date and place of your birth. Then a
history of the amateur teams with which you played before turning
professional and then of course a history of yourself with the
Black Hawks.

        Mr. Dunn said you have the Stick and the three Pucks
with which you made the record and I would like very much to have
these for display in the Hall.

        The pictures-- head and full length-- and the story on
yourself I would like as quickly as possible so work may start
on them.   We use same in our New Book which I am working on and
this I hope to have out in time for the Exhibition-- mid-August/
So you can see we do not have too much time much time to spare.

        Hoping you will help me out without delay, I remain,

                                Yours sincerely,
                                Hockey Hall of Fame

The letter notifying Bill of his induction into the Hockey Hall of Fame in 1965.

with the Winnipeg Warriors very much. And now, the honour of being inducted into the Manitoba Sports Hall of Fame with these great athletes is a memory I will always cherish. I am most humbled and grateful to the Manitoba Sports Federation and the selection committee. It is a great honour."

In 1990, Mosienko was named 'Ukrainian Sportsman of the last 25 years.' He was also named 'Ukrainian Sportsman of the Year' in 1979-80. He was then inducted into the United States-based Ukrainian Sports Hall of Fame in 2018.

In the year 2000, the Manitoba Hockey Foundation (now the Manitoba Hockey Hall of Fame) spearheaded an initiative to recognize a century of hockey excellence in Manitoba. A dinner that honoured Manitoba hockey players, builders, officials, media, sponsors, and supporters was held at the Winnipeg Convention Centre. The highlight of the evening was the announcement of the province's player, coach, and referee of the century along with first and second all-star teams:

Player of the Century: Terry Sawchuk
Coach of the Century: Dick Irvin
Referee of the Century: Andy Van Hellemond

FIRST ALL-STAR TEAM
Goal: Terry Sawchuk
Defence: Babe Pratt, Black Jack Stewart
Forwards: Andy Bathgate, Bobby Clarke, **Bill Mosienko**
Coach: Dick Irvin

SECOND ALL-STAR TEAM
Goal: Charlie Gardiner
Defence: Ching Johnson, Ken Reardon
Forwards: Frank Fredrickson, Bryan Hextall Sr., Reggie Leach
Coach: Billy Reay

Mosienko's hockey career did not end when he stopped playing professionally. Shortly after, he became an active member of various Oldtimers hockey teams, which assisted in fundraising events throughout Manitoba. This participation helped lead to the establishment of the Manitoba Hockey Player's Foundation Incorporated, which took an active role in helping charities and organizations.

His love for the sport of hockey carried on with his performance in Oldtimers games. He was also an avid participant in the Hockey Players Foundation as well as the Hockey Golf events.

Bill was invited to play for the Montreal Canadiens Oldtimers team against various Canadian Armed Forces teams in Germany and Switzerland. Frank Selke Sr., the Habs' long-time manager, always wanted Mosie on his team when he was playing, so having him on his Oldtimers squad was the next best thing for Selke.

"Selke called Bill and asked if he'd come out and play for the Canadiens. My dad said that he didn't think he could go because he had just bought out his partner at the bowling alley, and there would be no one to run it if he left," recalled Brian Mosienko. "We told him that he has to go as he'd never been to Europe before, and that the family would run the alley somehow. So, he went with all those great Habs players like Maurice Richard, Elmer Lach, Butch Bouchard, and Doug Harvey, to name a few. Dickie Moore had just retired from playing hockey, and my dad finished second behind him in scoring over there. Not too bad for the old man!"

Mosie and nineteen former Montreal Canadiens embarked on a twelve-day tour. They notably visited the Canadian Armed Forces base at Lahr, Germany. The old pros played five games against teams representing Canada's Air Division and Mechanized Brigade in Germany. They also put on a pair of clinics and played a game in Trenton, Ontario, on their way home.

A few years later, Max Bentley phoned Bill to come out to Ponoka, Alberta, for an Oldtimers game as the Bentleys and Bill hadn't gotten together in a few years. This was just after Doug's first cancer operation. "We'll get the old line together!" Max had said. He was raising money for the local team he was coaching. So out Mosienko went, playing alongside Max, and even Doug went out for a few shifts. "He was a little peaked," Mosienko told the local paper, "but he was feeling high because the doctors had told him they'd gotten all the cancer. What a treat it was for us all to be out there together again like old brothers."

Although Billy was starting to get up there in years, one thing is for certain—Mosienko still had his stride and could still fly out on the ice as he got older.

"One cool winter night before an Oldtimers hockey game, dad said, 'Let's go for a skate,'" recalled Bill Jr. "'Sure,' I said as a teenager. 'I'll skate circles around you!' Dad was in his forties, and I was a snotty teenager. We jumped in the car about 10 p.m. and headed for the outdoor rink at C.U.A.C. (now Sinclair Park Community Centre). The rink was lit only by streetlights, a skin of snow blowing across the ice, and no one around. On went the old tube skates, out came the sticks and puck. I chuckled as he went onto the ice. We started with a few lazy rushes up, and down the ice, then we went into the next gear for a couple more rushes. Then Dad went into another high gear for another dozen or so rushes while I sucked wind leaning on the goal. I learned that day that I was not the best skater in the family!"

Mosie and the rest of the players were always trying to entertain the fans in these Oldtimers games. One time they put a number 9 jersey on Bill and "Golden Jet" in very visible letters on his back to imitate Bobby Hull. On a string you couldn't see, attached to his hockey stick, was the puck. Bill would scoot around the rink, zigzagging and rambling all over, and the opposing team couldn't do a thing, which brought a massive roar from the crowd. He scored by throwing the whole stick and puck into the net!

"I saw the Bentleys and Dad play once at an Oldtimers Game at the Winnipeg Arena, and Maurice Richard was there," recalled Brian Mosienko. "And when the old Pony Line went on the ice, it was like that famous Winnipeg Jets line of Ulf Nilsson, Anders Hedberg and Bobby Hull. You couldn't keep track of them as they were all over the ice. I'll never forget it—man could they move."

"I took my friend to the game with me, and I'm sitting with my dad in the dressing room afterwards, and he says, 'Hey Brian, do you and your pal wanna go meet Maurice Richard?' And I said, 'No, we're okay,

The Manitoba Oldtimers (Left-to-right: Bill Juzda, Ted Green, Bill Mosienko).
COURTESY MOSIENKO FAMILY

I'm good here with the Bentleys.' My friend blasted me, saying, 'Are you crazy? We could have met the Rocket!'"

During the 1972 Summit Series between Canada and the Soviet Union, Mosienko dropped the puck during the pre-game ceremonies before the game that was played in Winnipeg. He got a massive standing ovation from the local fans who certainly hadn't forgotten who he was! Bill was also asked to drop the puck at future Canada Cup games.

In 1981, Mosienko went down to Santa Rosa, California, with the Manitoba Oldtimers at age sixty for the Senior Olympics tournament that was being put on by Charles Schulz, the creator of the *Peanuts* comic strip.

"At the time, I played a little bit on a team," recalled Brian, "and Dad asked if he thought it would be all right with the rest of the guys if he skated with us (as a tune-up for the Snoopy). I said, 'Yeah, Dad, I'm sure they won't mind at all.' He came in; his skates were so old, the blades were rotting off the boot. And everyone was saying, 'Hey Mosie, you can't wear skates like that.' But he went out there, and he was still flying past guys. He just loved to play."

The Manitoba Oldtimers at Snoopy's Senior Olympics in 1981.
COURTESY MOSIENKO FAMILY

When one fellow died on the ice that year, Mosienko figured it was time to hang the skates up.

Bill never talked much about his hockey career to his kids and wasn't one to brag about it. However, the stories would come out when he was visiting with fellow retired hockey players. Especially the guys that Mosie grew up in the North End with way back when.

"Fred Shero was a good family friend," said Brian Mosienko. "After he won the two Stanley Cups in Philadelphia, he was approached to coach one of the WHA teams. Freddy phoned my dad, asking what he should do, jump ship and start all over again in the WHA, which was an unproven league then. He wanted my dad's advice on the situation, and he advised Mr. Shero to stay in the established NHL because who knows what would happen if the WHA league failed. He ultimately listened to Dad and stayed put in Philly."

It turned out to be the right decision as the WHA folded after a few years, while Shero continued coaching in the NHL with Philadelphia and the New York Rangers until 1981.

Alex Shibicky also stayed a lifelong friend of Bill's. In his later life, Alex split his time between Vancouver and his big thousand-acre farm just outside the perimeter of Winnipeg. He would usually be in town during the summer months, and that's when he would catch up with Mosie.

"He'd come in almost every year, and when the pair got together, the hockey stories would fly," recalled Brian Mosienko. "Alex would get my dad going because you'd never know he played professional hockey as he never talked about it unless you asked him a few questions."

"Shibicky was a real good guy. After my dad passed away, he'd still come in and see me at the bowling alley. My son even got to meet him one day during lunchtime at school. A cool memory."

Alex Shibicky passed away in South Surrey, British Columbia, in 2005 at the age of ninety-one.

They say blood is thicker than water, and that was certainly the case in the Mosienko family. Bill and his siblings were always close and supported each other in times of need. They vacationed together and partied together on festive occasions like Thanksgiving and Christmas.

But what happens when you get more than two Ukrainians together? They argue! About anything and everything. You could tell how late it was in the evening by the intensity of their voices. But no matter what, they always left on good terms at the end of the night!

Bill picked up some hobbies later in life to keep himself occupied. He was a fabulous woodworker, building state-of-the-art cabinets and dressers.

Bill and Wanda always had a lovely big garden at their home on Cathedral Avenue, and they loved growing big oxheart tomatoes. He enjoyed fishing a great deal and would go up to Lockport, fish for the day, and come home with tons of pickerel.

"Dad and Mom were honestly the best chefs in the kitchen," said Brian Mosienko. "Mom did most of the cooking, and Dad would pick out recipes and add his special touches to them. We always had fabulous meals together on all the special occasions. There were always uncles, aunties, or friends invited over to share the festive occasion, and everybody could barely wait for the meal to be served."

Bill and Wanda also enjoyed travelling. They went to Hawaii for their twenty-fifth wedding anniversary. Other places travelled to include Spain, Morocco, and Disneyland. Bill and Wanda would also visit with old friends they had in Chicago that were involved with the team's fan club.

Through everything, Mosienko stayed a fan of the game of hockey for the rest of his life.

"It was truly a sight to behold to watch a hockey game with my dad. He became so animated and got so involved that he was always actively coaching from off the couch," recalled Brian Mosienko. "You'd have to wear earplugs to bleep out some of his instructions! And mom would be off watching the game in a different room."

"His greatest passion was hockey on or off the ice," said Bill Jr. "The intensity he had while watching hockey was unreal. I can't even imagine the intensity with which he played the game. We would sit at the kitchen table to watch the games while mom had the TV in the living room. Dad was pretty amusing at times with comments like, 'Pass the puck, you idiot, the man's open!' 'What kind of a stupid play was that?' 'Where did he learn to play hockey?'"

"But Dad never swore in front of us. I think I only heard him let loose with some explicit words once, but I don't understand Ukrainian!"

Mosie conceded to a *Winnipeg Free Press* reporter in the 1980s that the players of those times were likely faster than the guys of his era.

"For one thing, the equipment is so much lighter," said Mosienko. "The skates, the gloves and padding all weigh far less than when I played. The jerseys we wore would absorb a couple of pounds of sweat during the course of a game. That doesn't happen with today's synthetic materials."

Players were also becoming better conditioned over time.

"In my day, a lot of guys weren't really in top playing condition until after Christmas. I always put in a lot of work before camp opened. I always figured it was an edge I had to have, but today all the players show up at camp ready to play. That's something else we've learned from the Russians."

And unlike most oldtimers of his day, Bill seemed to prefer the modern style of play. "The game has opened up. The defencemen are playing like forwards, rushing with the puck. And there's less hitting. I like that."

Bill was always proud of the Pony Line and what he and the Bentleys accomplished together, despite their pairing only lasting two seasons.

"It seemed like so much longer. Everyone thinks it was four, five years or more. But I broke my leg at the start of our third season together, and by the time I got back, Max had been traded."

The number-one hockey question that Mosienko would get asked post-retirement was about that storied night in 1952 when he scored his three goals in 21 seconds.

"I've been asked to replay that three-goal night so many times. I don't get tired of talking about it. I hope it's one record that stays in the book." And it did. "Records are a big honour. It's every player's ambition to get into the record books. Staying there is another thing."

"When I think back to those days and how I wanted to leave some sort of mark in hockey, I never dreamed it would be by scoring the three fastest goals. It seems everybody remembers me for that. Hardly a day goes by without somebody wanting me to talk about it. And I'm sorry I helped end the career of the kid goalie, Anderson. He never played another game."

In the early 1980s, a group from the North Winnipeg Minor Hockey Association (NWMHA) approached Bill to determine if his name could be used to sponsor a Hockey Tournament involving three different age groups. He was delighted to be honoured in this manner.

Thus, the Billy Mosienko Hockey Tournament was born.

It all started in 1982 with the first tournament, and North Ender Gord Saydack was the first tournament chairman.

"I lived just down the street from Bill for many years," recalled Saydack. "And at the NWMHA, we wanted to do something that would give the kids more ice time around Christmas time, and so the idea for putting on a tournament came up. I approached Bill about having the tournament in his name, and he gave us approval instantly, which was great."

Over the years, lots of upcoming pro hockey players played in this tournament. A twelve-year-old Jonathan Toews was one of those future pros.

"Bill was just an everyday guy that lived on Cathedral Avenue with Wanda. He was really nice and always came out when we wanted him to come and never complained about anything."

"The type of guy Bill was, after the tournament finals were done in that first year, we went over to Sinclair Park Community Club for the volunteer windup, and so anyways, Bill asked 'How much do I owe?' He was ready to kick in. And I said, 'Billy, we made money!' The proceeds went to the North Winnipeg Minor Program. We even sent referees to Calgary for a referee school and created the Billy Mosienko scholarship for the University of Manitoba."

Saydack was chairman for the first ten years of the tournament before passing the reins on to Warren Chubey.

"The tournament started out for odd age groups like nine-year olds and Minor Midget," said Chubey. "We started off with only two divisions, and it was a success from the start. It then went up to three divisions, and later four. We just used one arena at the start (Keewatin Arena), and then later we got into Old Exhibition Arena. After we went to Pioneer Arena (now Charlie Gardiner Arena) and also Maples Arena."

After the tournament's final games each year, Bill would hand out MVP awards to the players that consisted of a Chicago Black Hawks jersey with Mosienko stitched on the back.

The tournament was a real highlight for Bill each year. He wouldn't miss it for anything as long as his health allowed it.

"He really enjoyed it and got a big kick out of watching the younger kids play. Bill would then sign autographs until everyone got one. We would have a bunch of programs made, and he signed every one."

"He was always easy to get along with. A real gentleman that I admired dearly."

If it weren't for the volunteers, the world-class tournament could never have been put on, but everyone was willing to give a hand, and things ran smoothly each year.

"The volunteers put huge hours into organizing and running the tournament to make it such a world-class tournament!" said Brian Mosienko. "My dad was very proud of the organization and how they ran it. At the end of the tournament, the organizers would invite Dad to their end of the tournament party, and he always enjoyed the comradery."

The tournament lasted nearly thirty years, from 1982 to 2010.

After the 'Incinarena' in East Kildonan was renamed after Terry Sawchuk in early 1991, the NWMHA sought to rename the Keewatin Arena after Mosienko.

It was fitting as the Keewatin Arena was in the North End, near where Mosienko had grown up.

It started with the arena renaming having to go through the Lord Selkirk-West Kildonan Community Committee. And then by the City's Parks, Protection and Culture Committee and city council. The NWMHA's goal was to make the official change in December 1991 for the tenth anniversary of the Billy Mosienko Hockey Tournament.

City council approved the name change almost instantly. Mosienko was elated upon hearing the news.

"It's an honour. I feel proud. Somehow, they don't forget about the old guys," Mosienko said. "I froze a lot of toes and noses learning to play hockey in that area. I'm just happy they did it while I'm still alive so I can enjoy it with my family."

"The next move should be to rename the arena in West Kildonan the Andy Bathgate Arena," Mosienko suggested. "Andy's in the Hall of Fame, and that's the area where he grew up."

Thirty years later and we are still waiting for that Andy Bathgate Arena. Get on it, City of Winnipeg!

The tenth annual tournament ran from December 26-30, 1991. On the evening of the 30th, just prior to the tournament's final game, was the dedication ceremony of the Billy Mosienko Arena renaming.

A limousine was sent to pick up Bill and Wanda at their house. The grandchildren piled into the limo with them. They tried every seat in the car because the driver told them that this same limo took John Candy and Wayne Gretzky to the Grey Cup game in Winnipeg. So much for their famous grandfather!

At 7:00 p.m., the limousine pulled up to the arena.

Flanked by his wife, Wanda, sons Bill Jr. and Brian, daughter Wendy, and grandchildren Kenny, Laura, Kyla, Ainsley and Tyler, the man they call "Mosie" strode proudly onto the arena's ice to the skirl of bagpipes from the Winnipeg Police Pipe Band.

Ron O'Donovan (Master of Ceremonies) introduced the Mosienko family, guest speakers, Mayor William Norrie. Bill's old hockey friends Ab McDonald and Eddie Mazur were also present.

"This is the last time we refer to this arena as 709 Keewatin," said O'Donovan, a public relations officer with the city's parks and recreation department. "We now call this the Billy Mosienko Arena. A name that will live forever and ever."

At one point, a plaque (which was mounted inside the arena) was unveiled, hailing Mosienko as "The Pride of the North End" to recognize his outstanding hockey career and his contributions to the National Hockey League. The plaque listed off his accomplishments during his fourteen NHL seasons with the Chicago Black Hawks and four seasons with the Winnipeg Warriors of the Western Hockey League.

Mayor Bill Norrie, who brought greetings on behalf of the city and the Winnipeg Jets, said that the young players of today could learn a thing or two from the sportsmanship exhibited by Mosienko, who won the Lady Byng Trophy as the NHL's most sportsmanlike player in 1945 when he went a full season without taking a single penalty.

"For the young people here tonight, Billy Mosienko serves as a positive role model," Norrie said.

When Mosienko finally took to the podium, some people in the crowd—both young and old—were choking back tears. "I am grateful and honoured," Mosienko said. "We will cherish this forever."

Later, Mosienko, in characteristic fashion, summed up what the evening meant to him. "Oh, gosh, it was really something," he said, with his wide grin. "So many nice things were said. It was just incredible. What more can I say?"

"What a thrill the arena dedication was to Dad," said Brian Mosienko. "It stood right up there at the top of Dad's list of great moments."

The Billy Mosienko Arena continues to live on in his name today and is home to all kinds of minor hockey, just how Mosie would have wanted.

In his later years, Bill had perhaps the biggest battle of his life when he was diagnosed with stomach cancer in 1986. In December of that year, he had an operation done to remove two-thirds of his stomach along with a malignant ulcer.

"The doctors were confident they'd got everything," Bill said at the time, "and they had, but they wanted to run more tests just to be sure. I went in for what was supposed to be the last test on January 8. Then on January 14, the day before my wife and I were getting ready to leave for Phoenix on holidays, I got the news. They'd found a trace of cancer in my bone marrow. They told me I'd have to have chemotherapy treatments."

Mosienko's reaction was typical. No disease was going to rule his life. His vacation plans might have to be altered slightly, but they certainly weren't going to be cancelled.

He had his first treatment in Winnipeg on January 15. On January 17, he and his wife were in the family car headed for Phoenix.

"I drove all the way to Sioux Falls, South Dakota that first day."

He fitted two more treatments in Phoenix around eighteen golf games and then had his final three treatments back in Winnipeg.

"When I went in for my last tests on June 22, they couldn't find a trace of the cancer anywhere in my system. It looks like I'm cured. I'm a lucky guy. I had great doctors, and they caught it in time. I still have to go in for a checkup every six months. I'm very fortunate. I'm feeling stronger all the time. I had a doctor who knew what he was doing, and everything seems to be okay."

"After that, he told me if he got another five years that he'd be happy," said Bill Jr.

Bill was almost at the critical five-year stage when on his last series of scheduled tests for cancer, they did a spinal tap on him and discovered precancerous cells in his spinal fluid again.

The first thing he said to the doctor after receiving the news was, "How do we fight this?"

Unfortunately, this time it was brain cancer, and it was inoperable. A series of chemotherapy sessions followed. Right to the end, Bill's hopes stayed high, and he fought as hard as he could.

Towards the end, though, Bill lost the ability to speak his thoughts.

"One time, he came back from Phoenix, and you could tell his memory was blank," said Bill Jr. "He forgot what we were talking about, and finally my mom took him to the doctor. He went to the hospital, and the cancer was in his brain. They gave him some medication which reduced the swelling and started doing spinal taps, drawing fluid from the spine, which is an excruciating procedure."

Eventually, it got to the point where Bill had to stay 24-7 at the King George Hospital (now Riverview). Wanda was right there at the hospital every day by her husband's side.

While Bill was at the hospital, old hockey guys like Bill Juzda, Danny Summers, and his old Warriors trainer Gordie Mackie would come and visit and talk to each other even though he could not participate. By that time, he had lost his sight, speech, and some of his hearing.

"You could just look in his eyes, and that's the only emotion he could show was in his eyes," said Bill Jr. "They would go in there every day and just talk, and he enjoyed it as much as he could."

"We then brought dad home one time on Easter. We had a BBQ steak for dinner, and he was disappointed when he had to go back to the hospital at the end of the night. That was the last time he was at his house."

Bill Mosienko passed away at the age of seventy-two on July 9, 1994.

"When Dad passed, I spent the night with him," recalled Bill Jr. "During the night, he sat up and grabbed the air in front of him. When Mom and my wife came back in the morning, we went for breakfast or lunch. When we returned, Dad had passed away."

Bill's funeral was held a few days later, on the morning of July 13, at St. John's Anglican Cathedral. It was a large funeral attended by many former hockey players, bowlers, relatives, friends, and fans.

Sam Fabio gave the eulogy at the funeral. Bill and Sam had helped set up the Manitoba Hockey Foundation together, which later became the Manitoba Hockey Hall of Fame. They travelled around together for years to different towns in the province to help raise money for the foundation.

"Mosie always operated as a professional," said Jack Fitzsimmons, a close friend and secretary of the Blackhawks' Alumni Association. "He displayed class and dignity, on and off the ice. I dare you to find one disparaging word ever written or said about him during or after his career."

Bill was interred in Winnipeg's Brookside Cemetery, where his parents and most of his siblings have all been interred. In the past, Bill helped tend the gravesites of his relatives at Brookside by planting and watering flowers whenever he could.

In 2003, a plaque was put up near his tombstone by the City of Winnipeg, giving a brief biography of Bill's hockey career and life.

Bill and Wanda had been married for forty-eight years. Wanda would pass away just two years later, in 1996, also from cancer.

"His influence on me as a father and role model will last forever," said Bill Jr. "A day does not go by when I don't think about my parents."

"When they were opening up the new Hockey Hall of Fame location in Toronto, my dad had gone for the celebration," recalled Brian Mosienko. "They were handing out the NHL Awards one evening there, and it was on CBC, so we were all watching from back home and looking for Dad on the television. Well, Ron MacLean is talking, and behind him, my dad is talking to Mario Lemieux, who had also battled cancer. I could read his lips, and he said, "Mario, I got it beat too," as Dad's most recent test had come back negative for cancer. But it came back and killed him."

"I was blessed having a father that was such a role model for any boy. When I worked with him at the bowling lanes, he treated me like I was a part-owner. But the most important part of this was I spent so much quality time with my dad! He wasn't just my dad; he was my best friend too."

Although the Mosienko hockey gene might have skipped a generation with Bill Jr. and Brian, it returned with Bill's grandson, Tyler Mosienko. Tyler was a highly talented centreman out of Winnipeg who went on to have a successful junior and professional hockey career around the world.

Born in Winnipeg in 1984, Tyler remembers his grandpa showing him the ropes in the game of hockey early on.

"I remember when I was about seven or eight years old, my dad and I would always build a rink in our backyard," said Tyler Mosienko. "So Bill would come out and show me a couple skating tips and help me smooth my stride out a little bit and show me some things to work on. That was pretty cool. Ever since I can remember, he was always such a big deal in Winnipeg. Everywhere he went, people talked really highly of him, so it was interesting to grow up in that environment."

"On the ice, grandpa showed me more physical stuff like how to skate properly. He would always tell me to try and anticipate the play and understand where the puck is going to end up and tips like that."

As a young kid, Tyler used to go watch games in the youth hockey tournament that was named after his grandfather.

"I remember we'd go watch him drop the puck, and that was a pretty big deal. When I got a little older, I actually played in the tournament too, which was neat. I played a few years in it, and although I never won it, I came in second once and got a silver medal!"

Sadly, Tyler was only ten years old when his grandfather passed away.

"It would have been awesome to have him around for a few more years to get to know him a little better as I grew older and got more mature. That's the way things go sometimes, I guess."

Tyler went on to play five seasons of junior hockey in the Western Hockey League (WHL) with the Kelowna Rockets. He then joined the Chicago Black Hawks organization for his first season of professional hockey. After attending Chicago's training camp, Mosienko spent that season with the Greenville Grrrowl of the East Coast Hockey League (ECHL).

"In Chicago, I met Denis Savard, who was the assistant coach of the team at that time, and he told me that he knew my grandpa a little bit, so we chatted about that. Later on, I got to meet Bobby Hull and Stan Mikita, and they both had some cool things to say about my grandpa, about how well respected he was as a person and as a hockey player as well."

Although he never cracked an NHL lineup, Tyler Mosienko went on to an illustrious pro career in leagues such as the ECHL and AHL. He then went over to Europe and played in Germany, Denmark, England, and France.

"It would have been great if grandpa to have lived long enough to have watched me play pro hockey. But I know deep down, he would have been very proud of me for getting as far as I did in the game."

Nowadays, Mosienko is back living in the Kelowna area, where he had played his five seasons of junior hockey.

"Tyler reminds me of my dad so much," said Brian Mosienko. "He's a real go-getter and gave it his all wherever he played."

In addition to his record of three goals in 21 seconds, another record that Bill Mosienko might have is most songs written about them for an NHL player. Since he has passed, there has been not one, but two songs dedicated to him.

First off, a Winnipegger by the name of Brian Cherwick and his Ukrainian fusion folk band, The Kubasonics, wrote a song in 2002 called "Billy Mosienko," which details Bill's three goals in 21 seconds. It's the closest thing to play-by-play you will hear in a song.

Here's Brian Cherwick telling the story of his song:

> I grew up just a few blocks from where Billy lived in the North End of Winnipeg. One of my school friends lived directly across the back lane from him. We knew that he had been a famous hockey player, but we were equally impressed with him because he was the owner of a bowling alley. My Dad was a fan of the Chicago Black Hawks and often told me about Mosienko having the record for the fastest hat trick. I think my dad became a fan of the Black Hawks because Metro Prystai also played for them, and he was from my Dad's hometown of Yorkton, Saskatchewan.
>
> Later in life, I began writing songs for my band, The Kubasonics. I had been reading a book of hockey stories, and one of the stories was about the night that Mosienko scored the famous hat trick. As I was reading the story, the song started forming in my head. I basically took the details of how each of the goals

was scored and rearranged them so that they fit the structure of song lyrics and had a rhyming scheme. I was trying to think of a musical style for the song and decided that since the events took place in the 1950s, it should have a bit of that flavour. We made it a rockabilly style, a style which, coincidentally, included the subject's name (Billy).

I had been reading that hockey book in the summer of 2001. The song came together soon after that. Once I had it ready, I realized that the fiftieth anniversary of the event was coming up in March 2002. I got my band together, and we made the recording of the song. At the time, my next-door neighbour was a news anchor for the local CBC television station. I told her about my song and asked what the procedure would be to contact the producers of Hockey Night in Canada. I had no illusions that they would use the piece but thought it would be good that they were aware that it existed. Coincidentally, my neighbour had worked with HNIC host Ron MacLean on a TV special and contacted him directly. The next day a CBC producer called me asking for a copy of the song. To my surprise, they liked it and were going to use it as part of a tribute to Billy on their Saturday night broadcast, which happened to fall on March 23 that year! When the show opened that night, it did with our music playing and an archival film of Billy skating down the ice. After that, as Ron MacLean introduced the games that would be featured for the rest of the evening, he held up the package of our CD that had the song on it and mentioned our band and me personally as the writer of the song. That was a very cool moment.

Billy's son, Brian Mosienko, was a friend of my uncle. They had both been drummers in Winnipeg bands. I knew that Brian was still running the bowling alley, so I sent a copy to him at that address. I explained to him who I was (I had met him when I was a kid but did not know if he would remember me). I explained that I used to see his dad in his yard while we were playing street hockey behind my friend's house. And I explained that I thought his dad's story was a remarkable one and should be told more often. I had hoped that my song would help a little bit. Brian got my phone number from my uncle and gave me a call. He told me how much he appreciated the song and that he played it regularly at the bowling alley. Whenever the song mentioned Billy scoring a goal, all the bowlers would cheer! He and his family later sent me a framed portrait of Billy as a token of thanks.

BILLY MOSIENKO (Lyrics)
Words and Music by Brian Cherwick

Well, it was March 23, in the year of '52
When the Blackhawks and the Rangers dropped the puck
The remarkable record set there on that day
Was a combination of speed and skill and luck

From the frozen Red River in the North End of Winnipeg
To the City of Chicago off afar
A speedy right winger named Billy Mosienko
Became one of the Blackhawks' biggest stars

Each time that he saw the NHL Book of Records
Billy dreamed of seeing his name among the greats
That night in March, when the Blackhawks skated out into
*   The Gardens*
Billy would not have long to wait

>*Billy, Billy, Billy Mosienko*
>*He'd get the fastest hat trick ever scored*
>*Billy, Billy, Billy Mosienko*
>*His record would live on forever more*

In the early minutes of the game's third period
As the Blackhawks burst in across the line
Billy took a pass from his centre, Gus Bodnar
And slapped in a goal at 6:09

After that goal there was a face-off at centre
Bodnar won the draw and hit Bill with a pass
Billy streaked across the blueline, shot and scored at 6:20
Just eleven seconds had elapsed

Bodnar won the next draw and passed the puck to George Gee
Who spotted Billy breaking in towards the net
Billy fired the puck again, the red-light flashed at 6:30
Twenty-one seconds, the fastest hat-trick yet!

> *Billy, Billy, Billy Mosienko*
> *He got the fastest hat trick ever scored*
> *Billy, Billy, Billy Mosienko*
> *His record would live on forever more*

By the time that Billy's hockey playing days were done
258 goals were his life-time tally
Then he went into business in his hometown of Winnipeg
Opening his own bowling alley

Now there's a life-sized photo of Billy at the entrance
To the world-famous Hockey Hall of Fame
And there's a giant bowling pin in Winnipeg's North End
Advertising "Billy Mosienko Lanes"

> *Billy, Billy, Billy Mosienko*
> *He got the fastest hat trick ever scored*
> *Billy, Billy, Billy Mosienko*
> *His record would live on forever more*

> *Billy, Billy, Billy Mosienko*
> *Just 21 seconds earned him fame*
> *Billy, Billy, Billy Mosienko*
> *The hockey world will always know his name*

> *Billy, Billy, Billy Mosienko*

In 2015, an alternative hip-hop artist and rapper from Halifax, Nova Scotia who goes by the name Wordburglar (AKA Sean Jordan), also released a song about Bill called "Bill Mosienko: 21 Seconds".

Here's the Wordburglar discussing his song:

> I first heard the name Bill Mosienko from my dad—coincidentally also named Bill—an avid hockey fan and unlimited resource of historical fun facts and obscurities. I played a lot of sports growing up, and my dad would use the tale of Mosienko's 21-second hat trick as a rallying speech to inspire my friends and I when the chips were down. I believe the first time I heard the story, I was in a hockey tournament, and we were losing. Kids were acting like the game was over and were checking out, so Dad told us how Mosienko scored the fastest hat trick in NHL history, and it really did motivate us. After that, I never forgot about Mosienko's 21-second hat trick. And neither did the rest of my family, as "Mosienko" went on to become a call-to-action rallying codeword for any challenge that presented itself—hockey-related or not. Don't think you have a chance at succeeding? My Dad would just say "Mosienko!" and my sister and I knew that meant to think positive, work hard and keep going.
>
> It's one of those obscure sports trivia questions that you can't believe is real, but it's also very inspiring in that anything-can-happen way. I've carried this story with me through life, and people enjoy learning about it when I play the song live—hockey fans or not. Sure, as a sports fan, it's a great reminder to never give up on the game until it's over—everybody loves a comeback, right? But it's also just an inspiring story to apply anytime the odds are stacked against you. Push on, persevere, never say quit—all that stuff. It's a timeless message. And that's what inspired me to write the song.
>
> With the song, I guess I'm carrying on my dad's tradition of metaphorically linking life to sports trivia—and hopefully sharing this awesome record with a new generation of listeners who may take some inspiration from it too. Mosienko!

BILL MOSIENKO (21 Seconds) lyrics by Wordburglar
  (Sean Jordan)

VERSE 1
It was Sunday March 23, 1952 /
Chicago vs. NY, down 6 to 2 /
4 goals behind just a few minutes left /
But the Pony Line right-winger wasn't finished yet /
Yes Bill Mosienko wasn't playing for show /
One of the greats on skates and a name you should know /
Hall of fame record holder—no one's making it close /
21 seconds—3 goals made in a row /
Whoa! See the game ain't over till you hear the Buzzer man /
Like you know the home team from the colours in the stands /
Something you can understand—never quit /
Bill brought 'em back and they won seven-six /
It wasn't the championship or even the playoffs /
It was hard work and not believing in days off /
It pays off, you won't win you don't try first /
He had a hat trick in half my verse! /

CHORUS
3 goals, 21 seconds /
True story it anyone's guessing /
My Dad always told me "Bill Mosienko"
Never give up. Mosienko! /

VERSE 2
Get open, catch a pass and give it a slap /
Small puck. Big net. Simple as that /
If there's time on the clock you got time for a shot Word to
  Bill Mosienko that guy on the Hawks /
While the iron is hot, lace your skates, take your place /
Get your game face straight, no plays to waste /
Cause where the puck drops is where big breaks await
Whether you're making crazy saves or taking breakaways /

Hey! Amazing grace! That's how greats are made /
Blades of steel but no razors don't shave your face /
In the race, stay focused keep your stick on the ice /
That's exactly I how I feel when I'm the ripping the mic /
Right? Right. I know you're probably like "What, c'mon!" /
Was it a timeout? Did the other team know the game was on? /
21 seconds for 3 that's the top score /
But what's crazy they say he almost got 4!
CHORUS Repeats

I find it very interesting that in writing this book and all the research and interviews that was put into it, I can confidently say that not one person has ever spoken a bad word about Bill Mosienko. It cannot be overstated how rare it is to have someone so genuinely liked by everybody.

Bill was a people person and cherished talking to all the individuals he met throughout his life. He was a huge believer in people and that everybody deserves a chance and to listen to their story.

"I wanted to get ahead, really wanted to get ahead in hockey," said Mosienko towards the end of his life. "That was my one ambition. I wanted to succeed so badly."

He succeeded not only at hockey, but at life. And twenty-seven years after his death, his memory has never faded. Not for twenty-one seconds.

ACKNOWLEDGEMENTS

Some people say that writing a book is similar to completing a puzzle. I would tend to agree with that.

I feel that preparing this book was not a solo project in the slightest. So many people contributed to the final product that I don't necessarily feel like the author, but more or less the guy who meshed all of the stories together and put it into a book format.

Now please bear with me while I thank a bunch of people that helped make this book possible!

First off, I would like to thank Bill Mosienko's sons, Bill Jr. and Brian, for being so open and helpful throughout this entire project.

To Bill Jr. and Frances—Thank you for having me up at your place a couple of times to talk about your dad and for sharing everything with me on that USB drive! You really helped get this project off the ground. And also, many thanks for taking me on a tour of the North End of Winnipeg to see where your dad had grown up. That was a memorable afternoon!

To Brian—Thank you for all of our phone calls and text messages over the past year as you regaled me with all of the tales about your father. You were always there instantly for me if I needed help with something, and I greatly appreciate that. I look forward to finally meeting you in person one day soon!

I'd also like to thank my beautiful fiancée Anastasia for her undying love and support that she gives me every day. I love you so much. Thank you for putting up with all the late nights that writing this book entailed!

Thank you to my family and friends that have supported me in my writing career. In particular, my grandparents Roy and Iris, to whom this book is dedicated. You are my two favourite people on earth, and I cherish every minute I get to spend with you.

I didn't think my research for this book would lead me to Delisle, Saskatchewan, at first. But I'm delighted that it did. I can't thank Lynn Bentley and his wife Gloria enough for their warm hospitality. They are salt of the earth people, and I'm grateful to have met them.

Thanks, Spinner, for the fun afternoons of golf at your fantastic course in Delisle. And for sharing your family's story with me. I'm very appreciative and look forward to my next visit to Delisle!

I'm also truly fortunate that I was able to interview over a dozen of Bill's former teammates/opponents for this book. Thank you all for sharing your stories and memories of Mosie.

All of these former players are in their 80s and 90s, and so a couple of them, such as Howie Meeker, have since passed away. I'm grateful I was able to get their stories in this book while they were still alive.

To Tyler Mosienko—Thank you for sharing the recollections of your grandpa, and congrats on a wonderful professional hockey career yourself.

To Jen Mosienko—You are an incredible artist, and I will never be able to thank you enough for your amazing portrait of Bill that is featured on this book's cover.

A special thanks to all the people I talked to for this book that had known Bill through the bowling alley or from the minor hockey tournament in his name. I appreciate you all for your stories about Mosie. And to Warren Chubey—it was great meeting you while I was in Regina.

Thank you to Marianne Swarek, who was able to dig out a small book about the Tobans Rink that her late husband, Joe Swarek, had written before he passed. I am very grateful to you.

I'm pleased I was able to meet up and chat with 92-year-old Borden Semenchuk, who lived across the street from Mosienko growing up. And with a great memory, was able to remember those early days like it was yesterday. Thank you to Ron and Elizabeth Semenchuk, who helped facilitate the interview, as Borden is hard of hearing these days.

In hearing the stories of Borden Semenchuk and Joe Swarek, I really got a feel for what a special time it was on Selkirk Avenue during the 1920s and 1930s. It seemed to be a block blessed by families with multiple boys who, despite living during the Depression, made the most of things and had a lot of fun.

A big thanks to Kirby Ross, a Nova Scotia historian, who tracked down when Bill's parents had come over by ship from Ukraine to Canada.

A pair of books, *Max Bentley: Hockey's Dipsy-Doodle Dandy* by Ed Fitkin and *Shero: The Man Behind the System* by Vijay S. Kothare, were essential for the first-hand stories of the Bentley brothers and Fred Shero.

The *Winnipeg Free Press* and *Winnipeg Tribune* archives were also essential in my research, as was the *Society for International Hockey Research (SIHR)* and its extensive database. I have to say that endless hours were spent digging through all those archives in the last year!

Finally, I would like to thank Great Plains Publications for taking another chance on me and believing in this project. I am so grateful that this book was published by such a top-rate publisher here in Manitoba.

At the end of the day, writing *Mosienko: The Man Who Caught Lightning in A Bottle* was a labour of love, and although it felt like a challenging journey at times, it is undoubtedly the most satisfying accomplishment of my writing career, getting it finished and in your hands. Thank you for reading Bill's story.

APPENDIX

Statistics

Career Statistics

Season	Club	League	REGULAR SEASON						PLAYOFFS				
			GP	G	A	TP	PIM	+/-	GP	G	A	TP	PIM
1938-39	Winnipeg Sherburn AC	MAHA											
1939-40	Winnipeg Monarchs	MJHL	24	21	8	29	14		7	8	3	11	2
1940-41	Providence Reds	AHL	36	14	19	33	8						
1940-41	Kansas City Americans	AHA	7	2	2	4	0		8	4	1	5	2
1941-42	Chicago Black Hawks	NHL	12	6	8	14	4		3	2	0	2	0
1941-42	Kansas City Americans	AHA	33	12	19	31	9						
1942-43	Chicago Black Hawks	NHL	2	2	0	2	0						
1942-43	Quebec Aces	QSHL	8	5	3	8	2		4	2	2	4	2
1943-44	Chicago Black Hawks	NHL	50	32	38	70	10		8	2	2	4	6
1944-45	Chicago Black Hawks	NHL	50	28	26	54	0						
1945-46	Chicago Black Hawks	NHL	40	18	30	48	12		4	2	0	2	2
1946-47	Chicago Black Hawks	NHL	59	25	27	52	2						
1947-48	Chicago Black Hawks	NHL	40	16	9	25	0						
1948-49	Chicago Black Hawks	NHL	60	17	25	42	6						
1949-50	Chicago Black Hawks	NHL	69	18	28	46	10						
1950-51	Chicago Black Hawks	NHL	65	21	15	36	18						
1951-52	Chicago Black Hawks	NHL	70	31	22	53	10						
1952-53	Chicago Black Hawks	NHL	65	17	20	37	8		7	4	2	6	7
1953-54	Chicago Black Hawks	NHL	65	15	19	34	17						
1954-55	Chicago Black Hawks	NHL	64	12	15	27	24						
1955-56	Winnipeg Warriors	WHL	64	22	23	45	37		14	6	12	18	4
1955-56	Winnipeg Warriors	Ed-Cup							6	6	3	9	6
1956-57	Winnipeg Warriors	WHL	61	27	26	53	25						
1957-58	Winnipeg Warriors	WHL	65	38	36	74	43		7	1	0	1	6
1958-59	Winnipeg Warriors	WHL	63	42	46	88	55		7	1	3	4	10
1959-60	Winnipeg Warriors	WHL											
	NHL Totals		711	258	282	540	121		22	10	4	14	15

Awards & Achievements

- NHL Second All-Star Team (1945 & 1946)
- Lady Byng Memorial Trophy (1945)
- NHL All Star Game (1947, 1949, 1950, 1952, 1953)
- Lester Patrick Trophy—WHL Championship (1956)
- Edinburgh Trophy Championship (1956)
- WHL All-Star Team (1957, 1958, & 1959)
- Manitoba Athlete of the Year (1957)
- "Honoured Member" of the Hockey Hall of Fame (1965)
- "Honoured Member" of the Manitoba Sports Hall of Fame (1980) and Manitoba Sports Hall of Fame (1985)